21644

D0687132

Albuquerque Academy.

WOODWORKING
TECHNIQUES
Joints and Their Applications

WOODWORKING
TECHNIQUES
Joints and Their Applications

R.J. DeCristoforo

Reston Publishing Company, Inc.
A Prentice-Hall Company
Reston, Virginia

Library of Congress Cataloging in Publication Data

DeCristoforo, R J
  Woodworking techniques.
  Includes index.
  1. Woodwork (Manual training) 2. Joinery.
I. Title.
TT180.D34   684'.08   78-17242
ISBN 0-8359-8785-X

© 1979 by Reston Publishing Company, Inc.
A Prentice-Hall Company
Reston, Virginia 22090

All rights reserved. No part of this book may be reproduced in any way, or by any means, without permission in writing from the publisher.

10 9 8 7 6 5 4 3 2 1

Printed in the United States of America

684
Dec

CONTENTS

Albuquerque Academy

21644

PREFACE

There is more to a piece of furniture, or any woodworking project, than meets the eye. What you see affects your sense of beauty, a factor that eludes specific definition. But what is not visible is tangible and bears on the quality and permanence of the project and reflects the ego of the person who constructed it. All quality pieces, regardless of function and of how the design affects the viewer, must have one thing in common: joints that do the job and tell of thoughtful craftsmanship.

The classic period pieces, many of which are not in museums but still in use, are revered as examples of a particular historical period and style, but they have become valued antiques because they were assembled in a way that has resisted the tests of time and use and abuse. In addition to superior woodworking techniques, they reflect the character of the manufacturer.

Joint making is an art, and like most art it involves practical knowledge and a strong intent. We might take a cue from the word "joiner," a term that at one time was a title indicating a most highly skilled woodworker. It's possible that the term applied more to house construction than it did to furniture and cabinet making, but the point is that it indicated the cream of the crop—the person who did the visible interior work that required tight, artistic connections.

Many of the joints in furniture can't be seen so, unfortunately, both in commercial and custom work, this critical element of construction is approached haphazardly. The most elaborate project made with the most exotic wood is of little value if the project is poorly engineered. The best glue you can buy will not substitute for uneducated joint selection or for incorrect cuts. In terms of permanence and efficiency, the construction is more important than the materials used.

A thorough knowledge of joints, joint application, and cutting procedures is often the difference between superior, acceptable, and bad work. But there is yet another critical factor—the intimacy between the worker and the wood.

Enjoyment and pride in working is the exact opposite of commercialism or planned obsolescence to any degree. It has to do with the challenge *in the doing* that makes the final result an almost anticlimactic experience.

The choice of joints and the degree of expertise with which you choose to form them is a very personal thing regardless of the tools you work with. It is said by some that hand work can never match the precision of machine production. This may be true to some extent, but only in relation to mechanical monsters that spew out hundreds of bits and pieces that are exactly alike. Our main concern is with custom work by an individual and with the belief that works of art can't be duplicated.

The craftsperson in industry is becoming less visible because of the need for mass production. There are engineers and designers and architects who do the creative work and the planning, and there are in-the-shop people who tend the machines that are set up to edge a board, form a mortise, or drill a hole. However, the very fact that the machine must be organized to do a single particular thing with automatic consistency is to the advantage of the custom designer and worker. Production machines do not have talent and are completely disinterested in what they are programmed to do.

The individual, whether his activities are therapeutic or wage-earning, can use power and hand tools as partners in individualism. The quality project can't be discredited because it was executed with power tools. It takes less time to rip or crosscut a board on a table saw or radial arm saw than it does to do the job with a hand saw, and it certainly takes less energy. If a hole is done correctly with a bit and brace, it will not be distinctive from a similar hole done on a drill press or with a portable electric drill.

Dovetails made with a portable router will be precise and uniform and acceptable, but the same job can be done competitively on a quality basis by the dedicated craftsperson working with a dovetail saw and chisels. In this area there is an important point that can be made: The size and shape of the dovetails made with the router are determined by the cutter and by the finger template that is used with the tool. The difference between these and those made by hand is in the flexibility of design. The machine *must* make uniformly shaped and spaced tails and sockets. The custom worker doesn't have to. He can, for example, have two small dovetails about a large center one. He can decide that three wide dovetails are structurally adequate and more correct esthetically than the smaller and more numerous dovetails the machine would produce. This is typical of decisions the machine can't make.

A person can be spoiled by machines to the extent that he limits his creativity by the cuts he can make with power, but this is a choice rather than a requirement. It is not true that craftspeople become more scarce as machines increase—not if the machines are sanely viewed as servants and not masters.

Actually, the power tool is merely an extension of the hand tool. It will have built-in components that help make accuracy more automatic, but the worker must still organize the tool and guide the work. As many errors can be made with a power saw as with a hand saw.

Schools today have more machinery than the average homeworker or even the professional custom worker might even dream of owning, but this should not produce fewer or inferior craftspeople—not if the instructor can relate the mysticism of the tree with a table or a chair or any wood project. Wood is alive in more than the strictly organic sense. Being intimate with the material is as important as being skilled with tools. The person who works with clay feels the medium with his fingers and so establishes a very close bond. This should also apply to the woodworker, which is one reason why hand tools must never be discarded or scorned. They do bring the wood and the worker closer and can illustrate procedural problems and solutions more graphically. The philosophy must be established one way or another, but once accepted there is no reason why, if the worker chooses, his physical effort can't be minimized. The modern craftsperson establishes a sane and sensitive balance between hand and power tool production.

The worker can make choices that may be affected but not dictated by the tools he has available. "Old timers" made their own tools and no doubt this created a special atmosphere, a camaraderie between worker and tool that carried over to the job being done. But the fact that we buy our tools today doesn't mean we can't create the same workshop climate. It's all in the mind and the attitude.

The worker can also be mistaken by making a fetish of complicated joints. A good piece of advice is to choose the least elaborate joint that is suitable for the assembly. There seems little point in being more extreme than necessary when you are installing storage shelves against studs in a garage. The built-in shelves made with shop-grade fir plywood panels don't call for the joints that should go with a walnut grandfather's clock. Often, the material and the intent set the stage.

By way of example, I can relate the story of a kitchen table and chairs project I undertook strictly as an experiment—a table and six chairs made of knotty pine. The fanciest joint was a rabbet; the bonding agents were glue and nails. The chairs remained squeak-free for an impressive period of time, but then what could not be seen became vocal. As an experiment, however, the project was successful. It did not deliver any more than I expected. The moral is that you must be true to the purpose. If I had tried to pass off the project as an example of good craftsmanship, the whole episode would have been fraudulent.

It is important to be honest. No one can be criticized for the quickie job if the need justifies the means. After all, a heavy plank with cement blocks as legs does make a suitable if temporary bench for a patio. Fraud occurs when the project is visually pleasant but functionally and structurally deficient. Cosmetic additions have nothing to do with quality, even though they might add distinction and even serve to identify the maker.

People who buy or make custom designed and executed pieces are looking for more than a storage piece or something to sit on. They are truly enamored of quality work and materials. They find satisfaction in details that point up the rare attention given the project. They know that high construction standards usually go hand in hand with original and exclusive designs.

In all situations, what the worker produces is affected by his answer to two questions: How long should this project last? and Shall I make it so it might last forever?

Although it is not the purpose of this book to teach the use of tools, it is necessary, of course, to show tools being used to make various cuts. Whenever you are involved with tools, whether they are powered or not, you are in danger of being hurt. Showing a method with a photograph or a drawing often makes it necessary to illustrate the procedure without the safety guards that would ordinarily be used. We don't recommend that you work this way. Being careful is better than being sorry. Tools that can cut wood can cut you.

Maintaining a degree of reserve in your relationship with tools is a great safety factor. Working with the tool as a friend doesn't mean the tool can think. Only you can do that. Don't become overconfident with tools, for then you will be vulnerable.

WOODWORKING
TECHNIQUES
Joints and Their Applications

Chapter 1

FUNDAMENTALS OF WOOD JOINTS

There are two important factors to consider when choosing a wood joint—appearance and strength. Appearance decisions can go to opposite extremes. You can do the most to conceal the joint, or you can intentionally expose it as a design element or because it tells of quality work. Examples of the latter are dovetails, fingerlaps, or box joints, and mortise-tenons that are husked or pegged. Often, dowels are allowed to project from a surface, or screw holes are covered with wooden buttons (Figure 1-1) instead of plugs, which can be sanded flush for maximum concealment.

Quite often the design of the project dictates the appearance of joints even though this may not be the basic intent. Compare the sides of the mini-chest shown in Figure 1-2 with a similar project done with sides of unadorned plywood. Here, we have an assembly of rails, stiles, and raised solid wood panels. Various types of joints are involved. For example, the panel edges fit grooves formed in both the vertical frame pieces (stiles) and the horizontal ones (rails). The rails have a tenon at each end which also mate with the grooves in the stiles. To emphasize the carved or three dimensional design, the mating edges of the rails and stiles are chamfered to introduce additional planes.

The casual observer will be affected by the visual impact of only the design, but the trained eye will know that the joints and the method of assembly were actually part of the woodworker's creative process.

The strength factor should be easy to understand and accept. It applies to simple and complex projects and to all joints. Fortunately, there is such a variety of joints that the worker can make the optimum choice in relation to the job being done. Movable shelves in a cabinet or closet, or dividers in a chest or drawer justify a less demanding approach than the strong union there should be between the front of a drawer and its sides, or all the joints in any chair.

It is said, and is true, that if you can build a good, strong, durable chair, you can build just about anything. The design of the chair, whether like the rocker shown in Figure 1-3 or a more straightforward piece as a dining chair, doesn't matter. While most pieces of furniture must be assembled so the various components stay together and can support contents, chairs must be engineered to stay rigid under constant use, and abuse, by users of varying weights.

Figure 1-1. Projecting dowels and exposed wood buttons are compatible with the heavy appearance of the chair.

Figure 1-2. Three-dimensional side panels on the mini-chest contribute to the hand-carved look.

Figure 1-3. Chairs, especially rockers like this one, are among the projects that require durable joints.

The rocker, because of its design, must be assembled with what are essentially dowel joints. Other chairs, especially those with a conventional leg-rail assembly, can be joined with dowels or mortise-tenon joints. In any case, with all projects, while the design of the joint might be arbitrary, the execution is not. Good work must prevail. If you accept that joints are projects within a project, you will be striving toward enviable craftsmanship.

STRESSES

In addition to internal stresses caused by changes in moisture content that occur in any piece of wood, and which we will discuss from time to time, there are the more obvious physical stresses on joints and on glue lines. Figure 1-4 shows the most basic forces which tend to separate parts and gives examples of how modifications and additions can supply extra strength.

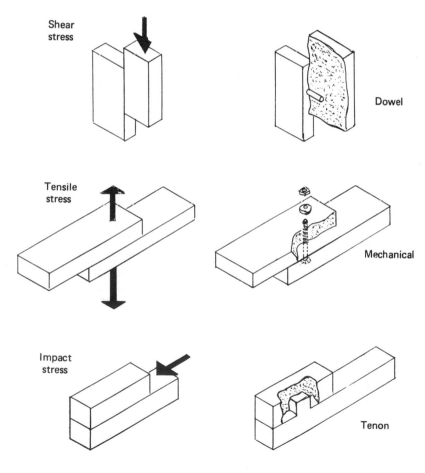

Figure 1-4. Some of the stresses that joints and glue lines are subjected to.

A first step in the design of any project is to view the construction and to judge what forces will contribute to its weakness. A mental picture may do for some but it's better to do a sketch, no matter how rough. Use arrows to indicate the direction of stresses on each joint.

The major stress on a trestle design, (Figure 1-5A) such as you might use to build a sawhorse, would occur when the project is used as legs for a temporary scaffold. While the connection between the top of the legs and the beam can be reinforced with heavy bolts, there is always the tendency for the legs to splay outward. The danger of failure will increase the longer the scaffold is used. A simple brace (Figure 1-5B) placed across the legs makes a major contribution toward a sounder, more durable project.

In this example the worker decided on the extent of his contribution. While the nailed-on brace will work, the half dovetail design shown in Figure 1-5C does a better job because it furnishes an interlock that holds parts together. The added support reveals that the maker took pride in his work even though it was just a sawhorse.

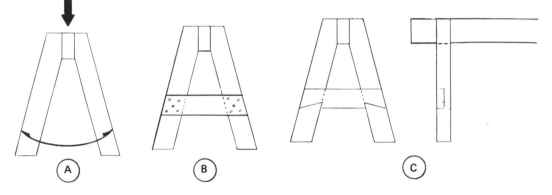

Figure 1-5. Trestle joints. The one at C will be most durable because it interlocks.

To a great extent the trestle idea applies to tables and benches. The leg-to-top joint is least likely to fail when the leg is symmetrical about a centerline which is at right angles to the top (Figure 1-6A). If you slant the legs in any direction (Figure 1-6B) you focus the stresses on the joint lines. It is likely that eventually the legs will loosen, especially if the project is a bench or any type of low table that people are apt to sit on.

To prevent loosening, most constructions in this area employ a substructure that includes rails and stretchers (Figure 1-6C). Often, only rails are used but it is preferable to have four of them so a top view of the leg-rail assembly is a closed frame. Regardless of how the job is designed it is best to view the substructure as a separate project that will stand rigidly and permanently on its own. View the top as a platform, not a structural member. Most times, especially when a top is solid lumber, the attachment should permit a degree of movement to guard against splits and cracks that can be caused by internal stresses.

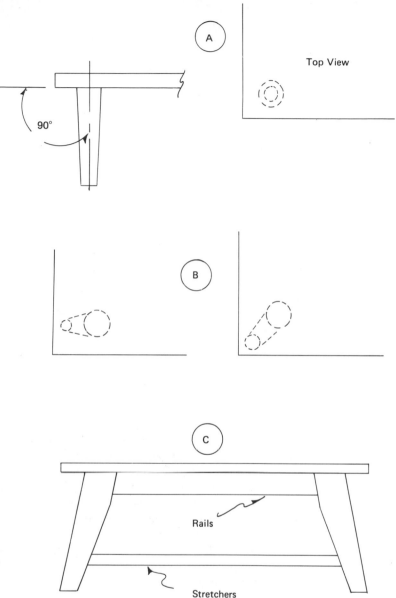

Figure 1-6. Rails and stretchers add considerable strength to bench and table assemblies.

STRESSES ON A DRAWER

A drawer is punished most at the places where the front of the drawer is joined to the sides (Figure 1-7). Each time you open the drawer you tend to separate the components at the joint line. The heavier the contents of the drawer, the greater the stress. That's why the dovetail is a good joint to use at those points. The sockets and tails form an interlock that will keep the parts together even if the glue should fail.

5

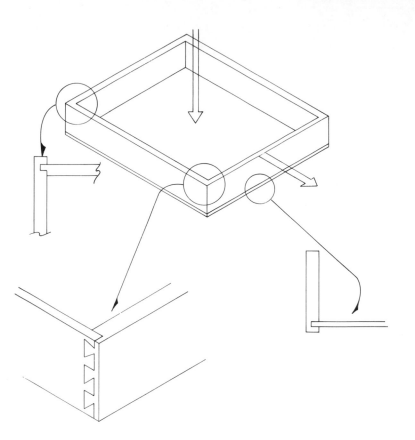

Figure 1-7. Major stresses on a drawer are shown by the arrows.

A reasonable substitute for the dovetail is shown in Figure 1-8. The drawer front is rabbeted to receive the sides, and short dowels are added as illustrated. View the joint without glue and you will see that the dowels fight the stresses applied when the drawer is pulled out. The diameter of the dowel should not be so great that wood surrounding it at points A and B (Figure 1-8) will be reduced to a very thin cross section.

Drawer bottoms are also likely to fail since they must support the contents. Inserting them in grooves cut in the sides and front—not necessarily the back—supplies additional strength.

The back of the drawer also takes punishment since drawer contents often slide to the rear. The back also contributes to the rigidity of the project as a whole. The joint used to connect the back to the sides is as critical as any.

The question is often asked, "Why use the more complicated joints on a drawer whose contents weigh only ounces rather than pounds, as with stamps, pencils or napkins?" Obviously the stresses will not be as great as those on a shop drawer that must hold tools.

The answer is twofold. The drawer itself must withstand hundreds of openings and closings and, again, the project tells of the dedication and pride of the woodworker. Perhaps the correct reaction to the material being used should also be mentioned. We don't react as negatively when simple joints, reinforced

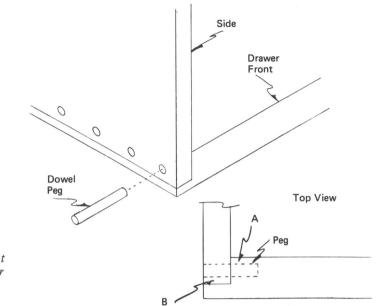

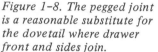

Figure 1–8. The pegged joint is a reasonable substitute for the dovetail where drawer front and sides join.

with mechanical fasteners, are used with shop grade plywood as we would if similar methods were used with walnut or Honduras mahogany.

JOINTS SHOULD MESH

Joint surfaces that mate loosely and do not make maximum contact will not produce strong bonds. No amount or kind of glue or wood dough will compensate for a sloppy fit. The contact points of even a simple butt joint should be viewed seriously before final assembly. If you hold the parts together against some backlighting and see some slivers of light coming through, you should accept that one or both of the pieces require some additional work.

Conversely, joint surfaces that do not come together without excessive clamp force or blows from a mallet, can cause serious problems. A dowel that fits too tightly, especially if it is not designed to allow for the escape of trapped air and excess glue, can cause splitting. It is not unknown for excess glue, unable to escape as it should, to travel through the pores of wood and emerge on a surface to cause blemishes in the finish. The same thought applies to a tenon in a blind mortise. An oversize tenon or tail in a dovetail joint also subjects the mating part to unnecessary strain, which merely adds to the stresses the area must withstand.

Joints that mesh as they should make it easier to do assembly work. It can be very frustrating and discouraging to set up parts and coat them with glue and then discover they will not mate nicely even under excessive clamp pressure.

The answer, of course, is to work carefully and accurately when cutting but even then, do a dry run. Assemble the parts without glue and with only as much pressure as you can exert by hand before you take the final step.

7

MEASURING AND MARKING

Acceptable tolerances in woodworking may not be as critical as those required in a machine shop yet the importance of accuracy when cutting and fitting wooden parts should not be viewed casually. It will not be a disaster if the shelves for a bookcase are 1/16 inch longer or shorter than they should be as long as the same error occurs on each. If the shelf lengths vary you will have trouble at assembly time. The sides of the case will be wavy when you pull parts together or some of the shelves will be weaker than others and will show gaps.

In the area of joints, however, inaccuracy is less tolerable. A hole that is 1/16 inch oversize or off-center will make a poor dowel joint. An oversize tenon can cause the mortised part to split. If the tenon is undersize it just won't do its job. Being accurate starts with measuring and marking carefully. There are a host of tools that will help, but they will be useless if the user isn't determined to be accurate. Measuring and checking more than once is a good approach.

BASIC MEASURING TOOLS

Flexible pull-push rules (Figure 1-9), often called steel tapes or flex tapes, are justifiably popular because they are easy to use, store and carry. Some, like the one shown, have a built-in device that keeps the tape locked at any extended position. Common graduations are in sixteenths and eighths of an inch but they are also available in metric or in inch-metric measures so you can make conversions as you work.

Lengths vary from three feet to 100 feet, blade widths from 1/4 inch to one inch. A tape used in a wood shop should not be under eight feet long since this is the longest dimension of a standard plywood panel. Choose a width of 1/2 inch or 3/4 inch since this will provide some necessary stiffness when the blade is extended.

Whether to choose a tape that has a recessing tip or one that swivels will be a personal decision. You can make mistakes with either. Be sure the recessing tip is kept clean so it will move smoothly when you are taking inside or outside dimensions. Be sure a swivel tip is moved aside when you take inside dimensions or you will add the thickness of the tip to the dimension.

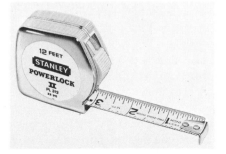

Figure 1-9. A flexible steel tape with a built-in lock that will hold the blade at any extended position.

The folding wood rule (Figure 1-10) or zigzag rule as it is often called because of the way it folds, has always been popular with carpenters and cabinetmakers. The most common length is six feet but they are available in eight foot lengths. Both fold to eight inches. Like the flex tapes, folding rules may be marked in inches, metric, or metric-inches. One advantage to folding rules is that you can set several of the blades at right angles to the remainder so you can reach inside a project for a measurement. Also, since metal joints lock the blades no matter how many are extended, you have a pretty rigid measuring device.

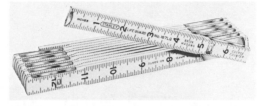

Figure 1-10. A folding or zig-zag rule.

Some folding rules have a built-in brass slide (Figure 1-11) so the rule can be used conveniently to take inside measurements as shown in Figure 1-12. Since the slide is removable, it can be used as a short bench rule or to take depth measurements.

Figure 1-11. A folding rule with a built-in slide that is removable.

Figure 1-12. A folding rule with a slide is used this way to take inside measurements.

A marking gauge (Figure 1-13) should be part of any woodworker's tool kit. Some of these are made with fixed pins. Others, like the one shown, have removable pins so they can be sharpened easily or replaced with a strip of lead. The latter type is recommended since there will be times when you will make a choice between marking with a steel point or a lead point.

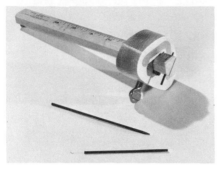

Figure 1-13. This type of marking gauge can be used with a steel or pencil-point.

A common mistake when using a marking gauge is shown in Figure 1-14. The position makes it easy to snag the point. It also increases drag and so causes a rough, inaccurate line. The right way to work is shown in Figure 1-15. Lay the beam flat on the work so the pin or lead drags naturally as you move the gauge. This position also provides a clear view of the point. Be sure you pull the gauge away from the point when marking. If you try to move in the opposite direction the point will dig in.

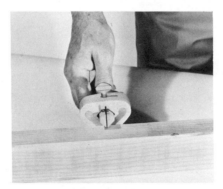

Figure 1-14. Don't use a marking gauge this way. The point, especially a steel one, will surely snag.

Figure 1-15. The correct way to use a marking gauge is shown here, with the beam flat on the work.

Figure 1-16. The head of the gauge will follow irregularities so the work edge should be smooth and straight to begin with.

      The beam is marked so you can set the head to a specific dimension, but this should always be checked with another rule before you mark the work. Testing the setting on a piece of scrap is also a good idea. Since the head of the gauge rides the edge of the work piece when you are marking (Figure 1-16), you won't get an accurate line unless the edge is smooth and straight to begin with.

      Squares, of course, are important layout tools especially when you need to mark right angles to a line or an edge. The All-In-One® square is a variation of the conventional combination square. As you can see in Figure 1-17, the head is designed so you can draw small circles, work with it as a protractor, and use it to gauge screw diameters. It also has a built-in scriber, and a vial so the head may be used as a level. The removable blade has equally spaced holes so, by using a scriber in one hole and a pencil in another, you can swing arcs or form circles. Like any square, it is used as shown in Figure 1-18 to mark lines at right angles to an edge. Be sure the blade is locked securely in the head and that the head is held snugly against the work edge as you mark.

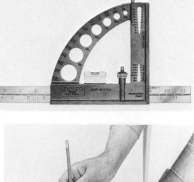

Figure 1-17. This type of square is for more than drawing lines. Tapered slots are used to check screw gauges.

Figure 1-18. Hold the head of the square firmly against the work. Rotate the pencil as you draw the line.

Other types of squares, which will be shown in use later, are the combination square, whose head permits drawing lines at 45 degrees as well as 90 degrees, and the try square, which has a fixed head. Some try squares have a handle that ends in a 45-degree angle where it meets the blade. In that case, the tool is called a miter square since it lets you check and mark 45-degree angles.

Steel squares are most often thought of in relation to house building and rough carpentry, yet they can be useful layout and checking tools. The longer blades enable you to mark longer lines than you could with a 12-inch square (Figure 1-19). Longer blade lengths are also an asset when you check joined components (Figure 1-20), something you should do before and after final assembly. The joints you construct should not only be sound, but should be accurate enough so adjacent pieces form the correct angle.

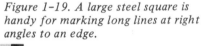

Figure 1-19. A large steel square is handy for marking long lines at right angles to an edge.

Figure 1-20. Large squares are also good to use when checking squareness of assemblies.

Most steel squares are called "rafter squares," "carpenter's squares," or "flat squares." While all can be useful in basic layout and checking work, the "homeowner's square" will be especially useful to the in-the-shop woodworker. It is stamped with information that includes decimal equivalents, a metric conversion table, wood-screw gauges, drill sizes, and other information. Since it is made of aluminum, it is not literally a steel square.

A tool you can use to strike arcs, form circles, or step off equal spaces will come in handy. Tools that fit this category are dividers or compasses; the difference being that dividers have two metal points and are considered metal working tools, and compasses employ a pencil as one point and so can be used

Figure 1-21. Dividers of this type have a removable steel point.

on wood or paper. The example shown in Figure 1-21 is called a wing divider and does come with two metal points. One, however, is removable and you can, as shown in Figure 1-22, substitute a regular pencil for one of the steel points. In effect, you have a compass and a divider in one tool.

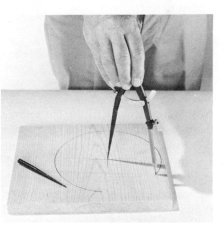

Figure 1-22. A regular pencil may be used instead of the steel point.

MARKING

Good tools help you to be accurate, but the best will be useless if you don't draw lines and mark dimension points correctly. Too often the measuring device is placed flat on the work and the dimension mark made by moving a pencil to and fro (Figure 1-23). The mark is more a blob than a sharp, clean indication. A better way, especially when the graduations on the rule are grooved, is to hold the instrument on edge as shown in Figure 1-24. Slide the point of the marker down the line so all you get on the work is a small dot. This is easy to do with any rule that has incised lines since they act as guide-grooves for the marker. Flex tapes can't be used this way. The guide mark you make should not be larger than the dot you get from a sharp, hard pencil. You will see heavy dots

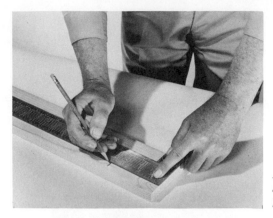

Figure 1-23. Scratching a dimension mark this way is not a good procedure.

Figure 1-24. It's much better to use a sharp, hard pencil this way so the dimension point is a small dot.

and broad lines in many of the illustrations in this book but they were done so for description purposes only.

The marker is as important as any other tool. The carpenter's pencil which has a heavy rectangular shape and a broad lead is okay as long as you expose a lot of the lead, sharpen it frequently, and maintain a chisel point by honing it on fine sandpaper. The No. 2 lead pencil, common in the home for writing tasks, may also be used if the worker accepts that it wears quickly and must be sharpened frequently for clear, sharp lines. Pencils with a No. 4H or No. 5H lead will hold points longer and will produce finer lines. In any case, when using conventional pencils to draw long lines, rotate the pencil in your fingers as you draw it along the guide. This avoids flats on the point which will result in broad lines.

The best way to mark cut lines is to work with a sharp knife (Figure 1-25). This has several advantages. The line you produce will be fine, and the knife will sever surface fibers so you will get a smoother cut when you saw.

Quite often, especially on wide material, two dimension points are established by measuring from one end of the stock. Then a straightedge to guide the marker is placed on the points. This is okay if you are careful but it does increase the possibility of human error. A more accurate way is to use a square that you place against one edge of the stock (Figure 1-26). If the stock is too wide to be spanned by the square, use the tool on opposite edges and connect the two lines by marking with a straightedge. You will know when you use the straightedge whether the first two marks are in line.

Figure 1-25. A knife is the best marker of all, makes a fine line, and will sever surface fibers for smoother cuts.

Figure 1-26. Try squares have fixed heads. Always use a square when you need a line at right angles to an edge.

Adjustable squares are good gauges to use when you must mark a line parallel to an edge (Figure 1-27). Work carefully to keep both square and marker moving steadily. Be sure the edge of the work is smooth and straight. If it isn't, you will just duplicate inaccuracies.

Locations for holes should be pinpointed by drawing intersecting lines. Then the intersection should be indented with an awl as shown in Figure 1-28, so there will be a seat for the bit you use to form the hole. When you set the awl, hold it at a slight angle for a clear view of the point and the mark. Place the tool vertically before you press down to form the indent. A good way to be accurate when drilling is to make a marked guide block like the one shown in Figure 1-29. The marks on the guide block are aligned with the intersecting lines on the work so the drill will be located correctly. The block also assures that you will be drilling at right angles to the work surface.

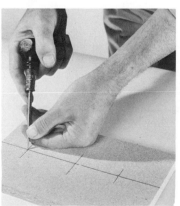

Figure 1-27. How to use a square to mark a line parallel to an edge. The tool is a "combination" square (left).

Figure 1-28. Use an awl to indent the intersection of lines you have marked to locate a hole (right).

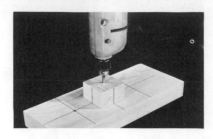

Figure 1-29. A simple guide block like this one will help you drill accurate holes.

If you drill a small hole through the guide block, say, 1/8 inch, then you can use it for many jobs. The primary hole can be enlarged to the size needed for the job.

SHARP TOOLS AND SMOOTH CUTS

Joint lines will be less visible if you make cuts as smooth as possible. Good tool handling, sharp tools, and the right tool, all make a contribution. Whether you get a coarse or a fine cut depends on the number of teeth on a saw blade and the style of the teeth. Generally, the more teeth per inch, the smoother the cut. The teeth on most saw blades are "set," which means that alternate teeth are bent in opposite directions. This is done so the blade will not bind in the work. The width of the cut made by the blade—the kerf—equals the gauge of the blade plus the amount of set (Figure 1-30). Smoother cuts are produced when the set is minimal or when the blade is taper ground. The latter type provides for blade freedom because the width across the tips of the teeth is less than the gauge of the blade. Most such blades are called "planers" and will produce the smoothest edges you can get with a saw.

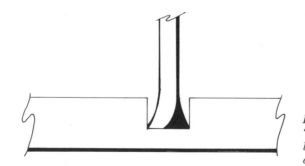

Figure 1-30. The width of a "kerf" is the gauge of the blade plus the amount of set on the teeth.

In all cases you should make a distinction between the saws you use for basic sizing cuts and those you use for the finesse touches required for good joints. The sample cuts shown in Figure 1-31 demonstrate the differences between textures and edge feathering obtained with different blades. Both cuts were made very carefully on a table saw; the one on the left with a combination blade, the other with a high-quality, carbide-tipped planer.

*Figure 1-31. Both cuts were carefully made.
The one on the left was cut with a combination blade and the other with a planer.*

The teeth on hand crosscut saws run from about 7 to 12 per inch. The
more teeth, the smoother the cut. When using such saws try to maintain an
angle of about 45 degrees between the teeth and the surface of the work (Figure
1-32). Make long, smooth strokes and do not hurry since this will only result in
tearing and splintering. Always saw to a marked line and keep the side of the
blade 90 degrees to the work. The *L*-shaped guide shown in Figure 1-33 will
minimize the possibility of human error. When clamped as shown it will assure
accuracy and square edges.

*Figure 1-32. Crosscut saws are
designed especially for sawing
across the grain of the wood.*

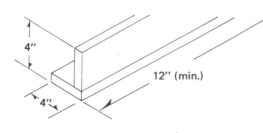

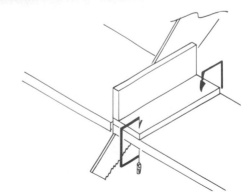

Figure 1-33. Guides like this will help you do better, more accurate sawing.

Ripsaws are designed for cutting with the grain and have fewer teeth per inch than crosscut saws. The angle between teeth and work surface (Figure 1–34) should be about 60 degrees unless you are cutting very thin stock in which case it should be reduced.

Figure 1–34. Ripsaws are for cutting with the grain of the wood. Don't use them on plywood or for cutting cross-grain.

Both types of saws will cut with or across the grain, but that does not make them interchangeable. In fact, the experienced woodworker, if he has but one choice, will always pick the crosscut blade since it makes the smoothest cuts. He will also use it on all plywood cuts but will work at a more acute angle since this does the least damage to surface fibers.

Backsaws (Figure 1–35) are used when smooth cuts and accuracy are critical, which automatically places them in the joint-forming category. They may be used freehand but most times are used with a miter box that you can make or buy. Chapter 5 on miters has a plan for making one.

Figure 1–35. The backsaw has many small teeth to produce smooth cuts.

The dovetail saw (Figure 1–36) is a light tool with a thin blade and many small teeth. While it is ideal for making the slanted shoulder cuts that are part of dovetail sockets and tails, it should not be limited to that use. It is a good tool to use on many cuts needed for tenons, dadoes, rabbets, and the like.

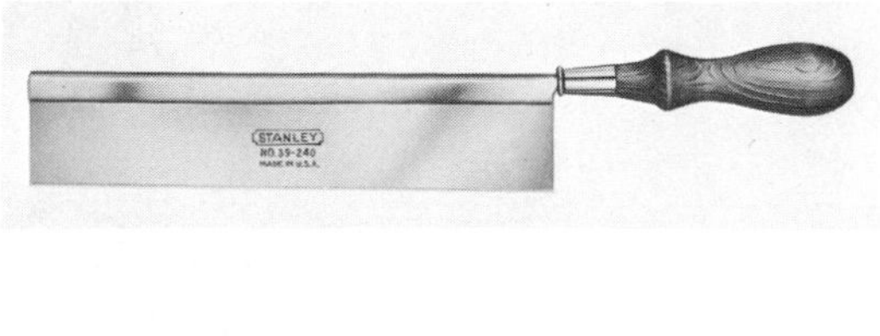

Figure 1–36. The dovetail saw is a fine tool and can be used with great precision.

You'll notice that both the backsaw and the dovetail saw have a heavy spine that runs along the top edge. The spine is there to stiffen comparatively thin-gauge blades, eliminating buckling and twisting when cutting.

All sawing operations can be improved by using guides or jigs that minimize the possibility of human error. There will be many to consider as we study the various types of joints but, by way of example, here are a couple that fit the category of "bench hooks." These are used with handsaws.

Figure 1-37 details a basic design for bench hooks. The item is gripped in a bench vise and serves as a guide for cross-cutting narrow or wide boards. The dimensions are not critical as there is no reason why the unit can't be longer than shown. The important element is the kerf in the vertical member. It should be cut with the saw that will be used and it must be perpendicular to the base and at right angles to the edge and surface of the upright.

A variation of the crosscut guide is shown in Figure 1-38. This is a much longer unit and has several kerf guides so you can opt for the best work position.

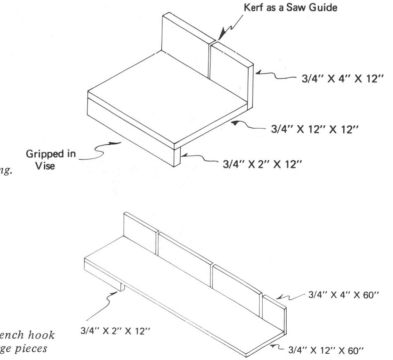

Figure 1-37. Bench hooks help you hold the work securely when you are sawing.

Kerf as a Saw Guide

3/4" X 4" X 12"

3/4" X 12" X 12"

Gripped in Vise

3/4" X 2" X 12"

Figure 1-38. This type of bench hook is long enough to handle large pieces of stock.

3/4" X 2" X 12"

3/4" X 4" X 60"

3/4" X 12" X 60"

Cutting techniques with power tools will differ yet the basic considerations are the same. Note in Figure 1-39, which shows a cut-off operation on a table saw, how the length of the part is gauged with stop rods and how the work will be held securely during the cutting because of the accessory hold-down on the miter gauge. The setup shown is an especially good one when you need many duplicate pieces.

Figure 1-39. Stop rods gauge the length of the work. The hold-down keeps the work secure during the cut.

Figure 1-40 shows a crosscutting operation on a radial arm saw. Here the free hand, which can't be seen in the picture, holds the work securely against the fence. The cut line on the work is there so the operator can tell right off whether the operation is being done accurately. If you have made the guide line with a square, as you should, and the saw is not following it, you will know that the tool requires some adjustment.

Figure 1-40. A line on the work will tell you how accurately you are sawing as you work.

DOWELS

The dowel commonly used in joints is a birch or maple or, sometimes, hickory peg which is chamfered at each end and grooved spirally or longitudinally (Figure 1-41) so glue and air can move when the joint parts are brought together. Joint pegs can be made from dowel rod which is available in lengths up to three or four feet but these may not be as precise in diameter as the preformed pegs made for the purpose. When you do make your own, be sure to provide the necessary chamfering and grooving. The grooves can be formed with a small *V*-chisel or you can do something similar by squeezing the pegs in the jaws of an ordinary pair of pliers as shown in Figure 1-42.

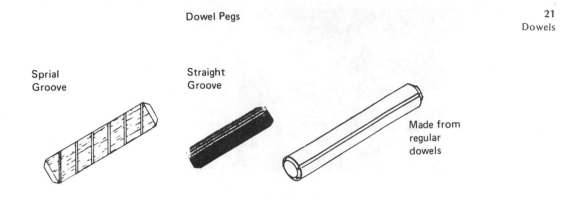

Sprial
Groove

Straight
Groove

Made from
regular
dowels

Typical Sizes

Diameter	Length
1/4''	1-1/2''
3/8''	1-1/2'' – 1-3/4'' – 2''
7/16''	2''
1/2''	

General Rules

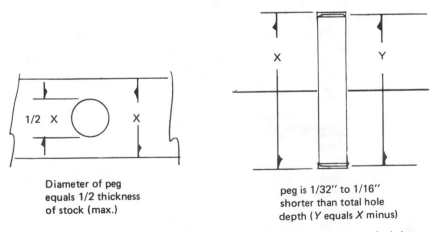

1/2 X   X

Diameter of peg
equals 1/2 thickness
of stock (max.)

X   Y

peg is 1/32'' to 1/16''
shorter than total hole
depth (Y equals X minus)

Figure 1-41. These are basic facts about dowel pegs that you can use in joints.

Figure 1–42. Use a pair of pliers to indent a dowel. The indents make room for air and glue that might otherwise be trapped in the hole.

If dowel holes are not drilled correctly and properly aligned, the joint parts will not mate as they should. Dowel centers can help, especially on the type of frame joint shown in Figure 1-43. The correct size dowel centers are placed in holes bored in one piece. The parts are then pressed together so the points on the centers mark the hole locations on the mating part.

Figure 1–43. Dowel centers are placed in drilled holes so the points will mark the position of the mating holes.

Most professional shops will use a drill press or a horizontal boring machine to form holes for dowels. Special jigs or fixtures are added to assure accuracy. Many of these, as we will show later, can be homemade for use in any vocational or avocational woodshop.

Holes bored by hand are best to use when only a few joints are needed. They are often done with a brace (Figure 1-44). A common set of screw-tipped bits used with the brace will include sizes from 1/4 inch to 1 inch with increases of 1/16 inch increments so you can form any size hole required in joint making.

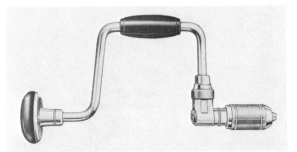

Figure 1–44. A typical brace.

Providing some mechanical means of gauging hole depth is a wise procedure. Power tools, like the drill press, have built-in stops; with a brace you can use an accessory called a bit gauge shown in use in Figure 1-45. This locks to the shank of the bit and can be adjusted to the depth of the hole you need.

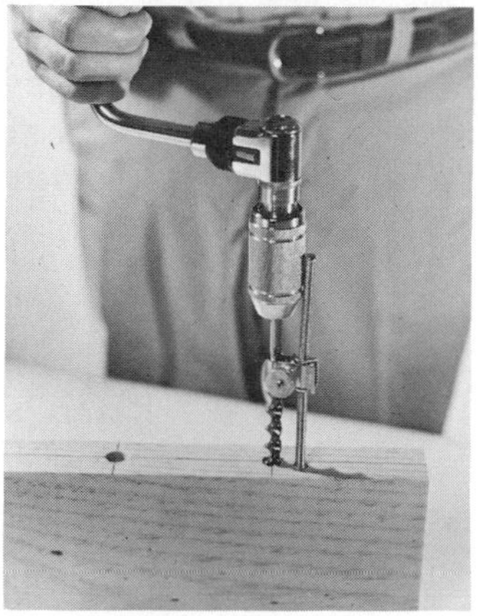

Figure 1-45. A bit gauge is used so any number of holes can be drilled to the same depth.

Working by hand calls for considerable care to keep the bit perpendicular to the work surface. There are, however, special jigs that can be used with a bit and brace (Figure 1-46). The one shown comes with a set of six guides to accommodate various sized bits. The tool is designed so it can be quickly clamped in place and is calibrated so the guide can be centered on various thicknesses of stock. Note the depth-control stop on the bit.

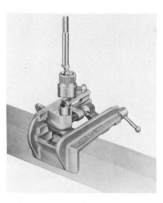

Figure 1-46. A typical doweling jig.

In order for a dowel peg to do its job effectively, its moisture content should not be more than five percent. A "wet" dowel will not absorb glue as it should and later will dry out and shrink, thus causing a poor joint and possible failure. Always keep joint dowels in a dry, warm place. It's a good idea to place them in a warm oven for a short time before using them. This reduces the moisture content as much as possible.

Always use at least two dowels in any joint as protection against stresses that might cause joint parts to pivot about a single one.

There will be more information about dowel applications in other chapters.

SPLINES

Splines (Figure 1-47) are strips of material used to strengthen joints and to hold parts in alignment during assembly. Applications range from edge-to-edge joints to short miters, but in all cases the important consideration is that the grain of the spline (Figure 1-47A) must run across the small dimension. This is easy to appreciate if you consider that wood is much easier to split *with* the grain than it is to crack it *across* the grain. When the spline is made and used as shown, its strength is at right angles to the joint line.

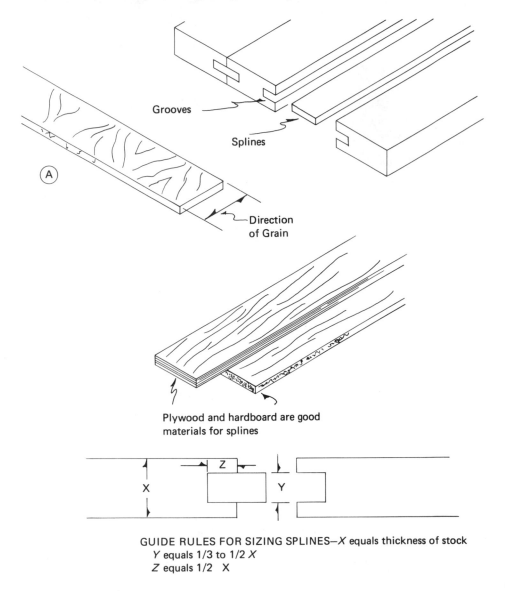

Grooves

Splines

(A)

Direction
of Grain

Plywood and hardboard are good
materials for splines

X

Z

Y

GUIDE RULES FOR SIZING SPLINES—*X* equals thickness of stock
Y equals 1/3 to 1/2 *X*
Z equals 1/2 *X*

Figure 1-47. The basics of splines.

24

Short splines are not difficult to make if you run kerfs through the end of a board and then slice off the pieces as shown in Figure 1-48. When long splines are needed, it's best to cut them from plywood or hardboard since hardboard is grainless and plywood has strength in any direction. Both materials are available in various thicknesses so you can choose what you want in relation to the thickness of the parts being joined.

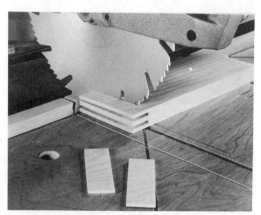

Figure 1-48. Short splines being cut on a radial arm saw.

A variation of the spline is shown in Figure 1-49. Here, the cross-shaped spline acts as a joiner between pieces, but also provides design value. This is particularly effective when the splines are made from a contrasting wood. In a following chapter we'll show how such splines are made and various ways they can be used.

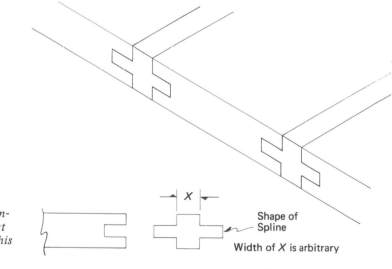

Figure 1-49. Splines contribute to an inlay effect when they are shaped this way.

X

Shape of Spline

Width of X is arbitrary

BUTTONS AND PLUGS

Dowels are often used to fill the holes through which mechanical fasteners, like screws, are driven. The dowels can be sanded flush or left to protrude as decorative details as shown in Figure 1-50.

Figure 1-50. The projecting dowels conceal the screws used in the joint and add a decorative detail.

Buttons and plugs like those shown in Figure 1-51 are used in the same way but have several advantages over dowels. Both products are more precisely made than the common dowel rod. They are available in a greater variety of wood species so there is a better chance of matching the project wood. The plugs and the oval head button are tapered so they will fit more tightly in the hole to minimize the joint line. The pieces are ready to use. All you have to do is glue them in place.

Buttons

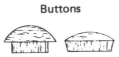

Plugs

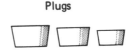

Typical sizes are 3/8″, 7/16″, 1/2″. Available in birch, oak, walnut, mahogany.

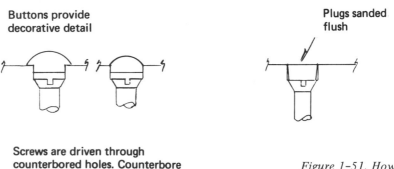

Buttons provide decorative detail

Plugs sanded flush

Screws are driven through counterbored holes. Counterbore should equal diameter of plug or button

Figure 1-51. How buttons and plugs may be used.

Many craftsmen prefer to make their own plugs and this has advantages. First, you can form the pieces from the same wood used in the project, getting a closer match than you could get in any other way. Also, by using a plug cutter

Figure 1-52. A type of plug cutter.

like the one shown in Figure 1-52, you can cut down through the surface of the wood or down through end grain, getting a grain direction that will match adjacent surfaces.

The best way to use the tool is in a drill press (Figure 1-53); drill as deep as the cutter will allow so the center cylinder will be rounded off at the top edge. After the plugs are separated from the stock, place them for flush sanding or for leaving the rounded end exposed.

Figure 1-53. The cutter forms plugs that are rounded off at the top edge.

You can break off the plugs by using a screwdriver as in Figure 1-54 or by working on a table saw as shown in Figure 1-55. An advantage of working the latter way is that the bottom of the plugs will be flat. Breaking them off with a screwdriver doesn't ensure this.

Figure 1-54. The plugs can be removed by snapping them off with a screwdriver.

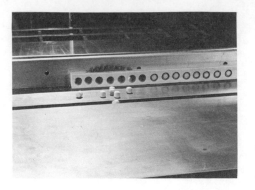

Figure 1-55. Another way to re-move the plugs is to saw them like this.

Another type of plug cutter, definitely for drill press application is shown in Figure 1-56. Because this plug cutter has greater depth of cut you can go right through 3/4 inch stock (Figure 1-57) or use it to form dowel pegs for joints as shown in Figure 1-58. Another use, which we will show later, is to use the tool to form an integral dowel on the end of a rail or stretcher to serve as a round tenon.

Figure 1-56. Another type of plug-cutting tool.

Figure 1-57. The plug cutter cuts deeply enough so you can go right through 3/4-inch stock.

Figure 1-58. The plug cutter may also be used to form dowel pegs for joints.

There are a variety of such tools available so be sure to use the driver and the speed that is recommended by the manufacturer.

WOOD SCREWS

Many pieces of quality furniture will use screws in some areas of the assembly if only to secure reinforcements or backs of cabinets. Actually, screws used judiciously add strength to some joints and, of course, they are used to attach pieces of hardware like hinges and pulls. The common screws, shown in Figure 1-59, are the flathead, roundhead, and ovalhead.

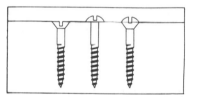

Figure 1-59. The three basic woodscrews are flathead, roundhead, and ovalhead.

The flathead screw, unless it will be concealed with a plug, is driven flush with the wood surface. The roundhead may also be driven in a counterbored hole for concealment, but is often left exposed. The ovalhead requires a partial countersink. Ideally, when parts are being joined, the length of the screw should be about 1/8 inch less than the total thickness of the pieces. In practice, though, the longest suitable screw is usually chosen.

In order for a screw to hold correctly, a hole should be drilled as shown in Figure 1-60. If the lead hole is too small, it will be difficult to drive the screw, especially in dense woods. If it is too large you may as well not use a screw. If the body hole is too large, the attached part will not be secure. If too small, the screw can cause splits, especially if you are driving through thin stock or near edges (Figure 1-61). The depth of the body hole may match the thickness of the part being fastened. The depth of the lead hole should be about half the length of the threaded portion of the screw.

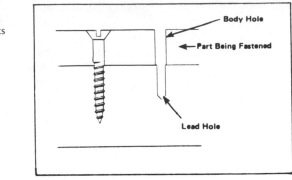

Figure 1-60. Screw holes must be drilled correctly if the screw is to hold with maximum strength.

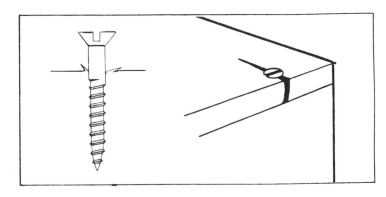

Figure 1-61. A shank hole that is too small can cause splits, especially on thin stock and near edges.

Correct sizes of drilling tools to use are shown in Figure 1-62. The only time you can ignore this information is when the screw is small and thin and the stock is soft. In that case you might be able to get the screw seated correctly by doing a starting hole with an awl.

SIZES OF DRILL POINTS TO USE WHEN DRILLING HOLES FOR WOOD SCREWS			
SIZE OF SCREW (No)	BODY DIAMETER OF SCREW (Inches)	BODY HOLE (Inches)	LEAD HOLE (Inches)
0	1/16	1/16	
1	5/64	5/64	
2	3/32	3/32	1/16
3	3/32	7/64	5/64
4	7/64	1/8	5/64
5	1/8	1/8	3/32
6	9/64	9/64	7/64
7	5/32	5/32	1/8
8	11/64	11/64	1/8

SIZES OF TWIST DRILLS TO USE WHEN FORMING SCREW HOLES			
NUMBER SIZE OF SCREW	SIZE OF SCREW (Inches)	BODY HOLE	LEAD HOLE
0	.060	53	
1	.073	49	
2	.086	44	56*
3	.099	40	52*
4	.112	33	51*
5	.125	1/8	49*
6	.138	28	47
7	.151	24	46
8	.164	19	42
9	.177	15	41
10	.190	10	38
11	.203	5	37
12	.216	7/32	36
14	.242	D	31
16	.268	I	28
18	.294	19/64	23
*may be necessary in hardwoods only			

Figure 1-62. The charts show the correct sizes of drilling tools to use when forming holes for screws.

Ordinarily you would have to go through several drilling procedures in order to establish a correct form for the screw, but there are some modern tools which make the job easier and even more accurate. The Screw-Mate® shown in Figure 1-63, will form both the pilot hole (lead hole) and the shank clearance hole (body hole), and will form a countersink for the screw head as well. The Screw-Sink® will form lead hole, body hole, and counterbore (Figure 1-64). Both tools are available in various sizes for screws from No. 6 × 3/4 inch up to No. 12 × 2 inch.

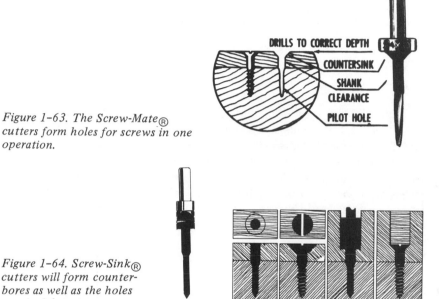

Figure 1-63. The Screw-Mate® cutters form holes for screws in one operation.

Figure 1-64. Screw-Sink® cutters will form counter-bores as well as the holes required for screws.

Counterbores are needed when using a plug to hide a screw, but they also make it possible to attach thick or wide stock with short screws (Figure 1-65). For example, if you need to attach a 3/4-inch thick slab to a 2-1/2-inch rail, you would need a screw more than 3 inches long. By providing a counterbore, you can cut the screw length by at least 50 percent.

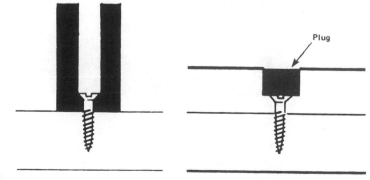

Figure 1-65. Counterbores are needed for plugs. Deep counterbores let you attach wide pieces with short screws.

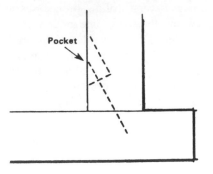

Pocket

Figure 1-66. Screws driven at an angle should have pockets so the screw head will seat correctly.

Screws driven at an angle will seat as they should if you counterbore to provide a flat for the screwhead (Figure 1-66). If the counterbore can't be accomplished with a conventional drilling tool, then do the job with a small, sharp chisel.

Countersinks are available for forming a seat for a flathead screw (Figure 1-67). Form a full countersink if the wood is hard. On softwoods, stop short of a full depression since driving the screw will complete the countersink.

Washers are often used with exposed screws (Figure 1-68) so the screw head will not bite into the wood, and to increase the bearing surface. Flat washers are always used with roundhead screws. The countersink types, whether depressed or raised, may be used with either flathead or ovalhead screws.

Figure 1-67. Countersinking for flathead screws. The arrow points to a seated screw.

Figure 1-68. Washers will keep screws from biting into the wood and increase the bearing surface of the screw head.

When you drive a screw into a counterbored hole, be sure to use a driver whose width is less than the diameter of the hole to prevent damaged edges (Figure 1-69). When you place plugs, use only as much glue as you need for the job. Wipe off excess glue immediately with a damp cloth. Sand the plug flush only when you are sure the glue is dry (Figure 1-70).

Figure 1-69. The width of the screwdriver's tip must not be greater than the diameter of the counterbore.

Figure 1-70. Do not sand plugs flush until after the glue is dry. Arrow indicates a sanded plug.

Screws that are driven correctly will hold as they should, but you can take one of the extra precautions shown in Figure 1-71 to be sure they don't "unwind." In one, a small hole is drilled through the screw head at an angle of about 45 degrees and then a brad is driven through the hole into the wood. In the second method, use a staple that fits the slot in the screw.

Steel screws will work okay with most woods except oak. The combination of the acid in oak with the steel will often cause stains. Substitute brass screws instead. These are softer than steel and can be marred or even broken when driven. Coat them with wax—an idea you can use with *any* screw to make driving easier.

Sometimes, even when you have drilled holes as you should, a screw will be difficult to drive, especially if the wood is very dense. To solve the problem you can make a tapping screw by filing off half the diameter of the screw in the threaded area. Drive this screw to form threads in the hole and then replace it with the permanent screw.

Figure 1-71. Two methods you can use to lock a screw; an extra precaution you can take so the screw won't "unwind."

Nails are often used to reinforce joints especially on rough work, utility projects, and cabinets that do not require the type of joints called for in quality furniture. Common nails and box nails, shown in Figure 1-72, are similar. Box nails have slimmer shanks than common nails and are a better choice if the wood being used has a tendency to split. Both have broad heads to provide good bearing surface and should be used only when an exposed nail is not critical in terms of appearance. A staggered pattern of nails (Figure 1-73) is always better than nails on the same centerline, which is more likely to cause splits.

Common nail

Box nail

Figure 1-72. Common and box nails are similar but the box nail has a slimmer shank.

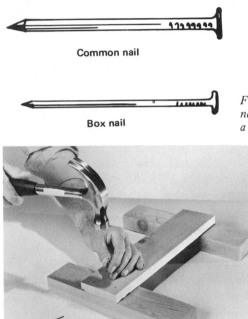

Figure 1-73. A staggered nailing pattern is always best since it's less likely to cause splitting.

Wire brads and finishing nails (Figure 1-74) are not uncommon on good, interior cabinetwork. In some areas of furniture they might even be used to attach backs to case goods and to secure trim. In most situations these nails are used when you don't want the head to show. To seat them correctly, drive them only until the head still projects above the wood surface. Then use a nail set as shown in Figure 1-75, to sink the head. The slight depression that remains is filled with wood dough.

Be aware that there are many sizes of nail sets and that you should work with the one whose point is not larger than the nail head. Self-centering nail sets, like the one shown in Figure 1-76, let you set nails and brads mechanically with less danger of marring the wood surface. The case of the tool sits over the nail head; tapping the plunger with a hammer does the setting.

WIRE BRADS	Length in Inches	Gauge
	3/16	20 to 24
	1/4	19 to 24
	3/8	18 to 24
	1/2	14 to 23
	5/8	13 to 22
	3/4	13 to 21
	7/8	13 to 20

Figure 1-74. Wire brads and finishing nails are designed to be set below the surface of the wood.

FINISHING NAILS	Size (d)	Length in Inches	Gauge	Approximate Number Per Pound
	2	1	16-1/2	1350
	3	1-1/4	15-1/2	880
	4	1-1/2	15	630
	6	2	13	290
	8	2-1/2	12-1/2	196
	10	3	11-1/2	125

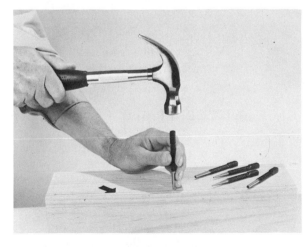

Figure 1-75. Setting is done with special tools, but be sure to choose a size that is right for the nail head.

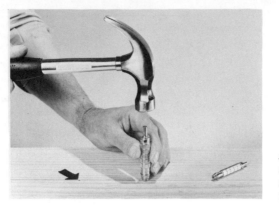

Figure 1-76. Self-centering nail sets are available in various sizes. The arrow points to a set nail.

Decorative wrought iron nails (Figure 1-77) are used when their exposed heads suit the design of the project. Many times, they do not serve a structural purpose. That is, joint design supplies the strength; the nails are added for appearance.

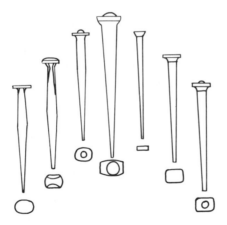

Figure 1-77. Decorative wrought iron nails are often used for the design they add to a project.

If the wood you are working with has a tendency to split, take the time to drill a small hole before driving the nail. Often, the nail itself with its head snipped off, can be used as a bit in a drill. It won't work like a twist drill, but it will serve to form a pilot hole.

GLUE AND CORNER BLOCKS

Check the hidden areas of any good cabinet or piece of furniture and you will find that glue blocks have been added to increase its strength. Even when intricate and interlocking joinery is part of the concept (Figure 1-78), a glue block is added to increase rigidity, making the project more durable.

Glue blocks (sometimes called rub blocks) can be square or triangular (Figure 1-79) and are always put in place with generous applications of glue. A good procedure is to coat the block and then put it in place with a slight sliding

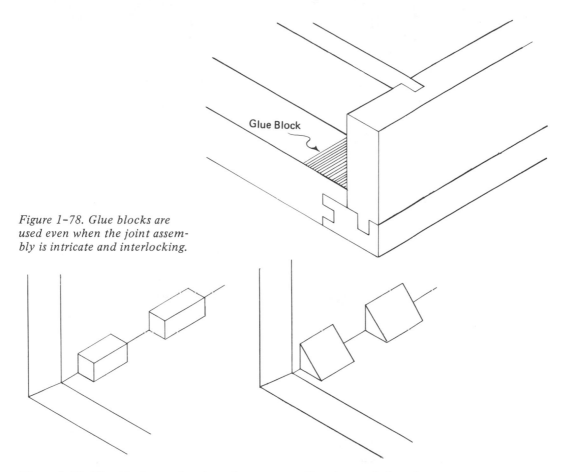

Figure 1-78. Glue blocks are used even when the joint assembly is intricate and interlocking.

Figure 1-79. Glue blocks can be triangular or square. Use plenty of glue when adding them.

action to make good contact with mating surfaces. The blocks can be secured further with nails, but screws will do a better job.

Sometimes, especially with projects of thin plywood, glue blocks play a more structural role. As shown in Figure 1-80, they actually serve as part of a structural frame.

Figure 1-80. Full-length glue blocks, used like this, become part of a structural frame.

Corner blocks will add considerable strength where, for example, legs and rails of tables and chairs meet. They are usually triangular in shape and are attached with glue and screws. Figure 1-81A shows a corner block which is shaped to provide shoulders so the screws can be more easily driven. The same illustration shows a corner brace, which is often used in place of a block. It does not, however, supply the strength you get with a full block.

Workers who really care, and manufacturers of high quality pieces, will often design corner reinforcements as shown in Figure 1-81B. This kind of attention requires time and effort, but it is one hallmark of craftsmanship. The hanger bolt shown is a standard item and may be tightened at any time should components loosen.

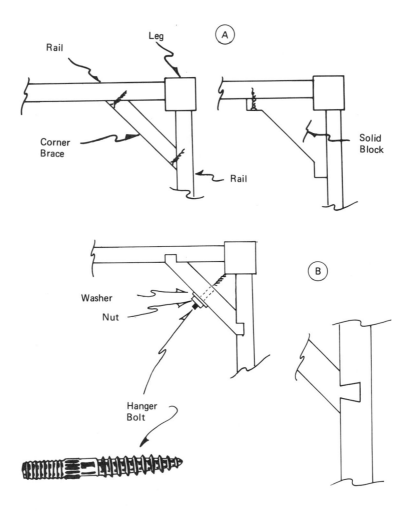

Figure 1-81. Corner blocks and braces do much to strengthen leg and rail assemblies.

Nuts and bolts (Figure 1-82) don't play a heavy role in furniture assemblies, but they can be useful in heavy, utility-type constructions because they have more strength than wood screws. They are a good choice for projects like outdoor furniture which you might want to disassemble for storage. Bolts do not thread into the wood, but pass through full-size shank holes. A good choice for wood assemblies is called a carriage bolt. These have oval or round heads that are not unattractive, and have a square shoulder underneath. The shoulder bites into the wood, preventing the bolt from turning when you tighten the nut.

Lag screws may be viewed as a combination wood screw and bolt. They are heavy-duty fasteners available with either square or hexagonal heads. Most times they are used in heavy constructions, but occasionally they can serve to add strength to furniture projects. The example assembly in Figure 1-83 shows a lag screw used to reinforce what would otherwise be a weak connection—end grain on the stretcher to surface grain on the rail. The lag screw was later hidden with a wooden rosette.

Figure 1-82. Nuts and bolts can be used on rough work and on projects you may wish to disassemble.

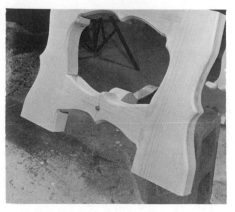

Figure 1-83. A lag screw was used to strengthen the joint. Later, a wooden rosette covered it.

T-nut   T-nut in use

Figure 1–84. The prongs on the flange of a Tee-Nut dig into the wood and keep the item from turning.

Tee-Nuts (Figure 1-84) should be used when you want to provide steel threads in wood to pull parts together with a machine screw or to make an assembly you can break down. The units are installed in holes that are drilled to match the outside diameter of the barrel. The prongs on the flange grip the wood when the Tee-Nut is pressed into place. They may be surface- or flush-mounted depending on whether you counterbore the hole to accommodate the flange.

Inserts, like the one shown in Figure 1-85, do a similar job, but can be used in blind, as well as through holes. Installation requires a hole that is the same size as the body diameter of the insert. Since the threads on the unit are designed as "knife threads" to cut into wood, the insert may be driven home with an ordinary screwdriver.

Both the Tee-Nut and inserts come in various sizes that may be used with standard machine screws or bolts.

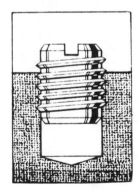

Figure 1–85. Threaded inserts form their own threads when they are driven into a hole with a screwdriver.

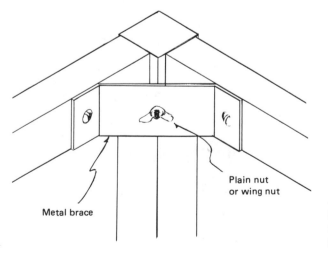

Plain nut
or wing nut

Metal brace

Figure 1–86. Ready-made metal braces are available for use in place of corner blocks.

There are many types of ready-made metal fasteners or reinforcement items that are usable to strengthen furniture joints. The one shown in Figure 1-86 is a reasonable substitute for a handmade corner block or brace. Some of these are made with end flanges bent to fit kerfs cut into the rails.

The chair brace shown in Figure 1-87 is usually thought of as a repair piece to stiffen wobbly assemblies, but there is no reason why it can't also be used on new work to reinforce the basic joint.

Figure 1-87. A chair brace, often used for repair work, may be used on new work as well.

Corner braces (Figure 1-88) and mending plates (Figure 1-89) are typical of the many pieces of hardware specially designed to strengthen simple joints. For example, they can be used on end-to-end joints or frame joints that are just butted together. Either can be surface mounted or set flush with wood surfaces by providing a mortise.

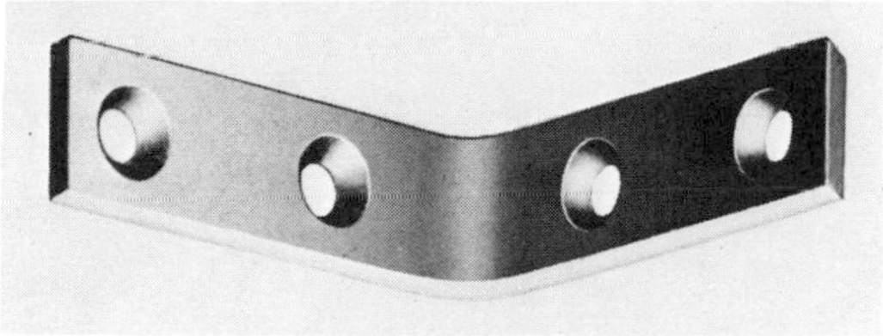

Figure 1-88. Metal corner irons are available in many sizes and in different materials like steel and brass.

Figure 1-89. Mending plates also come in different sizes and materials.

A new product in reinforcement hardware, shown in Figure 1-90, is a three-surface corner brace. The unit is steel, one piece, and bent so it will fit inside corners perfectly.

Figure 1-90. The three-surface corner brace is a new product in reinforcement hardware.

HIDING EDGES

Hiding edges applies mostly to projects made of plywood or to assemblies of various materials that will be covered with a wood or plastic laminate veneer. While the joints in the project must be strong, they do not have to be visually attractive since they will be covered anyway. Take, for example, the simple bookcase assembly shown in Figure 1-91. Lumber and plywood are combined; joints are rabbets and dadoes reinforced with glue, screws and nails. As is, it is not an example of prime workmanship, but it is as strong as it must be to do its job. When the unit is covered with a plastic laminate as is being done with a panel in Figure 1-92, or with a wood veneer, no one will know what joints were used. The durability of the joints will be their real test.

Figure 1-91. Combining different materials but providing strong joints is okay when you plan to add a cover material.

Figure 1-92. Plastic laminates are often used to cover assemblies like the one in the previous illustration.

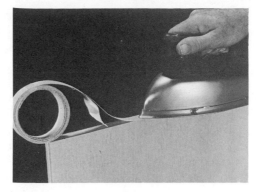

Figure 1-93. Some self-adhesive flexible edge-bands may be attached with the heat from an electric iron.

Plywood edges on any project can be covered with flexible bands of veneer. Some of these are self-adhesive, some require application with contact cement. Others have an adhesive coating that is activated when heated by an ordinary household pressing iron (Figure 1-93).

One of the problems with flexible edge-bands is that the grain runs longitudinally and this will match the run of the surface grain on only two edges. Many craftsmen will make their own veneer tapes by working along the lines shown in Figure 1-94. The cut is made to separate the surface veneer from the body of the plywood. A second cut removes the strip which is then applied to the panel's edge with contact cement. Note the same grain direction on both the surface and edge of the sample panel.

An excellent way to make a plywood joint is to use the "waterfall" technique shown in Figure 1-95. We'll show this in more detail later, but essentially, the idea is to remove a *V*-shaped piece from the panel so the surface piece and the edge piece as shown in the illustration, which originally were adjacent to each other, can be reassembled to form a 90-degree joint with minimum disruption of the grain flow.

Figure 1-94. Cutting a strip of surface veneer makes a band with matching grain direction.

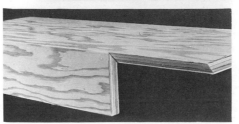

Figure 1-95. The "waterfall" joint lets the grain pattern flow smoothly over the edge.

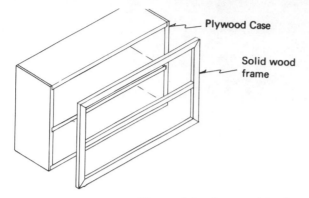

Plywood Case

Solid wood frame

Figure 1-96. A solid wood front hides the joints and the edges of the plywood.

Plywood is often used in the construction of wall-hung cabinets and similar projects. In such cases the *appearance* of the joints is not critical since a solid wood framing, like the one shown in Figure 1-96, can be used to cover frame edges and joint lines.

Some ideas for hiding edges when plywood is used as a slab for table tops or chests are shown in Figure 1-97. Note that some of the designs provide a lip, and bulk the edge so the panel will appear to be heavier.

Figure 1-97. Plywood edges may be concealed by using any of the methods shown here.

Figure 1-98. Typical of the round projects you can make by cutting and bevel-joining flat boards.

44

When you cut X number of segments at a particular joint angle, the pieces will assemble to form a circle. This leads to the construction of the barrel-type furniture shown in Figure 1-98. The cuts required are simple bevels, but accuracy is critical because of the number of joints involved. If you have a slight error on each of 24 pieces, imagine what the total error will be.

Segments can be cut consecutively from boards as shown in Figure 1-99A and they are assembled as shown in B of the same illustration. The narrower the segments and the more of them there are, the closer the assembly will come to being a true circle (Figure 1-99C).

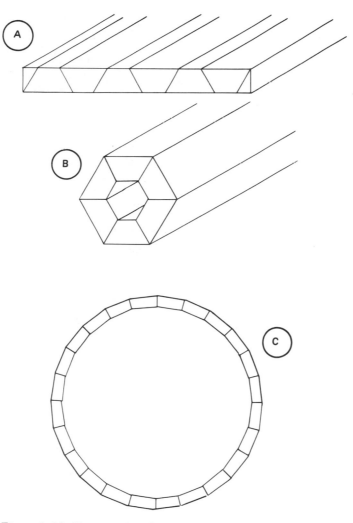

Figure 1-99. The more beveled segments you have and the narrower they are, the closer to a true circle you get.

The arithmetic is shown in Figure 1-100. It is important to understand that the cut-angle for the joints is one-half the included angle of the segments. Since segment joinery is important in many areas of woodworking, we'll go into it more deeply in a special chapter.

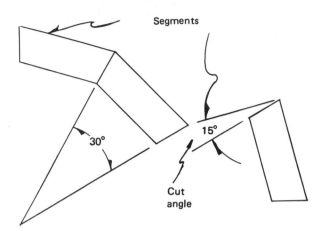

Use this formula to determine
the cut angle on each segment:

1. Decide on number of segments.
2. Divide 360 (number of degrees in
   a circle) by the number of
   segments.
3. Divide the answer by two.

EXAMPLE (for 24 segments)

$$\frac{360}{24} = 15$$

$15 \div 2 = 7\frac{1}{2}$ (the cut angle)

Figure 1-100. The arithmetic you should know to cut beveled segments accurately.

Chapter 2

BUTT JOINTS

Simple butt joints are classified as the weakest of the wood joints and are often shunned because they leave end grain exposed. Study the examples in Figure 2-1 and you will see that the joint supplies minimum contact area and that often, one surface is end grain. This does not contribute much strength in a glue joint.

In appearance the joint leaves little to be desired, since merely butting parts together results in the least amount of joint line. Even the cross-miter, while it does conceal end grain, has a longer joint line than the butt when the pieces are viewed from the front. A front view of a butt joint when compared with, for example, a dado or a rabbet, leaves no doubt about which joint looks better.

Many craftsmen and manufacturers will treat an end butt as shown in Figure 2-2. The idea will be successful only if the end grain is sanded and sealed sufficiently so it can be stained and polished for a slick look. The shallow kerf is sometimes added as a decorative detail. Be sure to keep the depth of the kerf shallow so you don't drastically reduce contact areas. The end grain of close-grained wood like maple or birch will not be difficult to treat in the manner described, but open-grained wood like oak will require more careful attention.

GRAIN DIRECTION

The grain direction of mating parts of all joints has a bearing on strength and appearance, but it is especially important with joints like the end butt. Dimensional changes along the length of a board, that is, *with* the grain don't occur enough to cause problems. Changes in the width of a board, *across* the grain, can actually be measured. That is why the grain direction of pieces joined in an end butt should be planned as shown in Figure 2-3. Hopefully, any change that does occur will be the same in both pieces. If a change happens in only one piece, the joint will be weakened and the part may split.

47

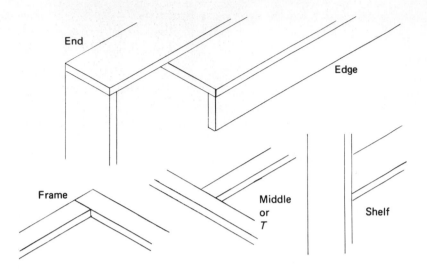

Figure 2-1. Types of butt joints.

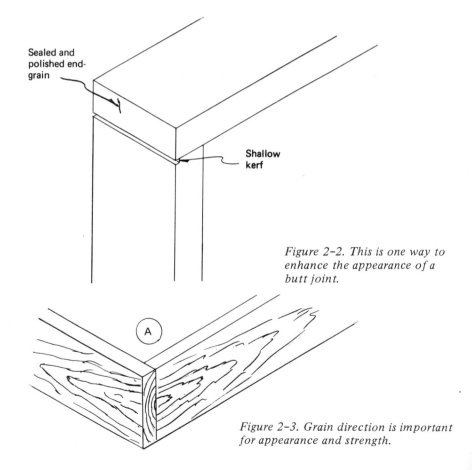

Figure 2-2. This is one way to enhance the appearance of a butt joint.

Figure 2-3. Grain direction is important for appearance and strength.

Take special precautions when you coat the end grain with glue. A good procedure is to dilute a small amount of glue and use it as a sizing. Check how much the wood soaks up and apply a second coat if necessary before using full-strength glue to do the final assembly.

REINFORCEMENT

Butt joints will be much stronger if they are reinforced in addition to being glued. The most common techniques involve nails, screws or dowels (Figure 2-4). Nails driven at an angle will hold much better than those hammered straight in. Drill a small pilot hole for the nail, at least through the part being attached, if needed to avoid splitting.

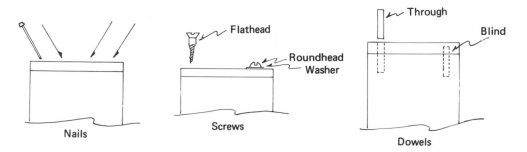

Figure 2-4. The basic methods of reinforcing end butt joints.

Screws can be used but they don't grip as well in end grain as they do in cross-grain. Choose a longer screw than you would ordinarily use and try working with a smaller lead hole than is technically correct. Figure 2-5 demonstrates how to decrease the weakness of screw threads in end grain. When the joint is organized as shown, the screws will bite into the cross-grain of the dowel, increasing their holding power considerably.

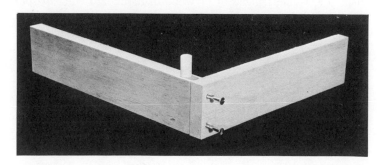

Figure 2-5. Screws in end grain will grip as they should if a dowel is installed as shown here.

Dowels can be used when the appearance of nails or screws is not acceptable. As shown in Figure 2-4, the dowels may be through or blind. The holes for the through dowels will be easier to do. Alignment will be exact if you hold or clamp the parts together and drill through both at the same time. When you work this way, be sure to disassemble the parts after drilling to clean out wood chips before applying glue and putting the parts together permanently.

Flat corner irons (Figure 2-6) can be added to increase strength. These are often thought of as mending materials or for use on utility or rough projects where appearance is not important. But they can also be used effectively on showpieces such as a well-executed open case painted white, and with corner irons finished in a flat black. The additional pieces add strength and contribute to appearance as well. As the illustration shows, the irons may be surface-mounted or set flush in a mortise.

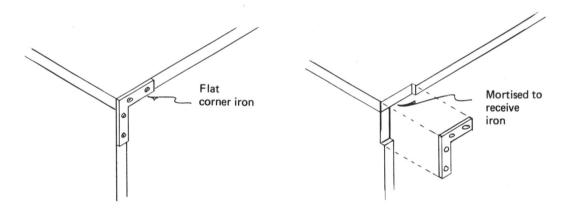

Flat
corner iron

Mortised to
receive
iron

Figure 2-6. Flat corner irons will add strength and can serve as decorative details.

One of the disadvantages of a butt joint is its weakness under lateral stress (Figure 2-7). Gusset plates will fight this if the purpose of the project permits their use. Gussets made of plywood or hardboard will not split and so will be more durable than any made from lumber. A one-piece back, placed on an open case (Figure 2-8) acts like gussets to combat lateral stresses.

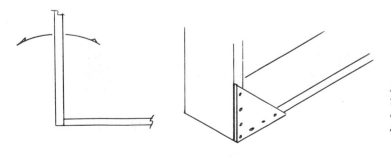

Figure 2-7. Gussets pre-vent failure that can be caused by lateral stresses.

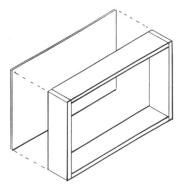

Figure 2-8. A one-piece back adds much rigidity to a simple case assembly.

GLUE BLOCKS AND STRIPS

Butt joints on plywood, whether the material is thick or thin (Figure 2-9), should always be reinforced to strengthen the glue joint. Follow the procedure already outlined for sizing end grain with thinned glue whenever a plywood edge is involved in a joint. On thin stock it's better to have a full-length reinforcement strip instead of individual glue blocks or corner irons (Figure 2-10).

Glue blocks will do a better job of pulling pieces together if you follow the installation procedure shown in Figure 2-11. The block is put in place with heavy paper or thin cardboard between it and the part that will be pulled in. The paper is removed after the block is secured with the first set of screws. The gap that remains lets the second set of screws pull the vertical piece tightly into place.

Glue blocks may be used on the outside of a joint (Figure 2-12) if conventional placement interferes with interior constructions.

Figure 2-9. Butt joints on plywood should always be reinforced. Use full-length glue blocks on thin material.

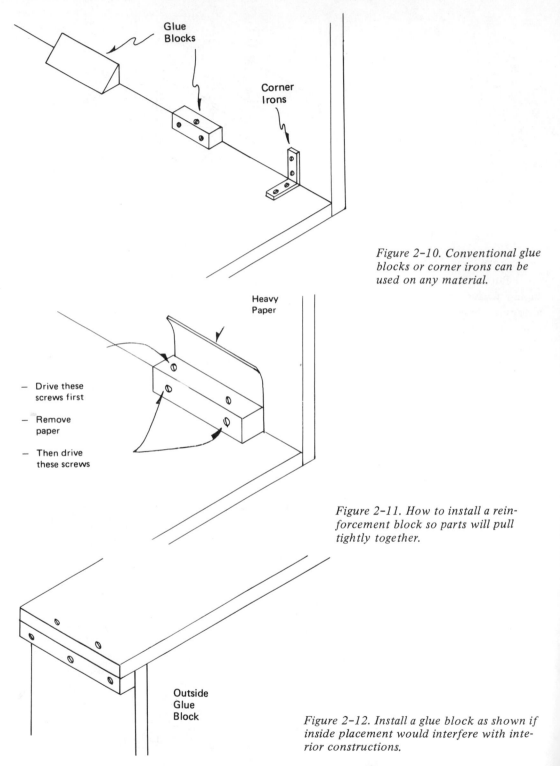

Glue
Blocks

Corner
Irons

Figure 2-10. Conventional glue blocks or corner irons can be used on any material.

Heavy
Paper

— Drive these screws first

— Remove paper

— Then drive these screws

Figure 2-11. How to install a reinforcement block so parts will pull tightly together.

Outside
Glue
Block

Figure 2-12. Install a glue block as shown if inside placement would interfere with interior constructions.

Shelf joints will be very weak unless cleats, which act like glue blocks (Figure 2-13) are added to provide support. The cleat may be fastened to the side and the shelf or to only the side if the shelf will be removable. Shelf joints may be reinforced with any of the methods that were shown for end butts (Figure 2-14).

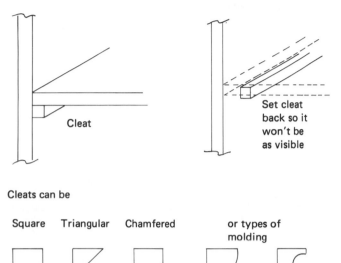

Figure 2-13. Cleats are used to reinforce shelf butts. Make them or use commercial moldings.

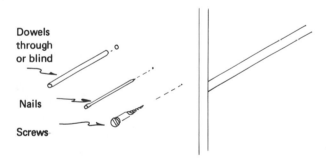

Figure 2-14. Dowels, nails, or screws may also be used to reinforce shelf butts.

FRAME BUTTS

Frame butts are reinforced by using the techniques shown in Figure 2-15. Corrugated nails are available in different sizes so you can choose the one that will work the best for the thickness of the material being used. Be sure the parts are clamped firmly together before you drive the nails. It's best to use one or two nails, depending on the width of the stock, on each side.

Both the through dowel and the dowel placed at an angle should be in-

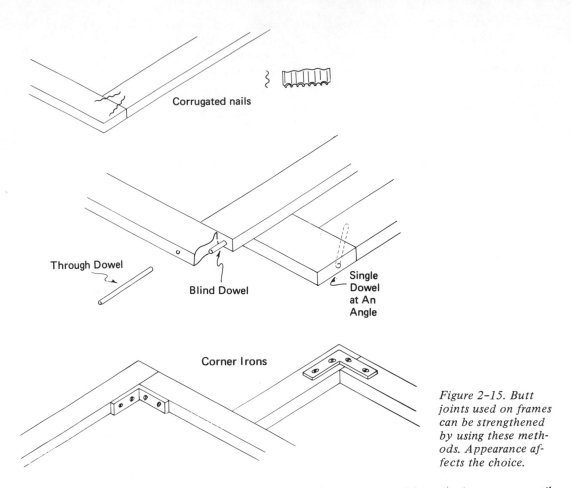

Corrugated nails

Through Dowel

Blind Dowel

Single Dowel at An Angle

Corner Irons

Figure 2-15. Butt joints used on frames can be strengthened by using these methods. Appearance affects the choice.

serted with the frame parts under clamp pressure. Maintain the pressure until the glue is dry.

The joints shown are used in many situations that call for a hollow core panel (Figure 2-16).

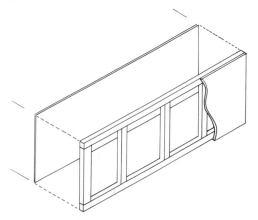

Figure 2-16. Reinforced butt joints will make a strong frame for a hollow core panel.

54

Reinforcement methods for middle or *T* butts are shown in Figure 2-17. How you design, and this applies to all types and variations of joints, depends on what the project will be used for and the general quality of the construction.

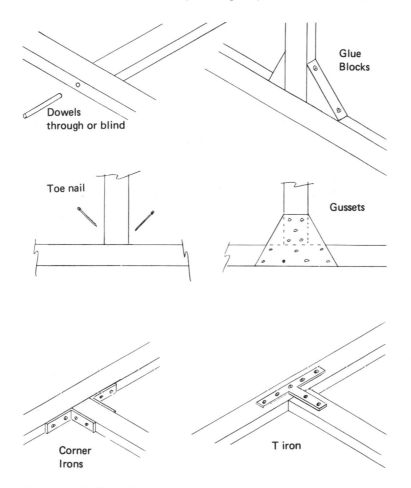

Figure 2-17. Methods you can use to reinforce a T or middle butt joint.

HIDING THE JOINT

Two methods of hiding the joint are shown in Figure 2-18 with covers that can be homemade. The piece in **A** is a square block with one chamfered edge; the piece in **B** is a strip that was rabbeted to fit the corner. Attach parts like this with glue and brads, or small finishing nails that can be set and then hidden with wood dough. There are various types of commercial moldings that can be used in place of pieces you make yourself.

55

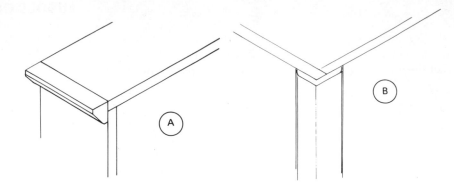

Figure 2-18. Two ways to hide a joint. You can make the pieces or use commercial moldings.

This kind of detail may add to the appearance of the project, but the parts should not be viewed as structural members even though they might contribute some reinforcement. The strength of the union must be in the joint itself.

INTERLOCKS

The example shown in Figure 2-19 is an assembly of butt joints which is quite strong because of the way the parts are put together. Notice that the nails, or screws if you choose to use them, that secure one piece do not interfere with those in the adjacent part.

The placement of fasteners does deserve some attention, especially on assemblies like the one shown in Figure 2-20. A careless layout can cause one fastener to act as a stop for another if it is driven at a right angle to the first one. Nails might slip by each other but they might also be diverted to the surface and cause damage.

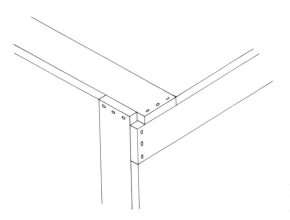

Figure 2-19. Butt joints, organized this way, make a strong corner assembly.

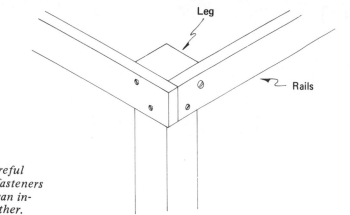

Figure 2-20. Be careful with layout when fasteners in adjacent pieces can interfere with each other.

Chapter 3

DADOES AND GROOVES

Dadoes and grooves are *U*-shaped cuts formed in one piece to receive the butt end of another component. The terms are often used interchangeably even though technically a dado is made *across* the grain and a groove is made *with* the grain (Figure 3-1). Many times, the act of forming a groove is called ploughing. The width of the cut matches the thickness of the insert; the cut depth is usually about one-half the thickness of the stock. It can be less, but going deeper may cause a weakness in the area.

The width of the cut should permit a nice, sliding fit for the insert (Figure 3-2). A forced fit can create stresses in the area and will interfere with assembly procedures. When you find the cut you have made does not permit an easy assembly, take the time to adjust it by wrapping a sheet of fine sandpaper around a suitable block of wood and using it as shown in Figure 3-3.

A major advantage of the joint is obvious when you compare it with a simple butt joint. Contact area is increased and so there is more surface for glue. The shape of the joint supplies a supporting ledge. This is an advantage when the insert will be, for example, a shelf. A disadvantage is the visible joint lines (Figure 3-4).

HIDING THE JOINT

There are techniques to use when you need the strength of the dado joint but want to eliminate the unattractive appearance. This objection is automatically eliminated if the case is designed with a front frame (or faceplate trim), as shown in Figure 3-5.

When trim is not used, and attractive appearance is wanted, you can use shelves that are wider than the case sides so they project at the front, as shown in Figure 3-6. This does not remove the joint lines, but they become less visible because the eye is attracted to the shelf instead. Note that the front edge of the insert can be treated in various ways. In addition to creating a form on the part itself you can add things like a solid strip of wood or a suitable molding. The latter methods should be used when the shelf is plywood.

58

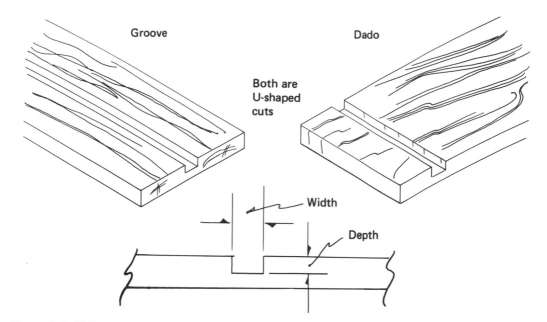

Groove

Dado

Both are
U-shaped
cuts

Width

Depth

Figure 3–1. U-shaped cuts across the grain are dadoes; with the grain, they are called grooves.

Figure 3–2. Inserted pieces should slide smoothly into place.

Figure 3–3. How to adjust when the dado width makes the joint too tight. Use very fine sandpaper.

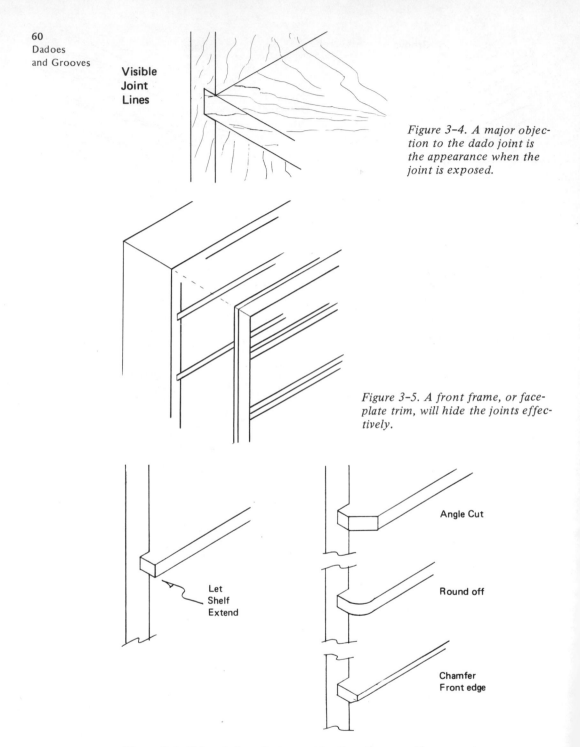

**Visible
Joint
Lines**

Figure 3-4. A major objection to the dado joint is the appearance when the joint is exposed.

Figure 3-5. A front frame, or faceplate trim, will hide the joints effectively.

Let
Shelf
Extend

Angle Cut

Round off

Chamfer
Front edge

Figure 3-6. Using shelves that are wider than the case sides serves to keep the eye away from the joint lines.

An alternative and very common method is to form a "stopped" dado. As shown in Figure 3-7, the *U*-cut does not run completely across the board so there are no visible joint lines. The inserts may be cut narrower than the case sides as in A, or they may be notched as in B.

The technique, done as shown, requires some handwork with chisels so the dado will be square where it is stopped. If you work with power tools you can eliminate some time and effort by designing the dado as shown in Figure 3-8. The power tool, since it cuts with a circular blade, will leave a radius at the end of the cut. The insert piece can be shaped as in A or B to fit.

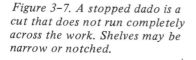

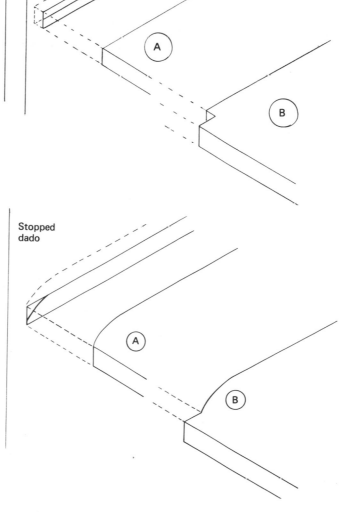

Figure 3-7. A stopped dado is a cut that does not run completely across the work. Shelves may be narrow or notched.

Figure 3-8. A stopped dado done on a power tool leaves a radius. Shelves can be shaped to match.

REINFORCEMENT

Quite often, especially when the shelf is solid lumber, it is not secured in the dado at all. This permits possible dimensional changes that might be caused by variations in moisture content to occur without damage. If reinforcements are included they can be the same as those used with a butt joint (Figure 3-9). If nails or screws are used, they can be added unobtrusively as shown in Figure 3-9A.

Loose shelves do not add much to the rigidity of a project. If they are installed loosely, the joints in the case itself become more critical since the unit must be strong enough to stand on its own.

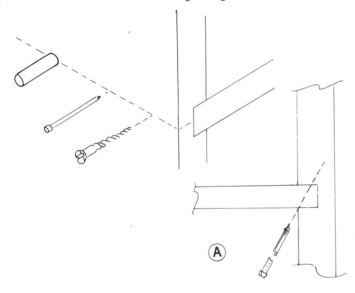

Figure 3-9. Methods of reinforcement for a dado joint. Nails or screws will be secrets if driven as in A.

CUTTING WITH HAND TOOLS

In cutting with hand tools, first make a careful layout with a square, marking lines across the stock and down both edges. A good procedure is to mark one line with the square and then to place the insert on the line so you can use its opposite edge as a guide for marking the second line. This will tell the exact width of the dado you need.

Make shoulder cuts first by using a backsaw as shown in Figure 3-10. The block of wood clamped to the saw acts as a depth gauge and assures that the shoulder cuts will be level. Remove the waste by using a chisel (Figure 3-11), working mostly from the edges toward the center and removing thinner shavings the closer you get to the bottom of the groove.

Another way to remove the waste is to work with a router plane (Figure 3-12), but do not set the cutter to the full depth of the groove right off. It's better to make a few shallow cuts than a single deep one. Often, the bulk of the waste is removed with a hand chisel and the job is finished with the plane.

Figure 3-10. Shoulder cuts made with a backsaw will be more accurate and of correct depth if a stop block is used.

Figure 3-11. Clean out the waste between the shoulder cuts by working with a sharp chisel.

Figure 3-12. A router plane will clean out the waste, but do the job in stages. Deep cuts lead to inaccuracies.

Stopped cuts can be formed by hand but you must first form a square cavity as indicated by the arrow in Figure 3-13. This can be all chisel work or you can bore blind holes to remove the bulk of the waste and then clean out with a chisel. The remainder of the job is done in routine fashion—shoulder cuts with a backsaw and waste removal with a chisel or the router plane.

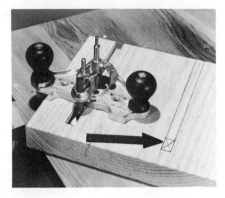

Figure 3-13. To do a stopped dado with hand tools, form a square cavity first.

POWER TOOL WORK

U-shaped cuts can be made quickly and precisely on a table saw (Figure 3-14) or a radial arm saw (Figure 3-15). The cuts shown, being across the grain, are dadoes. Figure 3-16 shows how a groove is formed on a radial arm saw. On a table saw, the rip fence is used as a gauge to set the distance from the cut to the edge of the stock.

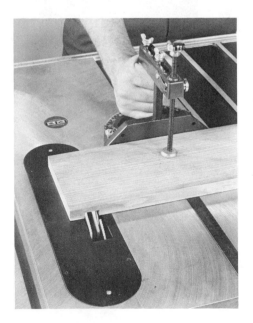

Figure 3-14. Forming a dado on a table saw. A miter gauge hold-down will help keep the work secure.

Figure 3-15. *Doing a dado on a radial arm saw.*

Figure 3-16. *A groove is done on the radial arm saw by securing the motor as shown.*

Quick and accurate work is possible because of special tools that are used in place of the conventional saw blade. A common one is known as a dado set or assembly (Figure 3-17) and consists of two outside blades and a number of chippers. Using one or more of the chippers between the blades lets you control the width of the cut. Quite often, since there is some variation in stock thicknesses, paper washers are used along with the chippers to bring the cut width to a precise dimension.

A similar tool is an adjustable dado and usually consists of a single, heavy blade mounted on a hub which is rotated to adjust for width-of-cut. Since the settings are infinite between minimum and maximum the tool can be organized to match exactly the thickness of any stock within its capacity.

Dado tools remove a lot of material so very deep cuts should not be made in a single pass regardless of the tool you use. Several cuts, with a depth adjustment after each, will make the job easier and will result in smoother, more accurate work.

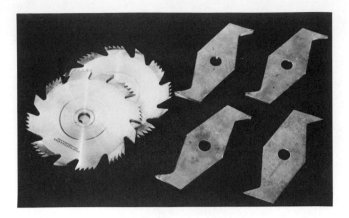

Figure 3-17. A dado set or assembly consists of two outside blades and a set of chippers.

Back-to-back dadoes are often required, as with a case with shelves that has an intermediate vertical member. This kind of work can be done to careful layout, but it's always better to construct a jig that will help handle the work and will make accuracy automatic. An example for use on a table saw is shown in Figure 3-18. The guide is held to the work with clamps and rides the edge of the table. After the cut is made on one side of the stock, the piece is flipped over and the opposite dado is cut. The position of the guide controls the distance between the cuts, but you must be sure to situate the work carefully so the dadoes will be at right angles to the work edge.

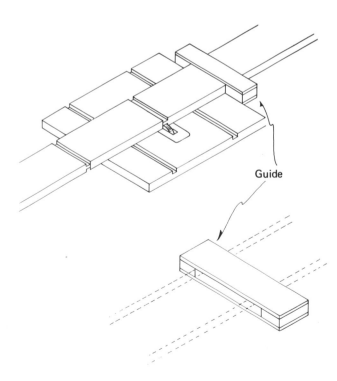

Guide

Figure 3-18. Here is a jig you can make to use when you need dadoes back-to-back.

Stopped dadoes are done on a radial arm saw as shown in Figure 3-19. The arrow points to the line which is marked on the work to tell how far forward to bring the cutter. Since the cut isn't visible on a table saw, the best procedure is to clamp a block of wood at the back of the table to act as a stop. The length of the cut would then be the distance from the forward edge of the stop block to the front edge of the cutter.

Figure 3-19. Stopped dadoes on a radial arm saw are done by moving the cutter to a line marked on the work.

CORNER DADOES

The corner dado is a *U*-shaped cut made across a corner of a furniture component. An example of where it can be used effectively is in the installation of a lower shelf on a table (Figure 3-20). The shape is accomplished routinely by making the shoulder cuts first (A) and then cleaning out the waste with a chisel (B). The corners of the insert piece are shaped to fit the dado cut. The addition of a dowel (C) will make the joint more secure.

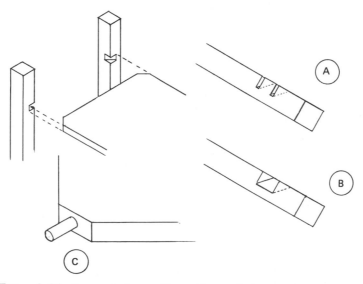

Figure 3-20. Corner dadoes will provide good support for a table shelf or shelves in open case work.

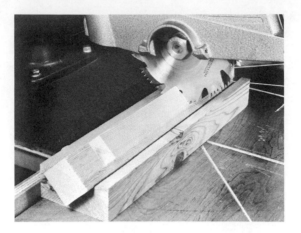

Figure 3-21. How to do corner dadoes on a radial arm saw.

Corner dadoes can be cut on power tools by using a method like the one shown in Figure 3-21. The base block, which has a *V*-cut down its center, supports the work and sets it in correct position for the cut.

OTHER METHODS

Dado sets are acceptable when you require many cuts, but if you need only one or two, the job can be accomplished with minimum fuss by making repeat passes with a regular saw blade (Figure 3-22). Mark the outline of the shape on the work and then make as many cuts as you need to remove the waste. Doing shoulder cuts first is a good idea.

Portable routers will form smooth, accurate dadoes and grooves but the operation must be organized to provide a guide for the tool. This can be, as shown in Figure 3-23, a straight piece of wood that is tack-nailed or clamped to the work, or you can use a commercial edge guide which is sold as an accessory for the tool.

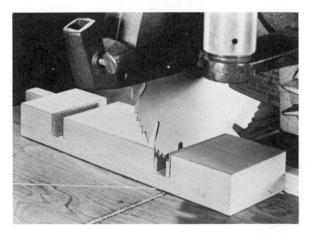

Figure 3-22. Dadoes or grooves can be formed by making repeat passes with a regular saw blade.

Figure 3-23. A portable router will make smooth, accurate cuts. The form at the end of the board is a rabbet.

Cutters should be the straight bit type like the one shown in Figure 3-24. This type of cutter may also be used on a drill press (Figure 3-25) but it's best to use an adapter that will take side thrust instead of the regular chuck. The arrow in the photograph shows the direction in which the work should be moved. The direction of rotation of the cutter will tend to keep the work snug against the fence. The same advice applies to the portable router even though you move the tool instead of the work. For example, in the setup shown in Figure 3-23, the pass should be made from left to right.

Figure 3-24. Straight bit cutters are used in a portable router to form U-shapes.

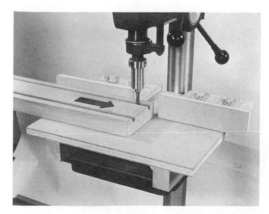

Figure 3-25. The same type of cutter may be used in a drill press. Use an adapter in place of the three-jaw chuck.

Most craftspeople are not aware that even a portable electric saw can be equipped with a special dado set that will form *U*-shaped cuts (Figure 3-26). The set is not available from the manufacturers of all saws and it may not even be suitable for a saw that you already own, so some checking is in order before you buy. The unit shown in the photograph is a Sears Roebuck product and while it is possible to mount it on non-Sears saws, you should proceed cautiously to be absolutely sure the setup will be safe. Read the instructions that come with the dado set before you make a purchase.

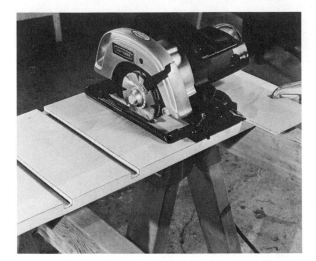

Figure 3-26. This is an unusual job for a portable saw, but practical if the special dado set can be used on the tool you own.

A new tool, called the Electrichisel® (Figure 3-27) can be used with a portable electric drill to form dadoes and grooves. It comes in 3/4-inch and 1/2-inch sizes but should not be used at speeds under 1700 rpms or over 3600 rpms. In all situations a guide strip (Figure 3-28) is essential to keep the tool from chattering or jumping. A small booklet comes with the tool and describes in detail how to use the unit to do mortises and rabbets in addition to *U*-shaped cuts.

Figure 3-27. The Electrichisel® is a new tool that can be used in a portable electric drill.

Figure 3-28. Always work with a guide so you can control the tool easily. Follow instructions that come with the product.

Chapter 4

RABBET JOINTS

The *L*-shaped cut required to form a rabbet joint is made in one of the pieces to be joined. It is called a rabbet regardless of whether it is done *with* or *across* the grain (Figure 4-1). The width of the cut usually matches the thickness of the insert. The cut depth can be one-half to two-thirds the thickness of the part in which it is made.

A good technique that will result in trim, smooth surfaces at the joint line is shown in Figure 4-2. Cut the rabbet a bit wider than necessary so that after the parts are joined and the glue is dry you can sand off the excess to make the edge perfectly flush with the adjacent surface.

Sometimes, especially when the project material is plywood, the rabbet is so deep that only the surface veneer remains on the part (Figure 4-3). This conceals unattractive plywood edges but establishes a weak point at the base of the shoulder. If you work this way, be sure that the case as a whole will be strong. When possible, glue blocks or similar reinforcements should be added to increase strength.

TYPICAL APPLICATIONS

Rabbet joints are common in basic box and case constructions. Usually, it's better to form the *L*-shape in the side members so the partial end grain that still remains will not be so visible. Much depends on the use of the project; whether, for example, it will be wall-hung or freestanding. Decide which parts will have the rabbet cut in relation to how the project will be seen.

Most cases and cabinets that are back sealed will have rabbet cuts along back edges so the back panel can be inset (Figure 4-4). Cut the rabbet a bit deeper than the panel thickness requires. When the project will be wall-hung it's better to make the rabbet 1/4-inch to 1/2-inch deeper than necessary so the

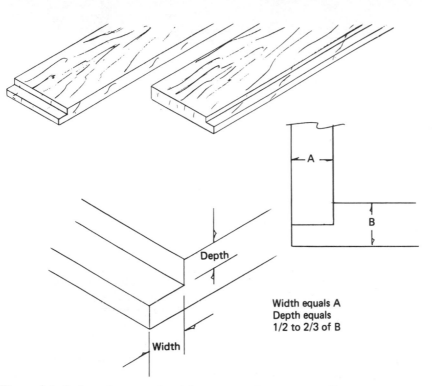

Figure 4–1. *L-shaped cuts made with or across the grain are called rabbets.*

Width equals A
Depth equals
1/2 to 2/3 of B

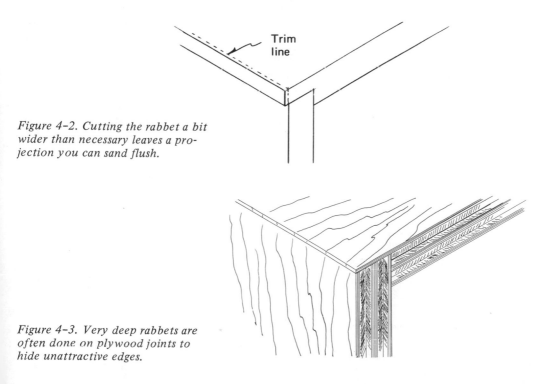

Figure 4–2. *Cutting the rabbet a bit wider than necessary leaves a projection you can sand flush.*

Trim
line

Figure 4–3. *Very deep rabbets are often done on plywood joints to hide unattractive edges.*

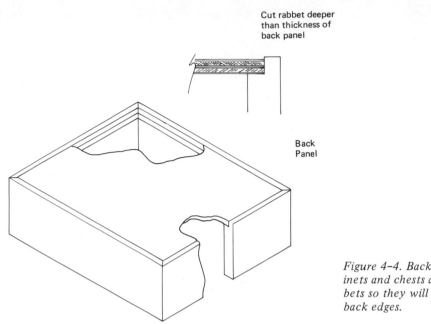

Cut rabbet deeper than thickness of back panel

Back Panel

Figure 4-4. Back panels of cabinets and chests are set in rabbets so they will be flush with back edges.

back edges of the cabinet can be trimmed to match irregularities in the wall.

A rabbet is often used as the front-to-sides joint in drawers. As you can see in Figure 4-5 the drawer side can be flush, or the rabbet can be cut wide enough so the drawer front will have a lip. This is not a very strong joint for its purpose if only glue is used. However, nails, screws, or wooden pegs driven through the side into the edge of the drawer front, will add considerable strength.

Rabbet cuts are often made in pieces that are added to a project to conceal a basic joint which might be another rabbet, a butt, or even a miter (Figure 4-6), or as additional adornment. When the latter objective is the motive the added pieces can be treated in various ways like the examples shown in Figure 4-7. Parts like this, when they are slight, do not add much strength and should

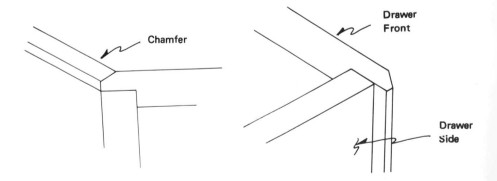

Chamfer

Drawer Front

Drawer Side

Figure 4-5. The joint that connects a drawer front and sides is often a rabbet. The joint should be reinforced.

74

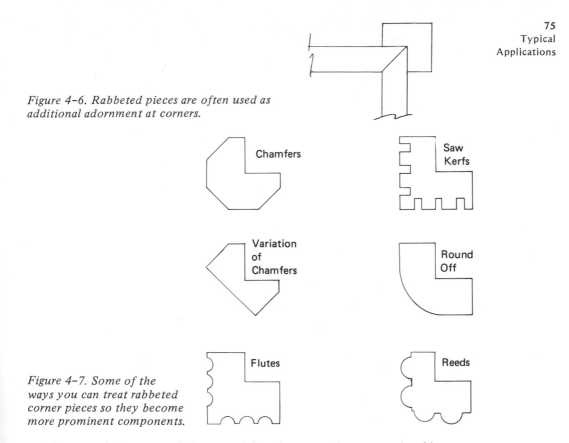

Figure 4-6. Rabbeted pieces are often used as additional adornment at corners.

Chamfers

Saw Kerfs

Variation of Chamfers

Round Off

Flutes

Reeds

Figure 4-7. Some of the ways you can treat rabbeted corner pieces so they become more prominent components.

not be viewed as structural elements. Often, however, they are made of heavy material and serve as panel framing, and can even extend below a case to act as legs or feet.

Rabbet cuts made in legs can serve as seats for rails as shown in Figure 4-8. Rabbet cuts that are a bit deeper than the insert piece will provide the shoulder indicated by A in the same illustration. This is a good way to use such assemblies, regardless of the type of joint used since any separation that might occur after the project has been in use will not be as visible as it would be if the parts were flush.

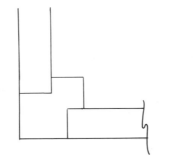
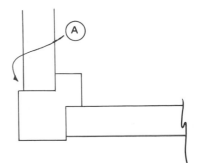

Figure 4-8. Rabbets are often formed to provide seats for other components. A setback (A) is a good idea.

Rabbet cuts formed in legs as seats for rails cannot, of course, run the full length of the leg. But rabbet cuts, like dadoes, can be "stopped" and we'll talk about the procedures a bit later.

FORMING WITH HAND TOOLS

Rabbets, especially short ones, can easily be formed by making two cuts with a saw as shown in Figure 4-9. First use the insert piece as a gauge to mark the width of the cut, adding, if you wish, the slight projection we talked about. Use a square to extend the guide lines down both edges and across the end of the stock. Work with a backsaw to make the shoulder cut using the same type of clamped-on guide described in Chapter 3 on dadoes. Then make a second cut to remove the waste. Accuracy is important, so careful sawing is in order. Some craftspeople will work with chisels to remove the waste after the shoulder cut is made with a saw. This is an option. Both methods are satisfactory if the results are acceptable.

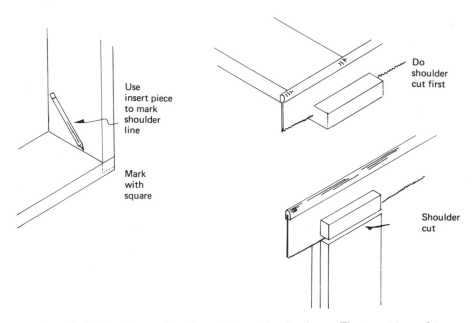

Use
insert piece
to mark
shoulder
line

Mark
with
square

Do
shoulder
cut first

Shoulder
cut

Figure 4-9. Forming a rabbet by cutting with a backsaw. The insert is used to mark the basic cut line.

Long rabbets, whether they are with or across the grain, are easier to form if you work with a rabbet plane (Figure 4-10). This is a special tool that is equipped with a fence to control the width of the cut and with a stop that is set to control its depth.

The plane will do its job precisely only if you use it correctly. Be sure to work so the fence on the tool is snug against the side of the work throughout

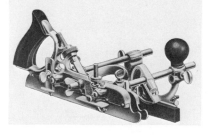

Figure 4-10. A rabbet plane provides gauges to control the width and the depth of the cut.

the pass (Figure 4-11). Adjust the projection of the blade so you have to make several passes to achieve full depth-of-cut. A few passes and good results is a better combination than a single cut and poor work.

The plane is equipped with a spur that severs surface fibers in front of the cutter when you are working across the grain. Be sure to set the spur correctly, as per instructions that come with the tool, to avoid the splintering and feathering that will result if the spur isn't precutting as it should.

Figure 4-11. Keep the plane's fence snug against the work throughout the pass.

POWER TOOL WORK

A rabbet can be cut on a table saw by using a two-pass technique, which is about the same as the procedure described for a backsaw. As shown in Figure 4-12, the shoulder cut is made with the work flat and with the rip fence used as a gauge. The width of the rabbet is measured from the *outside* surface of the blade to the fence. The saw-blade projection matches the depth of the rabbet. Remove the waste by making a second pass with the stock on edge as shown. The saw-blade projection is adjusted to match the width of the cut; the fence is set to control the depth. Do not make the second pass so the waste will be captured between the blade and the fence since this can result in a kickback.

A dado assembly can be used to form rabbets in a single pass as shown in Figure 4-13. If the setup shown is used, an auxiliary wooden fence must be

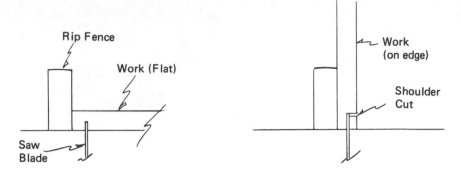

Figure 4-12. Two passes done this way on a table saw will produce a rabbet cut.

Figure 4-13. The job can be done in a single pass if you work with a dado set.

attached to the regular rip fence so the cutter won't damage the machine. The hold-downs, which are extra-cost accessories, increase safety on this and similar jobs, and help to keep the work stable for smoother cuts. Another way to do the job is to situate the fence so cuts are made on the free edge of the stock. This technique can be used without an extra wooden fence.

Rabbets that are too wide for a single pass with a dado can be accomplished by making repeat passes. An example being done on a radial arm saw is shown in Figure 4-14.

Another way to do clean, accurate rabbets is to work on a jointer as shown in Figure 4-15. Most jointers are equipped with a rabbeting ledge that makes this application possible. Set the fence on the machine to gauge the width of the cut. Lower the infeed table so you get the depth you want. Be aware that on such operations you can't use the machine's guard in normal fashion. This calls for extra careful work. A combination pusher hold-down, like the homemade one shown in the illustration, is a must.

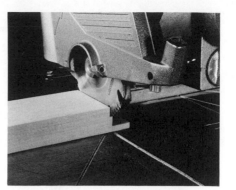

Figure 4-14. Make repeat passes if the rabbet is wider than the maximum setting of the dado set. Here, the job is being done on a radial arm saw.

Figure 4-15. Using a jointer to form a rabbet. Work with a pusher hold-down like the homemade one shown.

Figure 4-16 shows a rabbet being formed with a portable router. The bit has its own pilot which rides the edge of the work so no other guide is needed. When straight bits are used, like those which were shown in Chapter 3 on dadoes, a wood strip can be clamped to the work as a guide for the tool, or you can equip the router with an edge guide.

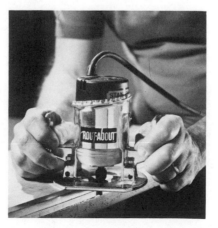

Figure 4-16. Forming a rabbet with a portable router. The pilot on the cutter rides the edge of the stock.

Figure 4-17. A cutter designed specifically for forming rabbets. The ball bearing pilot eliminates burning on edges.

The cutter shown in Figure 4-17 is specially designed for forming rabbets. The blades are carbide-tipped and the pilot is a ball bearing which turns independently of the cutter's shank. This eliminates the burning that can occur when an integral pilot is riding the edge of the stock.

The Electrichisel®, which was shown forming a dado, can also be organized to shape a rabbet. As shown in Figure 4-18, the work and a guide for the tool must be securely clamped.

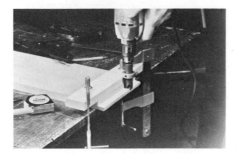

Figure 4-18. An Electrichisel®, driven by a portable drill, is used this way to form a rabbet.

STOPPED RABBETS

The procedure to follow for stopped rabbets is pretty much the same as the one described for stopped dadoes. The end of the cut, where the rabbet stops, is formed with a chisel and the balance of the job is done with a saw or a rabbet plane (Figure 4-19). For this work, the blade of the plane is set in the forward or "bullnose" position.

Figure 4-19. The arrow points to the notch that should be formed with chisels when a stopped rabbet is required.

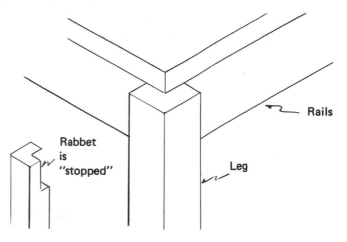

Figure 4-20. Typical application of a stopped rabbet. It forms a seat for the rails.

Short, stopped rabbets, often called notches, can be used in the type of joint shown in Figure 4-20. The shape probably can be formed just as easily with a backsaw and chisels as it can in any other way, but often, a router or a power saw equipped with a dado set is used to form the bulk of the cut, and the corner is cleaned out with a chisel.

You can fake a stopped rabbet by making the cut full length and then blocking one end with a filler as shown in Figure 4-21. This might reduce the effort involved for doing the job right but it also increases the number of visible joint lines and, depending on how the filler is cut, can create opposing grain patterns.

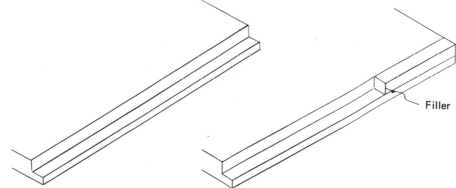

Figure 4-21. A full-length rabbet which is end-blocked with a filler becomes a stopped rabbet.

ANGLED RABBETS

Angled rabbets, like those shown in Figure 4-22, are used when adjacent parts do not make a 90-degree turn. Notice that the shoulders of the rabbet still form a right angle even though the form itself is not square to edges or surfaces.

A typical application is shown in Figure 4-23 where rabbeted connectors

81

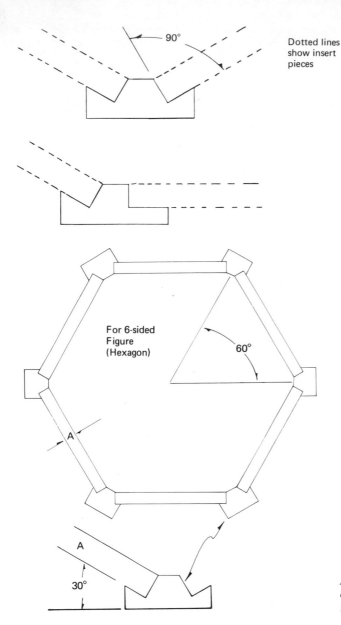

90°

Dotted lines
show insert
pieces

*Figure 4-22. Angled rabbets may
be used to join parts that do not
make a 90-degree turn.*

For 6-sided
Figure
(Hexagon)

60°

A

A

30°

*Figure 4-23. How angled rabbets in
connection pieces may be used to join
the parts of a segmented project.*

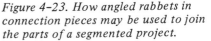

are used as joint parts in a segmented project. Many craftspeople find this technique easier to do than simple or splined miters, but a major reason for doing it this way is that the extra pieces provide a design element. Like the rabbeted corner pieces we have already talked about, these parts can be embellished with chamfers, reeds and other details.

One way to form angled rabbets is shown in Figure 4-24 where the job is being done on a radial arm saw that is equipped with a dado set. Once the setup is made, any number of similar pieces can be passed through; all cuts will be duplicates.

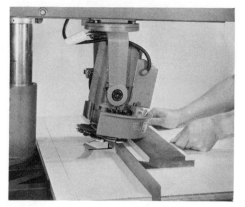

*Figure 4-24. How a radial arm saw
is organized to cut angled rabbets in
a single pass.*

Figure 4-25 shows how to work when many duplicate parts are needed.
Do the rabbeting in a long strip and then cut off as many pieces as you need for
the job. When the part you are working on is narrow, be sure you work with
ample guards and that you feed the stock with push sticks. Push sticks are easy
to replace. Your fingers are not.

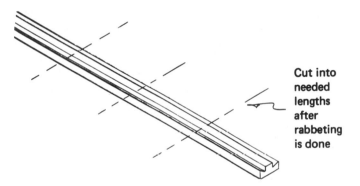

**Cut into
needed
lengths
after
rabbeting
is done**

*Figure 4-25. Procedure to follow when many similar pieces are
needed. Use push sticks instead of fingers when feeding narrow
stock.*

Chapter 5

MITER JOINTS

A well-executed miter joint is pleasing to the eye because it can leave a virtually unbroken grain line at the corner, and is revealed by only a fine line where the parts come together (Figure 5-1). Another advantage of the design is shown in Figure 5-2 where it is compared with a butt joint to show how it conceals unattractive end grain. This can be accomplished even when the mating parts have different widths as shown in Figure 5-3 by cutting miter angles that complement each other.

The best way to do this job accurately is to use a system that works regardless of the width of the pieces. Place one part on the other as shown in Figure 5-4A and make a mark where indicated. The cut line (Figure 5-4B) runs from the mark to the opposite corner. After the cut is made, the part is used as a pattern to mark the mating piece.

The simple miter, however, is not a very strong joint. For one thing, the mating surfaces of frame and cross miters are virtually end grain which doesn't contribute much to a strong glue bond. For another, the increase in contact surface, which is a variable that depends on the thickness and width of the stock, is not impressive. A comparison with a butt joint (Figure 5-5) bears this out. X is not much longer than Y. By actual measurement on a 10-inch board the difference is about four inches. On narrower pieces, which is usually the case with frame miters, the increase is, of course, much less.

Miter joints on projects like lightweight picture frames are usually done with glue and finishing nails. Heavier constructions, or any assembly you wish to make as durable as possible, call for more advanced reinforcement procedures. These often involve dowels or splines. Sometimes, as shown later, the joint is modified to include an interlock or to increase glue area.

ACCURACY IS CRITICAL

If the miter joint is to form a 90-degree corner, each of the cuts must be 45 degrees. Careless cutting can produce small mistakes that add up to an enormous error when you assemble the four sides of a frame, cabinet, or case. It will

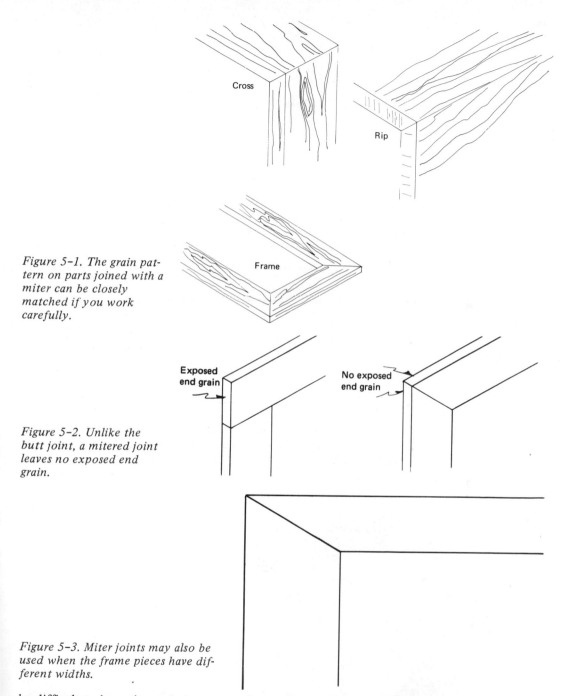

Figure 5-1. The grain pattern on parts joined with a miter can be closely matched if you work carefully.

Figure 5-2. Unlike the butt joint, a mitered joint leaves no exposed end grain.

Figure 5-3. Miter joints may also be used when the frame pieces have different widths.

be difficult to keep the project square and even if you manage it, there will be obvious gaps in the joint lines. The truth is, it's as easy to be accurate as not. Careful marking and careful cutting are not secret techniques. Don't assume, for example, that the settings you make on a power tool are precise. Make a cut on some scrap wood and check it carefully before you start cutting good stock.

85

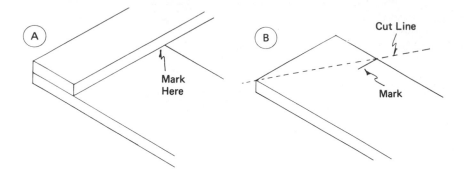

Figure 5-4. Use one of the parts this way to establish the cut line for the miter.

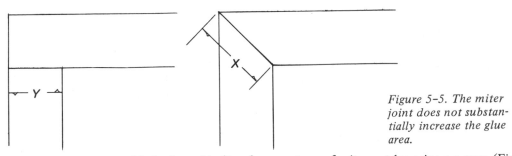

Figure 5-5. The miter joint does not substantially increase the glue area.

Mark the guide line for any type of miter cut by using a square (Figure 5-6). When the work is very wide and the blade of the tool isn't long enough for the line, remember that the diagonal of a square will form 45-degree angles with adjacent lines. By way of example, let's assume you need a 45-degree cut at the end of a piece of plywood 20 inches wide. Mark a line parallel to the end and 20 inches away. Connect opposite corners and you have a 45-degree guide line.

Figure 5-6. Miters must be cut accurately and the best way to start is with good layout procedures.

Marking a guide line gives you something to follow when you are sawing by hand, but it is also a check when you are power sawing. As shown in Figure 5-7, you will know immediately if the cut is accurate. Better to make adjustments when cutting than to realize the error at assembly time.

Whenever possible, especially when sawing by hand, set up a guide that will minimize the possibility of human error. This doesn't have to be a fancy arrangement. Just a straight strip of wood, clamped to the work as shown in Figure 5-8, will do. This will keep the saw on the cut line and will also help to achieve an edge that is square to surfaces.

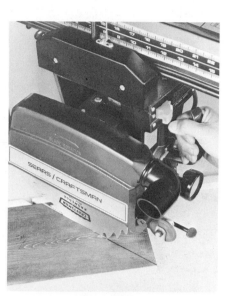

Figure 5-7. Layout marks on the work will reveal immediately whether the cut is correct.

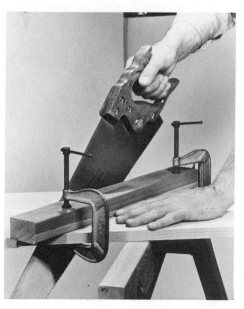

Figure 5-8. Always clamp a guide block to the work when you are cutting with a handsaw.

The common miter box is a wooden, *U*-shaped, holding device that has paired guide slots for a saw so you can cut left- or right-hand miters more accurately than you can do them freehand. Most units include an extra set of guide slots so you can also make 90-degree cuts (Figure 5-9). Some commercial units do not have the extra wide front that provides the bench hook. This, however, is not a good design since the hook is needed to keep the box steady, either by holding or clamping the hook against the edge of a workbench or by gripping it in a vise (Figure 5-10). A miter box is usually used with a backsaw.

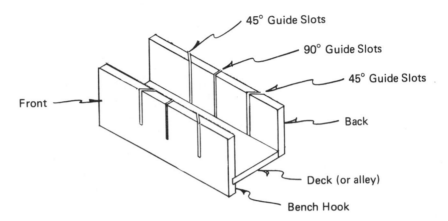

Figure 5-9. Nomenclature of a miter box. These can be purchased ready-made or you can make your own.

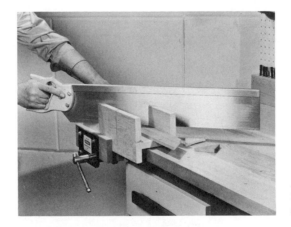

Figure 5-10. A well-made miter box, carefully used, will assure accurate miters.

The wooden units you can buy in a store, especially the less expensive ones, leave something to be desired in terms of their construction and accuracy. That's why most careful craftspeople will make their own, designing along the lines of the project shown in Figure 5-11. One dimension to check before making your own is the height of the front and the back when measured from

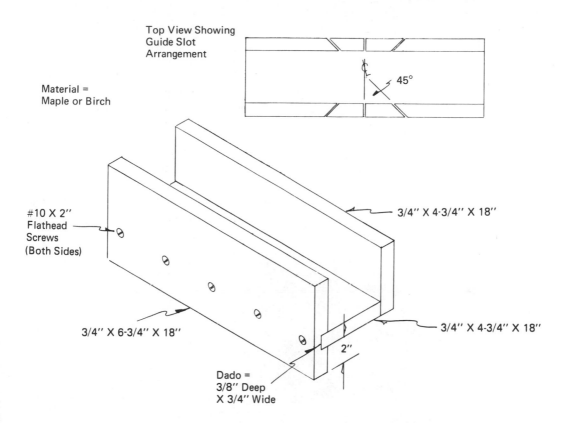

Top View Showing
Guide Slot
Arrangement

45°

Material =
Maple or Birch

#10 X 2"
Flathead
Screws
(Both Sides)

3/4" X 4-3/4" X 18"

3/4" X 6-3/4" X 18"

3/4" X 4-3/4" X 18"

2"

Dado =
3/8" Deep
X 3/4" Wide

Figure 5-11. Here are plans for a miter box you can make. Careful construction is essential.

the top surface of the deck. This can't be more—in fact, a bit less is better—than the width of the backsaw blade when measured from the bottom edge of the spine to the tips of the teeth. The reason is that otherwise the saw will not cut completely through the stock.

Cutting the guide slots is more important than anything. If they are not right, the tool will be useless. Mark the cut lines carefully across the top edges and down the sides of both the front and the back. Form the slots with the same saw you will use with the box. Work with a clamped-on guide to be sure the slots will be perpendicular. The slots may be formed by clamping the front and back together before assembling them to the deck. If so, be sure alignment is right before attaching parts permanently.

Figure 5-12 shows an alternate method of arranging the guide slots. An advantage of this design is that the vertical members of the box will be stronger because the slots are not as close. A disadvantage is that the work, on some cuts, will not have as much support as it gets when the slots are centered.

The miter box is most useful for cutting frame miters, cross miters on narrow stock, and miter joints on moldings. In all cases, the normal procedure is to hold or clamp the work tightly against the back and to keep it so until the cut is

89

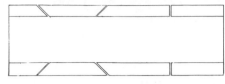

Figure 5-12. An alternate method of arranging the guide slots in a miter box.

complete. Don't rush to get the job done, concentrate on keeping the saw perpendicular. This will result in accurate cuts and also will eliminate damage to the box.

The tool shown in Figure 5-13 is also called a miter box, but is a high-quality product with built-in features that help make miter cutting easier and more accurate. Its index plate has positive locks that automatically position the saw for many miter angles other than the common 45 degrees. The saw guides are adjustable to accommodate backsaws of different thicknesses, and they keep the saw centered and vertical.

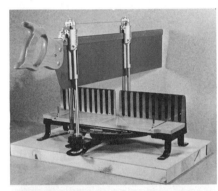

Figure 5-13. A high-quality unit has many built-in features that assure accuracy.

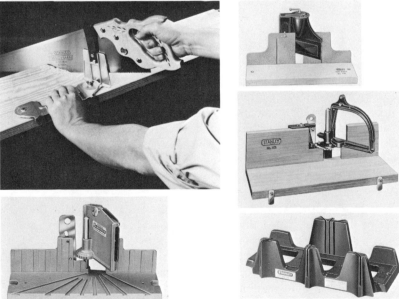

Figure 5-14. Other types of miter boxes and miter-cutting guides that are available commercially.

The products shown in Figure 5-14 are all miter boxes or miter-cutting guides that range from simple to complex and cover a broad price range. The one shown in Figure 5-15 is called a miter machine and is designed so the joint can be cut, glued, and nailed to form tight-fitting corners. It may be used for moldings or flat stock which is four inches or less in width.

Figure 5-15. The miter machine works like a miter box but includes clamps that hold work during assembly.

A newcomer in the field of miter cutting, shown in Figure 5-16, is called a power miter box. As you can see, it has an attached, adjustable motor that drives a circular saw blade. The advantages in minimizing physical effort are obvious and since the tool has various, built-in positive stops, there are gains in accuracy also.

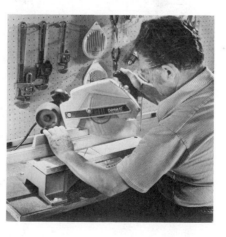

Figure 5-16. A relative newcomer in the miter cutting field has a power driven circular saw blade.

TABLE SAW WORK

Frame miters may be cut on a table saw by setting the miter gauge to the angle required and making the pass as shown in Figure 5-17. The operation is being done with the miter gauge in a closed position, but it can also be accomplished with an open setting—when the miter gauge is at the opposite 45-degree stop. The latter setup is preferred by some craftspeople since it keeps hands further away from the saw blade. In any case, it is critical to keep the work

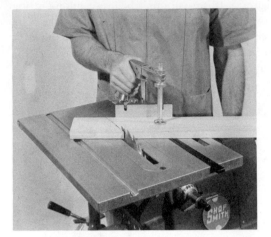

Figure 5-17. Doing a frame miter on a table saw. The miter gauge hold-down helps to keep the work secure.

firmly in place while the cut is made. When the stock is flat, there is no need to reset the miter gauge for the second cut. The same edge stays against the miter gauge, but the stock is flipped end for end as shown in Figure 5-18. The material is face up for the first cut, face down for the second one.

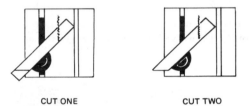

CUT ONE   CUT TWO

Figure 5-18. Frame miters on flat work can be done without changing the miter-gauge setting.

In any situation where the stock must remain face up, as with moldings, the second cut is made with the miter gauge reset to the opposite 45-degree stop and used on the other side of the saw blade (Figure 5-19). Resetting the miter gauge offers another opportunity to make a mistake, so work carefully. Make test cuts before cutting good stock.

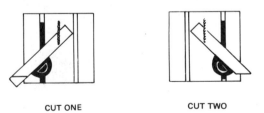

CUT ONE   CUT TWO

Figure 5-19. Extra care is required with shaped pieces since the position and setting of the gauge must be changed.

The rotation of the saw blade creates a force which tends to pivot the work or move it along the miter gauge. The technical term for this is creep. Holding the work firmly with your hands, or using a hold-down are basic procedures. Adding an extension, which you can make or buy, to the miter gauge is a wise additional precaution. The extension provides good support and when it is faced with fine sandpaper, as shown in detail B of Figure 5-20, will guard against creep.

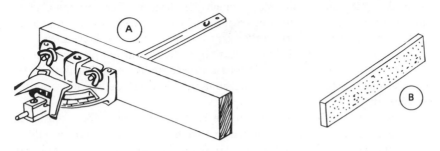

Figure 5-20. A miter-gauge extension, faced with fine sandpaper, helps do more accurate work.

Units known as sliding tables are easily made by the woodworker and will produce accurate cuts indefinitely if they are carefully made. This mechanical device helps eliminate the possibility of human error. Two examples of sliding tables which can be dimensioned to suit equipment on hand, are shown in Figure 5-21. The procedure for making either is the same.

Use 3/8-inch or 1/2-inch plywood for the platform; use a hardwood for the bars that will ride in the table slots normally used for the miter gauge bar. Size the bars for a good slip fit and put them in place in the slots. Place the platform so one edge is parallel to the table's edge and tack-nail it to the bars. These steps must be taken, of course, with the saw blade lowered beneath the surface of the table. The next step is to clamp the platform in position and raise

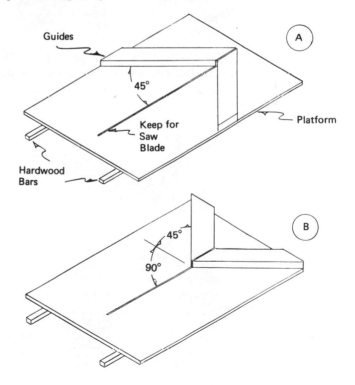

Figure 5-21. Sliding tables are worth making and can be used indefinitely for accurate miter work.

the blade so it cuts its own slot through the platform. Turn off the blade, remove the clamps, and then elongate the original slot. Work from the underside of the jig to permanently attach the bars to the platform with short screws.

The guides are positioned in relation to the slot in the platform and they must be positioned precisely. The best procedure is to tack-nail them temporarily, make a few trial cuts, and adjust if necessary before attaching them permanently.

There is a difference between the two sliding tables. The one shown in Figure 5-21A is for frame pieces which have been precut to exact length. The miter cuts are formed by placing the stock on the table and making the pass as shown in Figure 5-22.

Figure 5-22. One version of a sliding table is used for frame parts that have been cut to exact length.

The sliding table shown in Figure 5-21B permits cutting mitered pieces consecutively from one piece of stock. The work is placed and cut as shown in Figure 5-23. Either edge of the guide block, or blocks, can be used depending on the direction of the cut.

Figure 5-23. The other sliding table lets you cut consecutively on one piece of stock.

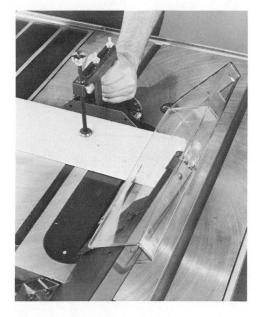

Figure 5-24. Cross miters are done by tilting the blade to the angle required.

Since the purpose of these tables is to produce a smooth, accurate miter, it is best to design them for use with a good, planer type saw blade.

Cross miters are formed as shown in Figure 5-24. The procedure is the same as you would use for a crosscut except that the blade is tilted. Keep the stock tight against the miter gauge. Make the pass slowly so you will get the smoothest cut possible. Place the work so its good side is up.

Doing a rip miter is the same as doing a simple rip cut (Figure 5-25). Be sure the edge of the stock that rides the rip fence is smooth and straight and that alignment of the fence to the saw blade is correct.

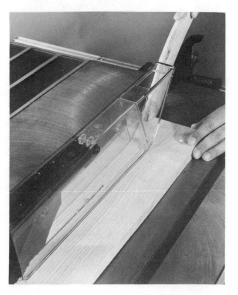

Figure 5-25. Rip miters are guided by the fence as for any rip cut, but with the blade tilted.

Cross and rip miters are not as difficult to do accurately as frame miters since the work pieces can be kept in firm position while cutting by using basic machine components. It is important, of course, to be sure the settings, especially the tilt of the blade, are right. Test cuts first are always wise.

RADIAL ARM SAW CUTS

Frame miters are done by setting the arm of the machine to the angle you want and then pulling the blade through the work as you would for an ordinary crosscut. An advantage of the radial arm machine is that the work stays put, held firmly against the fence. The saw blade is moved so there is little danger of creep. Once you have made test cuts to check out the angular setting, you can organize the machine as shown in Figure 5-26, using a stop block so you can cut any number of duplicate pieces. This will work whether you precut pieces to exact length or cut consecutively from a single piece. If the pieces are precut, you keep the same edge of the stock against the fence but flip it end for end for the second cut. When cutting from a single strip, you turn the stock over for each cut.

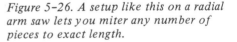

Figure 5-26. A setup like this on a radial arm saw lets you miter any number of pieces to exact length.

Many craftspeople prefer to work with a jig which looks like a sliding table but is tack-nailed or clamped to the machine's table as shown in Figure 5-27. In this setup you don't swing the arm of the tool, but use it in the routine crosscut position. The guides on the auxiliary table provide the accuracy for the miters. The jig may be used for flat pieces or moldings, but in each case the parts must first be cut to length.

The only difference between cross miters and rip miters and simple crosscuts and rips is that the blade is set at an angle for the miters. The actual cutting procedures are the same. You hold the work against the fence and pull the blade through to do a cross miter. For a rip miter, the blade is locked in position parallel to the fence and the work is pushed through.

Figure 5-27. A jig with 45-degree guides permits miter cuts with the tool in basic crosscut position.

REINFORCEMENTS

Corrugated nails may be used on some types of work, either on frame miters where they are driven through the surface of the stock, or on cross miters where they are driven at the end of the joint as shown in Figure 5-28. In this application the thickness of the stock will determine if they can be used. This is not an attractive reinforcement but it's acceptable on utility projects and where faceplate trim is used. The nails do add strength and also serve to hold parts together until the glue dries.

A more sophisticated mechanical fastener, shown in use in Figure 5-29, is a clamp nail. Its special design draws parts together and causes a tight miter joint. Its design, however, calls for a narrow groove which, in commercial practice, is usually formed with a special 22-gauge saw blade. An alternative when the size of the stock permits is to cut the grooves on a band saw since its blade forms a much finer kerf than you can get with a regular circular saw blade. Another suggestion is to cut the kerfs with a dovetail saw or backsaw. A simple

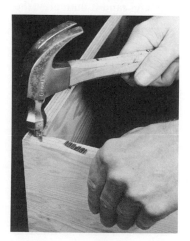

Figure 5-28. Corrugated nails are often used to reinforce miter joints.

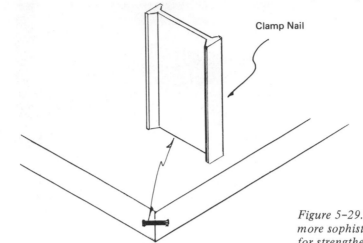

Clamp Nail

Figure 5-29. Clamp nails are more sophisticated devices for strengthening miter joints.

test will tell whether the kerfs are suitable. The average clamp nail is 9/16 inch wide so saw kerfs about 5/16-inches deep will accommodate them while providing a bit of clearance.

Clamp nails can be driven from both ends of the joint if the stock is wide and like finishing nails, they can be set beneath the surface of the wood and hidden with wood dough.

SPLINES

Splines (Figure 5-30) have many advantages. They add strength, keep parts in alignment during assembly, are not unattractive if you choose to leave them exposed, and they can be cut to suit any type of miter joint. As shown in Figure 5-31, the spline fits matched grooves which are cut in the joint parts. It's always best to work with a spline that is longer than necessary so you can trim and sand it flush after the glue is dry.

Figure 5-30. Splines will add much strength to any miter joint and also make it easier to do assembly work.

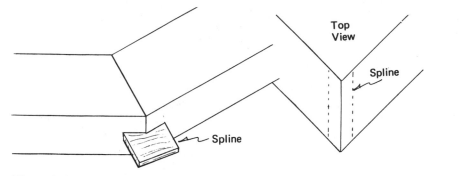

Figure 5-31. How splines are used in a frame miter. Excess is trimmed and sanded flush after the glue dries.

Splines used in cross and rip miters usually work well if their width is equal to the thickness of the stock (Figure 5-32). They are located to favor the inside corner of the joint as shown in the details A and B. Setting them closer to the outside corners will create weaknesses you don't need.

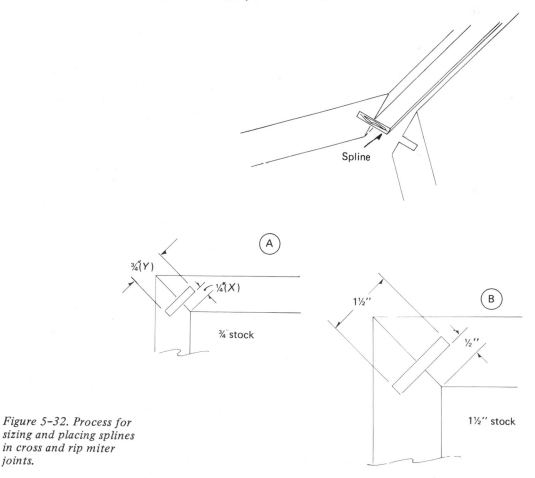

Figure 5-32. Process for sizing and placing splines in cross and rip miter joints.

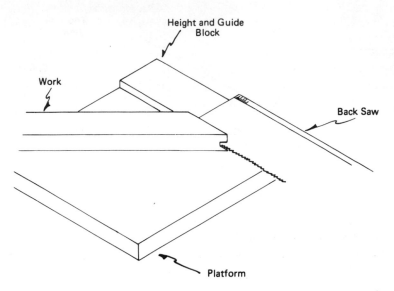

Figure 5-33. A system you can use to form accurate spline grooves when working with a backsaw.

Kerfs for splines in frame miters can be cut with a backsaw if you make a setup like the one shown in Figure 5-33. Note that the thickness of the guide block controls the position of the cut and that its width will control the cut depth. The saw won't cut deeper when the spine hits the guide block.

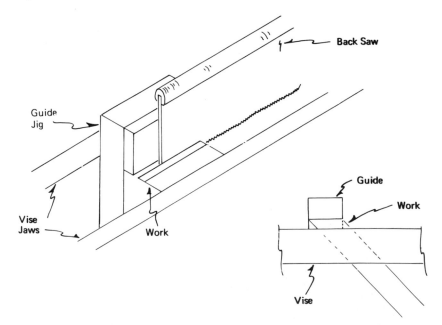

Figure 5-34. This alternate method lets you grip the work in a vise. Keep the guide jig for future use.

Another way to work is shown in Figure 5-34. Here, the guide jig and the work are clamped together in a vise. Again, the guide on the jig determines how deep the saw will cut.

Figure 5-35 shows how you can organize to saw spline grooves in cross and rip miters. The important consideration here is that the grooves must be perpendicular to the miter cut. The depth of the groove can be controlled by clamping a stop block to the saw.

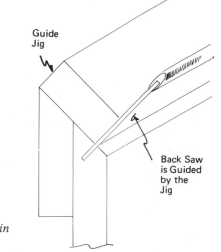

Guide
Jig

Back Saw
is Guided
by the
Jig

Figure 5-35. One way to organize when you hand-saw spline grooves in cross and rip miters.

Grooves formed with a backsaw are comparatively narrow, but you can widen them by redoing the initial cut with a crosscut saw or even a rip saw.

Figure 5-36 shows how to do spline grooves on a table saw. Detail A shows the setup for doing the miter cuts. To do the grooves (detail B), keep the saw blade at the same angle but adjust its projection for the groove depth you want.

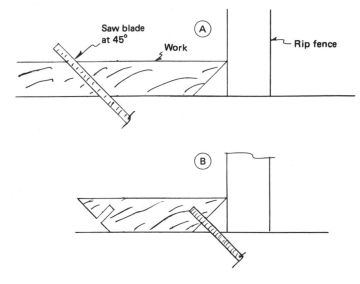

Saw blade
at 45°   Work   (A)   Rip fence

(B)

Figure 5-36. Forming spline grooves on a table saw for cross or rip miters. The blade angle is the same as for the miter cut.

If the groove is required for a frame miter, the work is done as shown in Figure 5-37. The first pass, shown in detail A is made with the work forming a closed angle with the table at the front of the blade. The second pass, in B, is made with the same side of the stock against the fence but with the angle open. Even though the depth of the cuts is usually shallow, this kind of freehand sawing must be done very carefully in order for the cuts to be accurate and for safe work. The procedure is done this way so the same surface of the work will be against the fence for each pass. This means the grooves will mate correctly even though they might not be exactly centered.

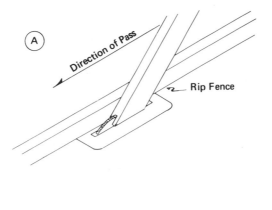

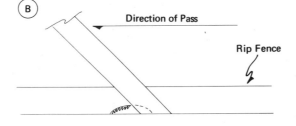

Figure 5-37. Spline grooves in frame miters are cut this way. This calls for careful handling or a special jig.

FEATHERING THE JOINT

Feathering is a type of partial spline that is used in a frame miter as shown in Figure 5-38. The feather shown is triangular but it's better to cut them as rectangles and trim and sand them flush after they have been installed and the glue is dry.

Whenever possible, hold the joint pieces together with clamps or in a vise so the feather-groove can be cut in both parts at the same time (Figure 5-39). The depth of the groove, while it should not be excessive, is really not too critical since you can cut the feathers to suit.

Figure 5-40 shows how feather-grooves can be cut in mating pieces with perfect accuracy and with safety on a table saw. The jig is made for a sliding fit

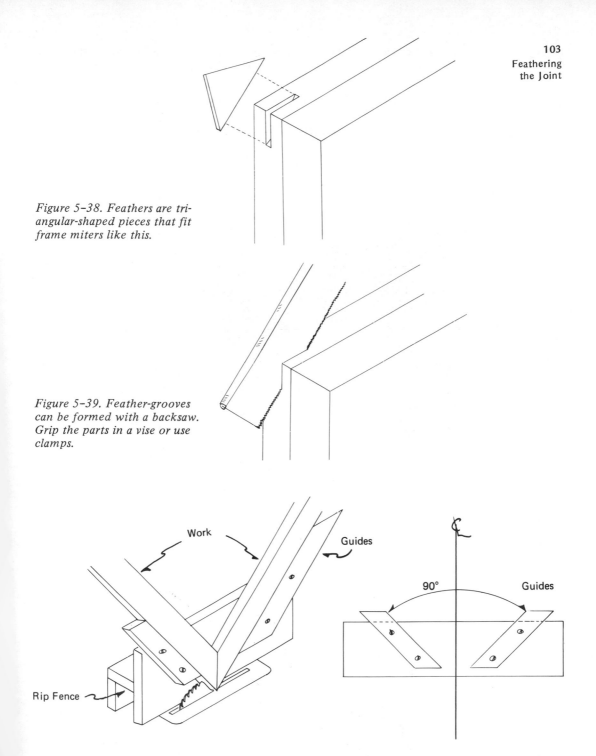

Figure 5–38. Feathers are tri-angular-shaped pieces that fit frame miters like this.

Figure 5–39. Feather-grooves can be formed with a backsaw. Grip the parts in a vise or use clamps.

Work

Guides

Rip Fence

90°

Guides

Figure 5–40. A jig you can make for doing feather-grooves on a table saw. It can also be used for spline grooves in frame miters.

over the rip fence. The work is clamped to the jig and positioned by the guides that are set at the angles shown in the drawing. The jig, with the forward guide removed, can also be used to do spline grooves in frame miters.

Grooves for feathers and for splines in frame miters can be cut on a radial arm saw by working as shown in Figure 5-41. The saw blade is set parallel to the machine's table; the work is elevated on a special table that has a guide block to position it for the cut. The table is an accessory that you can make by following the design shown in Figure 5-42. If the guide block is removable, the height table may be used for cutting grooves across the end of square stock and for doing other, similar operations, such as making cheek cuts for tenons and rabbets.

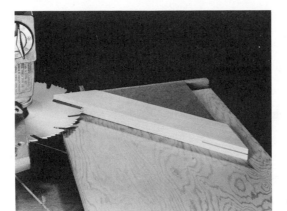

Figure 5-41. A special height table will make it easy to form feather or spline grooves on a radial arm saw.

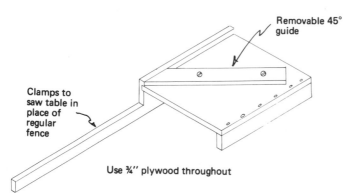

Removable 45°
guide

Clamps to
saw table in
place of
regular
fence

Use ¾" plywood throughout

Figure 5-42. A radial arm saw height table that you can make.

DOWELS

Holes for dowels that will be used to reinforce a frame miter must be perpendicular to the cut. This can be done freehand but it's always better to work with a mechanical guidance method which will assure accuracy. A doweling jig like the one that was shown in Chapter 1 can be used if you are working with a hand brace. With portable drills you can work with guide blocks. A good setup for drill press work is shown in Figure 5-43. The tilt of the table will place the work so the bit will be perpendicular to the mitered edge. The clamping device

Figure 5-43. This is one way to organize a drill press for forming dowel holes in a miter cut.

shown is actually a hold-down for a mortising accessory. A conventional clamp will do the job as well. Be sure to use a fence on the drill press table so the bit and the work will have a common centerline.

Conventional dowels, used on cross and rip miters, should be organized as shown in Figure 5-44. Like splines, they should be positioned to favor the inside corner of the joint. Figure 5-45 shows a drilling jig you can make to use with either a hand brace or a portable electric drill. Either way, a stop should be used on the bit to control the depth of the hole.

Figure 5-44. How to situate dowels when they are used in cross or rip miters.

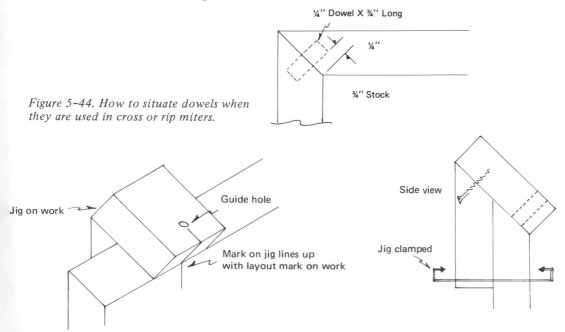

Figure 5-45. A jig like this can be used whether you are forming holes with a brace or a portable drill.

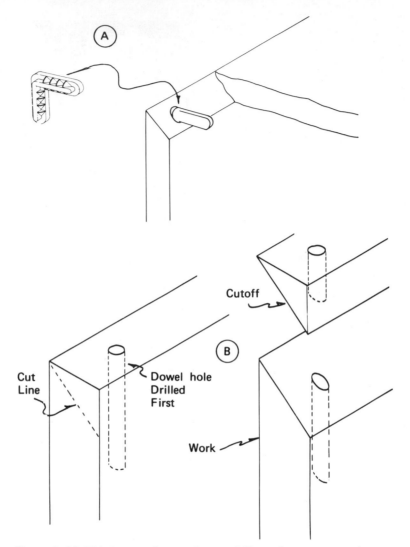

Figure 5-46. This is a good procedure to follow when you are using right angle or miter dowels.

Right angle dowels, shown in Figure 5-46A, are a relatively new item that make dowel reinforcement of all miter joints an easier chore. Since the special dowels make a 90-degree turn, the holes can be bored perpendicular to the edge of the stock instead of the miter cut. This permits you to work as shown in Figure 5-46B. Drill the holes first, which is easiest to do on a square edge, and then make the miter cut. Use the same technique when forming a frame miter (Figure 5-47).

Right angle dowels, or miter dowels as they are often called, make a strong joint because the strength of the plastic material from which they are made resists bending. Common sizes are 1/4-inch and 3/8-inch diameter.

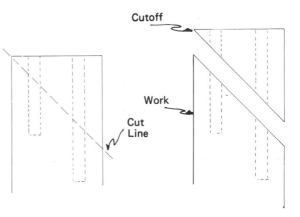

Figure 5-47. The same procedure works when you are using the special dowels in a frame miter.

COMPOUND MITER JOINTS

Compound miter joints, examples of which are shown in Figure 5-48, are required whenever a project has sloping sides, regardless of whether it is a four-sided peaked roof for a birdhouse, rails for a table with splayed legs, or a simple open box. This joint is actually more difficult to visualize than it is to put together.

The box with straight sides shown in Figure 5-49 doesn't require more than simple miter cuts at each corner. If the box is made with sloping sides, both a miter and a bevel are required at each corner for the joints to fit tightly. Figure 5-50 shows how the two cuts combine to form a compound miter. The two

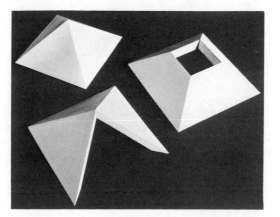

Figure 5-48. Compound miter joints are required whenever a project has sloping sides.

107

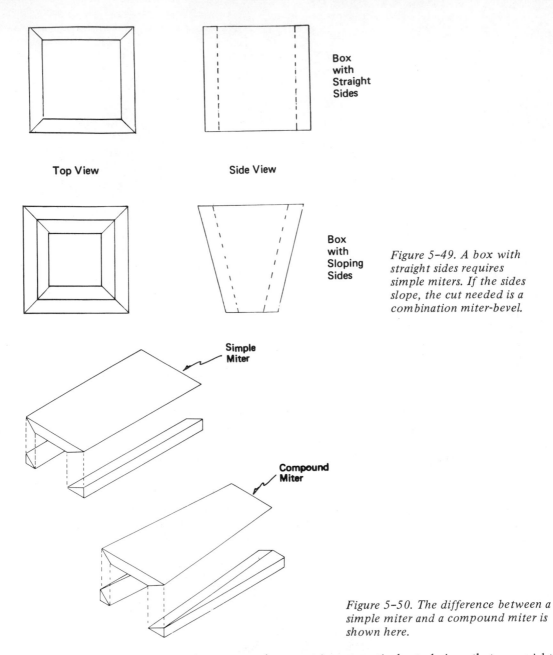

Box with Straight Sides

Top View

Side View

Box with Sloping Sides

Figure 5-49. A box with straight sides requires simple miters. If the sides slope, the cut needed is a combination miter-bevel.

Simple Miter

Compound Miter

Figure 5-50. The difference between a simple miter and a compound miter is shown here.

cuts are not done separately except in one particular technique that you might want to follow with hand tools. Usually, the two cuts are made at the same time.

Note that the top and bottom edges of the sloped sides will be off horizontal an amount equal to the tilt of the work (Figure 5-51). This won't matter on some work, but when it does, the edges of the parts can be beveled before assembly work. This kind of cutting is easier to do on one long board, so doing the beveling before cutting the compound miters is a good idea.

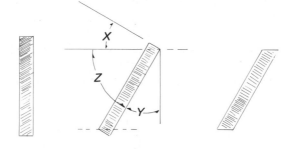

— The bevel angle (*X*)
equals the tilt angle
or slope (*Y*) of the
sides.
— If you add *Z* + *Y* or
Z + *X* you get 90 degrees

*Figure 5–51. The top and
bottom edges of sloping sides
can be prebeveled.*

The two-step procedure when using hand tools is shown in Figure 5–52. The first cut, done with a saw, forms the miter. The second step, done with a plane, produces the bevel. A better way is to work with a pre-beveled guide block (Figure 5–53) that is clamped to the work at the correct miter angle. Careful sawing will then result in a compound miter in one operation.

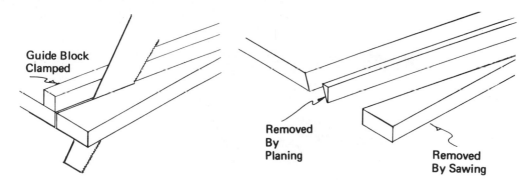

Guide Block
Clamped

Removed
By
Planing

Removed
By Sawing

Figure 5–52. One way to form a compound angle with a handsaw. Saw the miter and then plane the bevel.

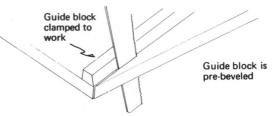

Guide block
clamped to
work

Guide block is
pre-beveled

Figure 5–53. Another, faster way is to prebevel a guide block so the cut is formed in one sawing operation.

Of course the angle of the miter and of the bevel can't be arbitrary if the slope of the work must be exact, but there are times—a shadow box picture frame is a case in point—when the slope can be arbitrary if it is visually acceptable. Figure 5-54, shows work being done in a miter box. A guide strip is clamped to the bed of the tool so it braces the frame piece at the tilt angle you feel will look right. The cut is made with the saw set at 45 degrees, just as if you were cutting a simple miter. The result will be a compound angle.

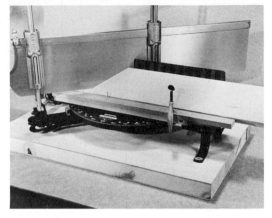

Figure 5-54. A regular miter cut with a miter box will form a compound angle if the work is sloped as shown.

Compound miters are cut on a table saw by using both a miter gauge setting and a blade tilt as shown in Figure 5-55. Since two settings are required the need to do them both correctly is critical. Being "off" just a bit will be detrimental, so make the adjustments carefully and test them by making cuts in scrap stock.

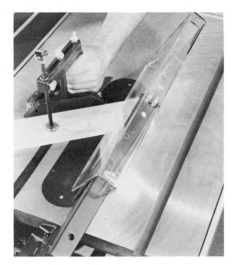

Figure 5-55. A compound angle cut on a table saw calls for both a miter gauge setting and a blade tilt.

The chart in Figure 5-56 shows the blade and miter gauge settings for the most commonly used slope angles. Notice that some of them are to a fraction of a degree, a precision that isn't easy to achieve by relying entirely on the tool's stamped markings. This is another reason to do test cuts.

Work Slope Angle	4-Sided Figure		6-Sided Figure		8-Sided Figure	
	Blade	Miter Gauge	Blade	Miter Gauge	Blade	Miter Gauge
10 deg.	44¼	80¼	29½	84½	22	86
20 deg.	41¾	71¼	28¼	79	21	82
30 deg.	37¾	63½	26	74	19½	78¼
40 deg.	32½	57¼	22¾	69¾	17	75
50 deg.	27	52½	19	66¼	14¼	72½
60 deg.	21	49	14½	63½	11	70¼

Notes:

    Blade and arm settings are in degrees
    Settings are called out to the closest ¼ degree

Figure 5-56. Blade and miter gauge settings to use when cutting compound angles on a table saw.

When the work is too wide to be handled easily and safely with a miter gauge, the cuts can be made by working with a taper jig as shown in Figure 5-57. The jig is guided by the rip fence and is set to produce the miter cut needed. This accessory is available commercially, but you can make your own by following the design shown in Figure 5-58. The mark that is made 12 inches from the hinged end (Figure 5-58A) is the guide you use to determine the amount of taper per foot as indicated by X in the same illustration.

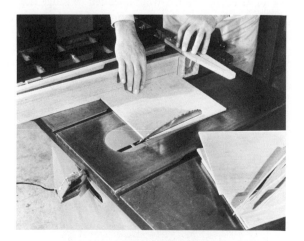

Figure 5-57. A taper jig comes in handy when the work is too large to be handled safely with a miter gauge.

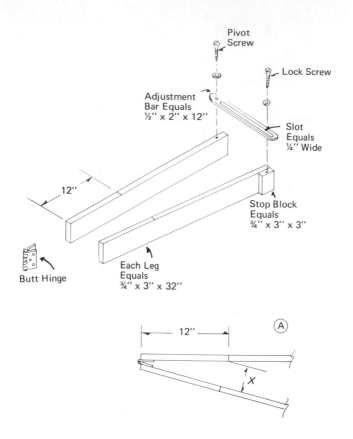

Pivot
Screw

Lock Screw

Adjustment
Bar Equals
½'' x 2'' x 12''

Slot
Equals
¼'' Wide

12''

Stop Block
Equals
¾'' x 3'' x 3''

Butt Hinge

Each Leg
Equals
¾'' x 3'' x 32''

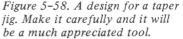

12''   (A)

X

*Figure 5-58. A design for a taper
jig. Make it carefully and it will
be a much appreciated tool.*

An easy way to do compound miters when you can be arbitrary with the
slope angle, is shown in Figure 5-59. The system uses a jig which is locked to
the miter gauge and supports the work at the slope angle you want. The gauge is
set at 45 degrees and the cut is made as you would a simple frame miter. Figure
5-60 shows how the jig is made and used. The stop does not have a fixed position, but is tack-nailed where needed to gauge the slope of the work. The jig can
be secured by driving screws through the holes or the slots that are in the miter
gauge.

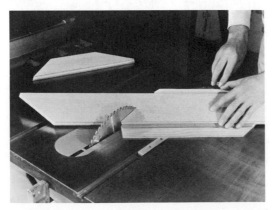

*Figure 5-59. An easy way to
cut compound angle joints
when the slope of the work is
not critical.*

112

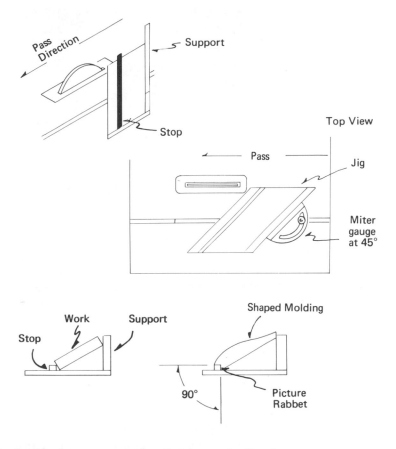

Figure 5-60. How to make
and use the jig that was
shown in Figure 5-59.

Splines will add a lot of strength to compound angle joints and will make it much easier to assemble the segments (Figure 5-61). The grooves for the splines will not be difficult to do if you follow the procedure shown in Figure 5-62.

Figure 5-61. Splines in compound miter joints will make it much easier to assemble the segments.

113

Figure 5-62. This is one way to cut spline grooves. Make a special insert if the work does not have sufficient bearing surface on the table.

Cut a bevel on a length of thick material at the same angle that is on the segments. Cut notches at each end of the guide so it can be clamped to the rip fence as shown. The guide will provide good support for the work and will hold it at the correct angle. Be sure, however, that the stock is thick enough to span the slot in the table insert so it will have adequate support when you are cutting. If it isn't, make a special insert of plywood or hardboard with a slot just wide enough for the saw blade to come through. Be sure to keep the work snugly against the guide. Make the pass slowly and with your hands well away from the blade.

Cuts for compound angle joints are done on a radial arm saw by swinging the arm for the miter and tilting the blade for the bevel (Figure 5-63). The correct settings for arm and blade for the most commonly used slope angles are shown in Figure 5-64.

One way to work so the job will be easier is to make an end cut first and then flip the stock for the second cut (Figure 5-65). This supplies a segment which you can then use as a pattern to mark other pieces when you work with it as shown in Figure 5-66. Be precise enough when you place the work for the cut so the saw blade will remove the pencil line.

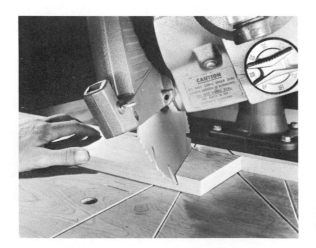

Figure 5-63. Compound angle cuts on a radial arm saw are done by swinging the arm for the miter and tilting the blade for the bevel.

Compound Angle Settings to Use on a Radial Arm Saw						
Work Slope Angle	4-Sided Figure		6-Sided Figure		8-Sided Figure	
	Blade	Arm	Blade	Arm	Blade	Arm
10 deg.	44¼	9¾	29½	5½	22	4
20 deg.	41¾	18¾	28¼	11	21	8
30 deg.	37¾	26½	26	16	19½	11¾
40 deg.	32½	32¾	22¾	20¼	17	15
50 deg.	27	37½	19	23¾	14¼	17½
60 deg.	21	41	14½	26½	11	19¾

Notes:
Blade and arm settings are in degrees
Settings are called out to the cloest ¼ degree

Figure 5-64. The arm and blade settings to use for compound angle cuts on a radial arm saw.

Figure 5-65. Segments can be cut consecutively from one board if the stock is flipped after each cut.

Figure 5-66. The first segment can be used as a pattern for the others.

Another way is to use the first piece as a gauge for locating a stop block that you clamp to the fence. The following cuts are made by butting the free end of the work against the stop block. Remember that when segments are cut consecutively from one board the work must be flipped for each cut.

Some easy ways to make cuts on a radial arm saw for compound angle joints when the slope of the work is not critical follow. Use the jig described

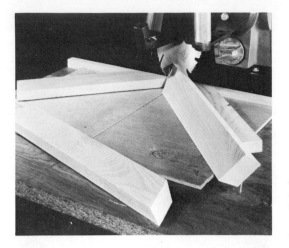

Figure 5-67. The jig made for sawing frame miters can be used for compound cuts also. The bevel on the stock establishes the slope angle.

earlier for cutting simple frame miters to position the work as shown in Figure 5-67. Notice that the base of the part has been beveled to establish the slope angle. The saw blade is set and pulled through as it would be for a simple crosscut.

A *U*-shaped jig, clamped to the table so it is 45 degrees to the line of a crosscut, is used as shown in Figure 5-68. The distance between the vertical members of the jig is suited to the angle at which the stock must be held. One jig will do for pieces of various widths if a height block is used under the work to establish the slope angle. Here too, the machine is set as it would be for a simple crosscut.

Figure 5-68. A U-shaped jig, set 45 degrees to the blade's normal crosscut position, holds stock for a compound angle cut.

A very quick method involves clamping a height block to the saw's table as shown in Figure 5-69. A thin strip of wood, which can't be seen in the illustration, is tack-nailed to the table to serve as a stop. A second stop block is clamped to the table to gauge the length of the work. The machine is organized as it would be to make a simple, 45-degree cut. In this situation, and in others we have discussed, the 45-degree setting indicates the project will have four sides. The cut angle, of course, must change in relation to the number of sides in the project. For example, for six sides, the cut angle would be 30 degrees.

Figure 5-69. A height block sets the slope angle; a stop, which can't be seen in the photo, secures the work. The blade is set for a 45-degree cut.

SPECIAL MITER JOINTS

The designs that follow are joints that can be used anywhere, but because they do require extra work and even more care than basic designs, they are usually limited to choice pieces of cabinet work and to high quality furniture. A major advantage, aside from strength and durability, is that the joint parts mesh. This can be a happy aid at assembly time.

Tongue and Groove Miter

A tongue and groove adds glue area in the joint but, more important, the tongue and the groove form an interlock so the parts can't slide. The joint is shown in Figure 5-70. The steps to follow after the mating edges have been cut at a 45-degree angle are outlined in Figure 5-71.

Step One: Assemble the parts of a dado set to cut the width of the groove you want. Tilt the dado to 45 degrees and form the groove in part one. The projection of the dado set above the saw table determines the depth of the groove.

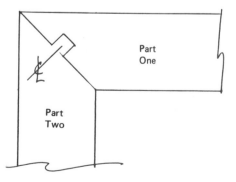

Part
One

Part
Two

Figure 5-70. A miter joint that incorporates a tongue and groove interlock.

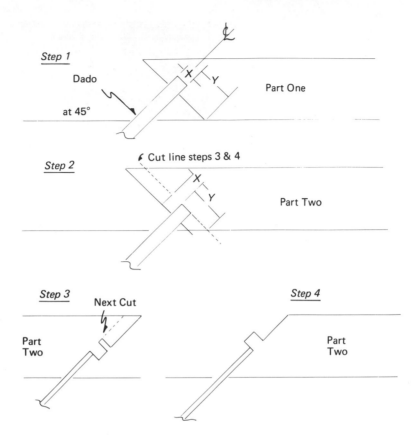

Figure 5-71. The steps to follow when forming the tongue and groove miter joint. Accuracy is critical.

Step Two: Cuts are made in part two with the dado at the same angle but with its projection adjusted as shown. A second projection adjustment is required to remove stock from the other side of the tongue.

Steps Three and Four: The remainder of the waste can be removed with the dado or you can switch to a saw blade as shown.

What is important here is that you make the saw settings carefully and that you make similar cuts in all pieces of stock before you change the setting for the next cut. Here, as with all joint cutting operations, it's wise to have test pieces on hand so you can make trial cuts before working on the good stock.

Housed Rabbet-Miter Joint

A housed rabbet-miter joint is a good joint to use (Figure 5-72) when you are joining parts that are not equal in thickness and need the good appearance of a miter plus the additional glue area afforded by a rabbet. As you can see in

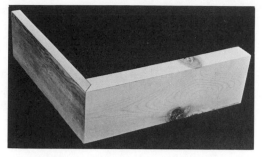

Figure 5-72. An example of a housed rabbet-miter joint.

Figure 5-73, the thinner piece requires only a simple cross miter cut. The thicker part is shaped as a combination rabbet-miter. The parts are cut as shown in Figure 5-74.

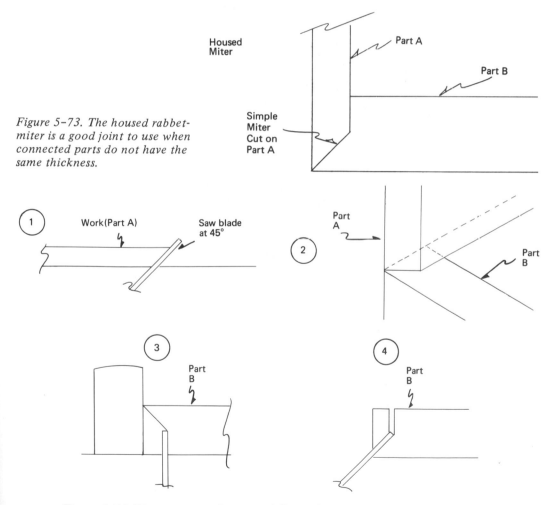

Figure 5-73. The housed rabbet-miter is a good joint to use when connected parts do not have the same thickness.

Housed Miter

Part A

Part B

Simple Miter Cut on Part A

1. Work(Part A)   Saw blade at 45°

2. Part A   Part B

3. Part B

4. Part B

Figure 5-74. The sequence of steps to follow when forming the housed rabbet-miter.

Step One: Do a simple cross miter cut on the thinner piece (part A).

Step Two: Use part A as a pattern to mark the shape of the cut you will need on part B.

Step Three: Set the rip fence so the distance from it to the *outside* of the saw blade will equal the thickness of part A. Set the projection of the saw blade so it will just meet the corner of the lines marked in step two, and make the cut as shown.

Step Four: The miter cut on part B starts exactly at the corner of the stock and just touches the bottom inside corner of the cut that was made in step three. Be very careful with blade projection so the joint will have clean lines.

True Rabbet-Miters

There are two basic types of rabbet-miters. The "simple" rabbet-miter is shown in Figure 5–75, and the more complicated "locked" rabbet-miter that incorporates a tongue and groove interlock is shown in Figure 5–76.

Figure 5–75. An example of a true rabbet-miter joint.

Figure 5–76. The locked rabbet-miter joint includes a tongue and groove interlock.

The best way to form the shapes required for the mating pieces is to use the formula shown in Figure 5–77, which will apply regardless of the thickness of the stock. You can't go wrong working this way but on the other hand, there's no reason why you can't deviate from the formula if you so desire or if some particular circumstance makes it necessary. Possible changes might be a deeper rabbet cut or a shorter tongue and groove pattern.

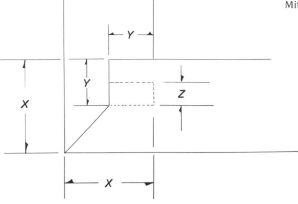

The Basics of Rabbet-Miter Joints
- All cuts fall within a square whose sides are equal to the thickness of the stock
- X equals the thickness of the stock
- Y equals $\frac{1}{2}(X)$
- Z equals $\frac{1}{2}(Y)$
- The diagonal line equals $\frac{1}{2}$ the full diagonal of the square
- When the lock tenon is included (dotted lines) its length equals Y, its width (Z) equals $\frac{1}{2}(Y)$

Figure 5-77. This formula for rabbet-miter joints will work regardless of the thickness of the stock.

To do the simple rabbet-miter, follow the program that is outlined in Figure 5-78.

Step One: Adjust the projection of the saw blade so it will equal one-half the thickness of the stock. Set the rip fence so the distance from it to the *outside* of the blade will equal the thickness of the stock.

Step Two: Make the first cut in part one by butting the squared end of the stock against the rip fence. Stock that is too narrow for safe work should be advanced with the miter gauge.

Step Three: Make a similar cut on the same piece, but with the stock pulled away from the rip fence so the cut will be more than halfway to the end of the work. The second cut must be to the left of the centerline, between the rip fence end of the work and the cut made in step two. Make repeat passes with the saw blade to remove the stock that remains between the two cuts. If you require very many pieces, it may pay to switch to a dado assembly for the clearing operation.

Step Four: Leave the projection of the saw blade unchanged but reset the rip fence so the distance from it to the *outside* of the blade is equal to one-half the thickness of the stock.

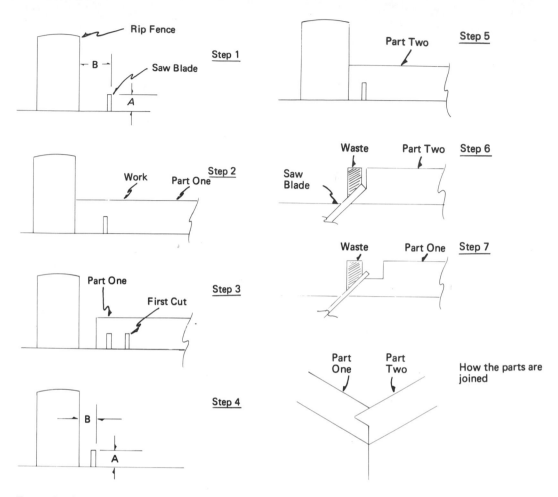

Figure 5-78. The sequence of steps to follow when forming the rabbet-miter joint.

Step Five: Butt the squared end of the mating piece against the rip fence and make the cut as shown. Use a miter gauge if the stock is too narrow to have adequate bearing against the fence.

Step Six: Tilt the saw blade to 45 degrees and make a miter cut on the part that was kerfed in step five. Be very careful with the projection of the blade since the miter cut must just meet the inside corner of the kerf. The best system is to make several passes, raising the blade a bit after each until the projection is perfect.

Step Seven: Make the same miter cut on the other joint piece. The projection of the blade is not critical in this step but the cut must start at the very corner of the work.

The rabbet-miter joint can be reinforced with dowels as shown in Figure 5-79. Locate the dowels on the centerline of the rabbet.

122

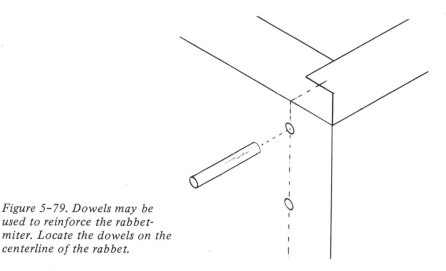

Figure 5-79. Dowels may be used to reinforce the rabbet-miter. Locate the dowels on the centerline of the rabbet.

Locked Rabbet-Miter

This joint incorporates a tongue and groove feature so the cutting procedure differs from those already described, even though the shapes are formed in a square whose sides are equal to the thickness of the stock.

The first steps on one piece are shown in Figure 5-80. There is no clearing out operation here. Instead, the distance from the rip fence to the blade is adjusted for the cuts so that a tongue remains on the work. The projection of the saw blade is still one-half the thickness of the stock. In the particular cut shown in the illustration, the distance from the rip fence to the outside surface of the blade is also one-half the stock thickness.

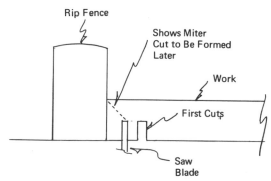

Figure 5-80. The first cut to make for a locked rabbet-miter.

The groove in the mating piece is formed with the stock on edge as shown in Figure 5-81. In the operation shown, the distance from the fence to the *inside* face of the blade equals one-half the stock thickness. The projection of the blade is *equal* to the stock thickness. Form the groove by making repeat passes or switch to a dado set. Be sure the width of the groove equals the thickness of the tongue formed on the first piece.

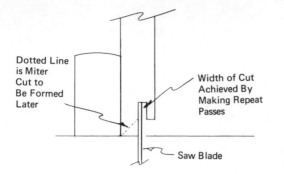

Dotted Line
is Miter
Cut to
Be Formed
Later

Width of Cut
Achieved By
Making Repeat
Passes

Saw Blade

Figure 5-81. The cuts on the mating piece are done this way.

Making cuts with the stock on edge is safe only if the work is large enough to provide good bearing surface on the table. When there is any doubt at all, or to be sure in any event, make the cuts by using a tenoning jig. This will provide extra safety and will also help you do a more accurate job.

A tongue and groove design can also be incorporated in the housed rabbet-miter (Figure 5-82).

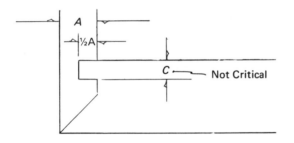

A

½A

C — Not Critical

Figure 5-82. A tongue and groove interlock can also be part of the housed rabbet-miter.

Chapter 6

LAP JOINTS

The term lap joints is often used too generally to describe a category of woodworking joints which are similar visually, but differ radically in relation to strength and how they are made. Literally, a lap joint is made by lapping one part of a project over another and fastening them together in the area of contact. Technically, such a connection is a *surface* lap. As shown in Figure 6-1, the strength of the joint when done only with glue would depend entirely on the area of contact. Unless mechanical reinforcements are added the joint will not resist lateral or twisting stresses for too long. This may be adequate for crate constructions and rough carpentry, but it won't be found too often in good cabinet work and furniture.

The lap joints that have more visual appeal and more strength are the half lap joints and the full lap joints. An example of a half lap joint is shown in Figure 6-2. Here, the thickness of each piece over the area of contact is reduced by one-half, so when the parts are put together the exterior surfaces will be flush and the joint will form an interlock. In the example, the connection is between one-piece back-and-leg and leg-and-seat components of a lounge chair. Since the joint will be severely tested, it is reinforced with screws that are concealed with plugs.

Full lap joints, examples of which will be shown as we go along, are usually done when one of the parts is thinner than the other. The seat cut, which is essentially a wide dado or rabbet, is formed in the thicker piece to suit the width and the thickness of the mating part.

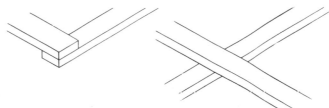

Figure 6-1. Surface laps do not make very strong joints unless they are reinforced.

Figure 6–2. Half laps form an interlock that resists stresses. Reinforcements may be added.

FRAME HALF-LAPS

Frame half-laps are often called end laps since they are used at the corners of frame constructions (Figure 6-3). The cuts required in both parts are rabbets that are sized according to the formula given in the illustration. The joint shown in Figure 6-3A is a full lap. In this case the rabbet cut is made only in the thicker piece and is dimensioned to suit the insert.

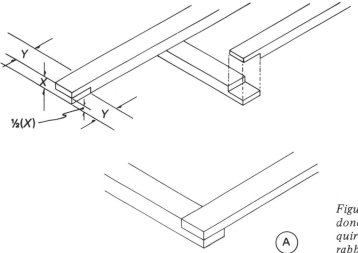

Figure 6–3. Frame half-laps are done at corners. The cuts required are actually matching rabbets.

The cuts can be made with a backsaw, as shown in Figure 6-4. First mark the work carefully with a square and then do the shoulder cut with a block clamped to the saw as a depth gauge. Make the second, or cheek cut, with the stock on edge. A good procedure is to clamp the mating pieces edge to edge so the saw cuts can be made in both in the one operation.

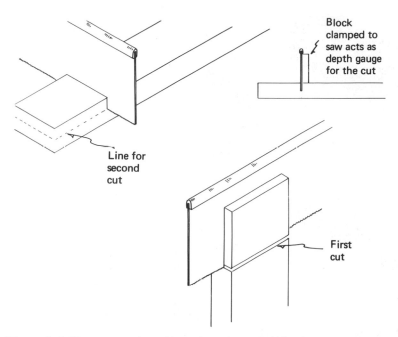

Figure 6–4. How to cut the rabbets for a frame half-lap by using a backsaw.

Sawing a fraction inside the line when doing the cheek cut is good practice. The cut is then cleaned out with a sharp chisel (Figure 6–5).

There are several ways to do the job on a table saw. Work with a dado assembly with its projection set to one-half the thickness of the stock. Clear out the shoulder area first and then make repeat passes to remove the rest of the waste. If you hold or clamp the mating pieces together, you can do the dado cuts across both at the same time.

A regular saw blade can also be used. Make the shoulder cut first with the stock flat on the table and then the cheek cut with the stock on edge. The latter

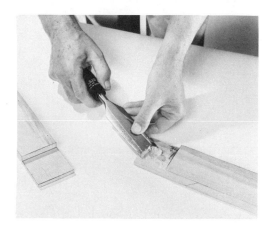

Figure 6–5. Finishing the cheek cut by working with a chisel. This is often done to assure smoothness and accuracy.

Figure 6–6. Use of a commercial tenoning jig on a table saw to form the shape for a frame half-lap.

cut is safer to do with a tenoning jig (Figure 6-6) since the work will be held securely with clamps. When you work this way you can skip the initial shoulder cut by making repeat passes to remove the waste. It's also possible to do a one-pass job if the dado assembly can be set high enough for the cut. Make the pass very slowly since you will be removing a lot of material.

Basically the same procedures can be followed on a radial arm saw. The

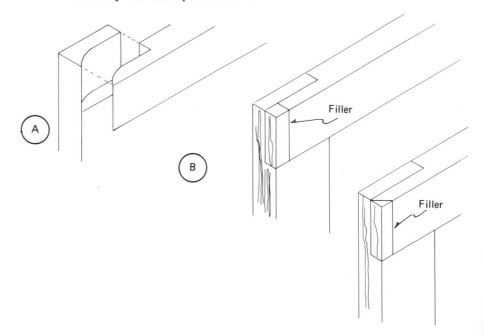

Figure 6–7. Modifying the cut as shown here lets you assemble parts with a minimum of exposed end grain.

work/machine relationship changes because of the characteristics of the tool. When doing the two-pass work, the shoulder cut is made with the stock flat on the table—the cheek cut by using a height table. If done with a dado set, the work is placed flat on the table and the cut is cleared out by making repeat passes.

The techniques shown in Figure 6-7 can be used to hide end grain. In A, the cut in one part is done with a dado set and stopped just at the edge of the work. The second piece has a full cut but the end is then rounded off so the two parts will mesh. In B, one of the pieces in the joint is cut short or end-mitered to accommodate small filler blocks. The results will be effective only if the fillers are made and installed very carefully. Match grain patterns as closely as possible.

Frame half-laps that do not make a 90-degree turn can be handled as shown in Figure 6-8. Make the shoulder cut at the necessary angle, but locate it so the cheek cut will be longer than necessary. Excess material can be trimmed and sanded flush after the glue is dry.

Figure 6-9 shows how you can design the joint to get the strength of a half-lap but the appearance of a miter on one side. Notice too that the end grain

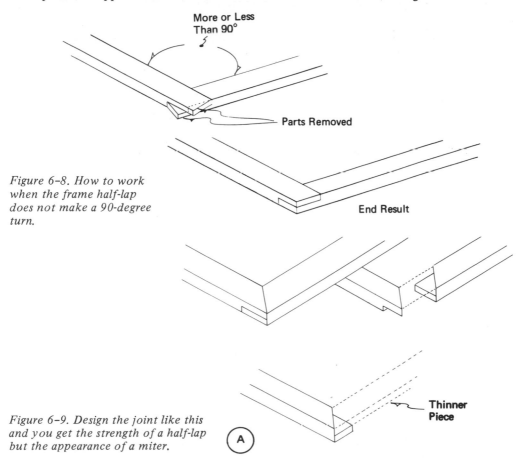

Figure 6-8. How to work when the frame half-lap does not make a 90-degree turn.

Figure 6-9. Design the joint like this and you get the strength of a half-lap but the appearance of a miter.

on one piece is visible only from a certain side. This is a good frame construction and is often used for cabinet doors, but be sure to plan so the mitered side will be the visible one when the project is finished. Figure 6-9A shows how to do the same thing when doing a full-lap joint.

Often, the cheek cuts on lap joints are sloped as shown in Figure 6-10. The mating bevels add a degree of interlock which strengthens the joint. The same illustration shows how the idea is applied to a middle or *T* half-lap.

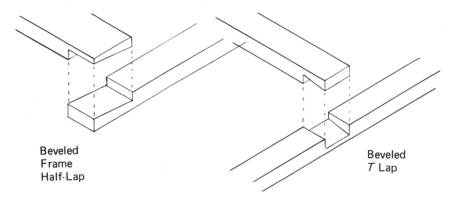

Beveled
Frame
Half-Lap

Beveled
T Lap

Figure 6-10. Incorporating a bevel provides some interlock so the joint will be stronger.

END-TO-END HALF-LAPS

An end-to-end half-lap isn't found too often on cabinets and furniture, but it can be handy for joining two pieces of wood which otherwise would be discarded to make a longer, usable board. The cuts (Figure 6-11) are the same as those needed for frame half-laps. The longer the joint line, the stronger the union will be.

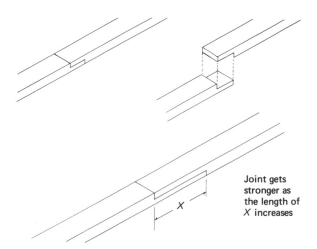

Joint gets
stronger as
the length of
X increases

X

Figure 6-11. Half-laps can be used to join parts end to end. The longer the lap, the stronger the joint.

A similar method can be used, as shown in Figure 6-12, when you need circular parts you can't cut from a single piece of stock. Straight segments are joined with end half-laps which are cut at the correct angle in relation to the number of pieces in the project. There are six segments in the illustration, so the joint angle is 30 degress. If mechanical reinforcements are used in the joints, be sure to situate them so they don't interfere with the circular cuts that will be made after the glue in the joints dries.

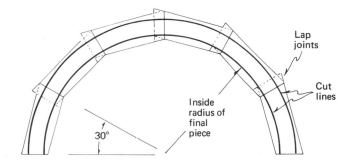

Figure 6-12. End half-laps can be used to join segments to "make" stock for circular forms.

MIDDLE OR *T* HALF-LAPS

Middle or *T* half-laps are used when one end of a project part connects to another component as shown in Figure 6-13. It does not necessarily have to connect at the *center* of the second piece. The cut in one piece is a dado whose depth equals one-half the stock thickness, and whose width matches the stock's width. The second piece is rabbeted so it will fit flush in the dado. The full-lap version is shown in the same illustration. Here, the dado is sized to match the dimensions of the insert.

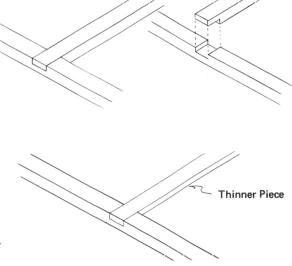

Figure 6-13. A middle or T lap calls for a dado in one part, a rabbet in the other.

Angled lap joints are used when the parts that join do not form a right angle. The major consideration here, of course, is that the dado and the shoulder of the rabbet be cut at the correct angle. Figure 6-14 shows a basic angled lap joint and a modified version which can make the connection stronger. In both cases, it's a good idea to form the rabbet so the insert will be longer than necessary. Sand the excess flush after the glue dries.

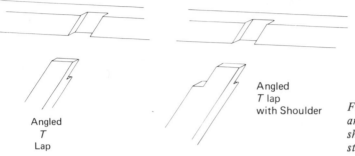

Angled
T
Lap

Angled
T lap
with Shoulder

Figure 6-14. T laps can be angled as shown. Providing a shoulder will make the joint stronger.

CROSS HALF-LAPS

This joint makes a strong connection when project components must cross each other (Figure 6-15). The cuts are duplicate dadoes which equal the width of the stock and one-half the stock's thickness. The joint can also be a full-lap when one of the parts is thinner than the other.

The dadoes can be cut quickly on a table saw or radial arm saw if you make repeat passes with a dado set. To form them by hand, follow the procedure shown in Figure 6-16. Use a backsaw to make shoulder cuts first, and then a series of relief cuts in between. The relief cuts will make it easier to remove the waste with a chisel. Work with the chisel from both edges of the stock as shown in the illustration, leaving a raised center area that will be removed last.

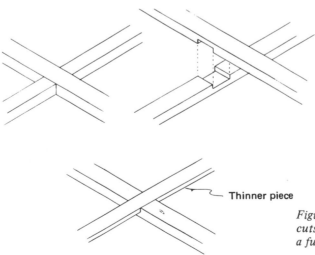

Thinner piece

Figure 6-15. Cross half-laps require dado cuts in both pieces. Bottom sketch shows a full-lap joint.

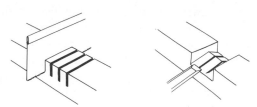

Figure 6-16. Dadoes for a cross half-lap joint can be formed with a backsaw and chisels.

Parts that cross often do so at an angle other than 90 degrees. The dadoes needed are cut in routine fashion but at the angle dictated by the project (Figure 6-17). A typical application of the cross half-lap is shown in detail A of the same illustration. This is a top view of diagonal stretchers used to strengthen the legs of a table project.

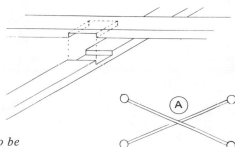

Figure 6-17. Cross half-laps can also be done at an angle. Diagonal stretchers are often joined this way.

EDGE HALF-LAPS

The difference between these joints and the cross half-laps is that the dadoes are cut into the edge of the stock instead of the surface (Figure 6-18). Because the dadoes are usually narrow and quite deep, they are often called notches. The formula for sizing the cuts departs from the way we've been working thus far. Here, the width of the dado equals the thickness of the stock, the depth of the dado equals one-half the width.

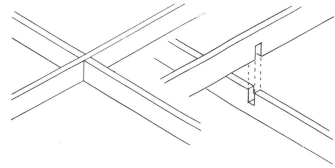

Figure 6-18. The cuts required for edge half-laps are often called notches because they are usually narrow and deep.

A miter box can be used when hand-sawing the shoulder cuts. Clamp a stop block to the saw (Figure 6-19) to control the depth of the cut. Let the stop block be long enough so it will span across the front and back of the box. Although the illustration shows one part being cut, there is no reason why you can't gang pieces so the same cut can be made on all of them. Work with a chisel as shown in Figure 6-20 to remove the waste. Remove it in sections, taking shallower bites the closer you get to the bottom of the notch. Do the final cleaning out by cutting from both sides of the work.

Figure 6-19. Shoulder cuts for notches can be formed this way. The clamp on the saw is securing a stop block.

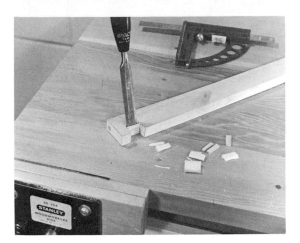

Figure 6-20. Clean out the waste between the shoulder cuts by working with a chisel.

This kind of cutting can be done easily and quickly on a table saw by using a dado set as shown in Figure 6-21. Be sure the width of the dado exactly matches the thickness of the stock and that its projection is exactly one-half the width of the stock. Here too, there is no reason why the same cut can't be made in many pieces at the same time. Clamp the parts together and pass them across the cutter as if they were a solid block.

Gang together pieces when using edge half-laps for egg crate or grid patterns (Figure 6-22). The formula shown in the illustration will apply regardless

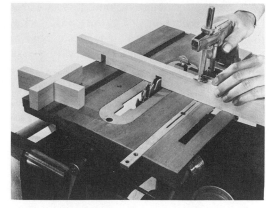

Figure 6-21. Notches can be cut very quickly and accurately by working with a dado set on a table saw.

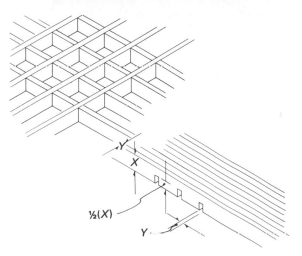

Figure 6-22. This is the formula to use when cutting notches for an egg crate pattern.

of the width or thickness of the stock. The cutting can be done freehand, guided by a careful layout on the front piece in the stack, but a better way, which provides a mechanical means of achieving accuracy, is to make a jig like the one shown in Figure 6-23.

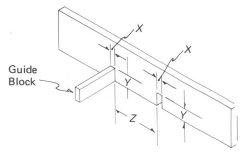

Figure 6-23. A jig like this, used with a miter gauge, helps you cut egg crate notches faster and more accurately.

X equals material thickness
Y equals ½ material width
Z equals spacing of partitions

The jig is secured to the miter gauge. Make the first cut by butting the edge of the stock against the side of the guide block. Other cuts are made by situating the last notch cut *over* the guide block. This organizes the procedure so the distance between notches on all parts will be exactly the same. No layout on the work is necessary.

Edge half-laps are often used to connect the sides of a project (Figure 6-24), as in an indoor or outdoor plant container. This joint forms a good interlock for a permanent project, but may also be used on units to be disassembled.

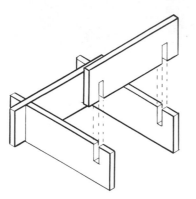

Figure 6-24. Notches are often used to form interlocking joints on the sides of projects.

THE FINGERLAP JOINT

The fingerlap joint (Figure 6-25) is often called a box joint. It is found on many classic pieces, sometimes exposed as an indication of craftsmanship, other times used in hidden areas simply because it has much strength. It does not have an interlock feature like the dovetail joint, but it has structural appeal because of the unusual amount of glue area. It also has visual appeal because of the way the shapes come together.

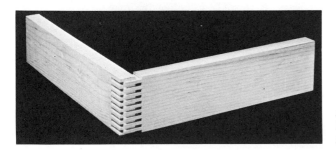

Figure 6-25. A fingerlap joint is good looking and very strong because of the substantial glue area.

A common recommendation for the design of the joint suggests that the width of the fingers and the notches should equal the thickness of the stock. This will work but it doesn't always produce the most attractive joint. Reducing the width of the fingers and notches to one-half the thickness of the stock (Figure 6-26) or even less often contributes to a better looking project. On shallow

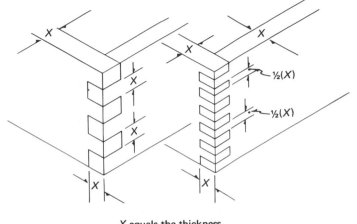

Figure 6-26. Two formulas you can use to dimension the fingers and grooves for a fingerlap joint.

X equals the thickness
of the stock

constructions—boxes, drawers, and the like—narrow fingers add to the total glue area and the project will be stronger.

The fingerlap joint may also be used to join parts that have different thicknesses (Figure 6-27). The result will be more appealing if the width of the fingers matches the thickness of the thinner part.

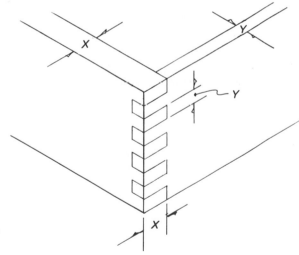

Figure 6-27. Work this way when one of the parts is thinner than the other.

CUTTING BY HAND

To cut by hand requires time and care, but these are craftmanship concerns under any circumstances. The joint should not be ignored just because hand tools must be used. A good procedure to follow is shown by the series of steps in Figure 6-28.

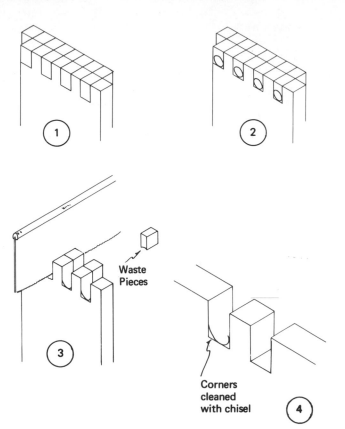

Waste
Pieces

Corners
cleaned
with chisel

Figure 6-28. A procedure to follow when forming a fingerlap joint with hand tools.

Step One: Clamp the pieces in a vise so they are offset by the width of one finger. Make a layout, as shown, to indicate the cuts across the edges and the depth of the cuts.

Step Two: Bore holes where indicated through both pieces of wood. Use a bit that matches or is a little smaller than the width of the notch. It's a good idea to clamp a piece of scrap against the back of the pieces so the bit won't cause splintering where it breaks through. Drill slowly and be sure the bit is perpendicular to the surface of the stock as you work.

Step Three: Use a backsaw or a dovetail saw to make the shoulder cuts. Stay a bit on the waste side of the line so you can use sandpaper or a chisel later to do the final cleaning out.

Step Four: Work with a chisel or a square-edge file to clean out the corners left by the bit. Some of this cleaning out can be done with the saw in step three.

CUTTING WITH POWER TOOLS

The fingerlap joint is cut on a radial arm saw by using an auxiliary height table as shown in Figure 6-29. The mating pieces are tack-nailed or clamped together to a backboard which is part of the table. The cuts shown in the illus-

*Figure 6-29. This is one way
to do the fingerlap on a radial
arm saw. Width of fingers and
grooves match the kerf width
of the saw blade.*

tration are no wider than the kerf made by the saw blade. This means that for
each cut you raise the saw blade a distance equal to twice the width of the kerf.
Careful settings and accurate tool adjustments are critical. Wider cuts are possible
when you substitute a dado assembly for the saw blade. Be sure the work is
locked firmly in position throughout the operation. Make the cuts slowly and
keep your hands away from the cut area.

Cuts can be made on a table saw to a layout on the work, but a much better way is to make a special jig (Figure 6-30). Notice that the jig is similar to the
one shown for cutting notches for egg crate patterns. This one, with its own bars,
is used independently of the miter gauge as shown in Figure 6-31. The distance
between the side of the guide block and the adjacent side of the kerf equals the
width of the fingers. The height of the guide block equals the depth of the cuts.
The length of the guide block is not critical, but it should not be less than twice
the thickness of the work. Use the jig as shown in the series of steps in Figure
6-32.

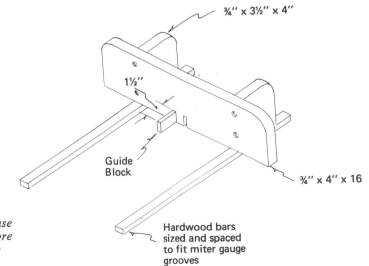

¾" x 3½" x 4"

1½"

Guide
Block

¾" x 4" x 16

Hardwood bars
sized and spaced
to fit miter gauge
grooves

*Figure 6-30. A jig you can use
on a table saw for faster, more
accurate cutting of fingerlap
joints.*

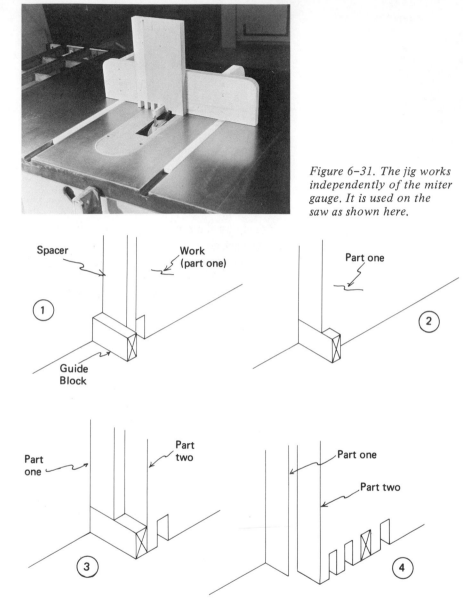

Figure 6–31. The jig works independently of the miter gauge. It is used on the saw as shown here.

Figure 6–32. These are the steps to follow when using the jig to form the shapes for a fingerlap joint.

Step One: Make a spacer strip with dimensions that match the groove width and place it between the guide block and the edge of one of the parts. Hold the work and spacer firmly in place and advance the jig to make the first cut.

Step Two: Remove the spacer and move the work so the first cut made will rest snugly against the guide block.

Step Three: Add the mating piece by butting it against the guide block. Then make a pass to form a groove in both pieces simultaneously.

Step Four: Continue to make cuts by placing the last groove formed over the guide block to position the work for the next cut.

Figure 6-33 shows the same type of jig, but made so it can be attached to the miter gauge. Figure 6-34 shows a version of the jig that can be adjusted for various groove widths. It, too, is attached to the miter gauge, but with screws that pass through a slot that permits lateral adjustments. Notice that the guide is a thin piece of hardboard instead of a full size block. This is so various groove widths can be handled. In practice, the cuts, as viewed from the operator's side of the machine should show the *left* side of the notch already formed, placed against the *left* side of the guide, which positions the work for the next cut.

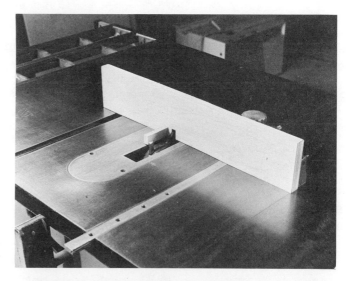

Figure 6-33. This version of the fingerlap jig is designed for attachment to the miter gauge.

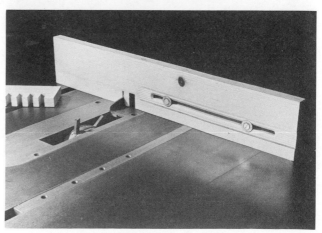

Figure 6-34. This jig also attaches to the miter gauge but is adjustable to suit various cut widths.

FINISHING THE JOINT

The fingerlap joint does have some exposed end grain. In order to minimize its impact, cut the notches just a bit deeper than they should be so the fingers will project a bit (Figure 6-35), and can be sanded perfectly flush later. Sanded end grain is always more attractive than the texture that remains after a saw cut.

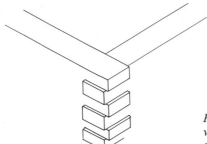

Figure 6-35. Design the cuts so the fingers will project a bit. Sand them flush when the glue is dry.

When the notches are cut deep enough so the fingers can remain projected as a design element (Figure 6-36) it has a unique appearance. In this case, the parts should be thoroughly sanded before assembly. Chamfering the corners of the fingers as shown in detail A of the same illustration can make the project even more attractive.

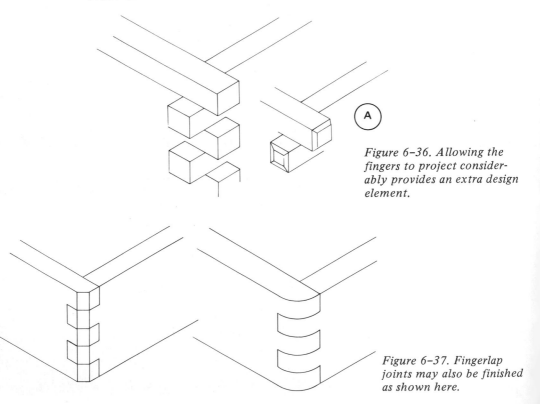

(A)

Figure 6-36. Allowing the fingers to project considerably provides an extra design element.

Figure 6-37. Fingerlap joints may also be finished as shown here.

142

Figure 6-37 shows two ways you can treat fingerlap joints after assembly is complete and the glue is dry. On large projects these jobs can be done with portable sanders. If the projects are small, the finishing can be done more easily on a stationary belt sander.

LOCKING THE JOINT

Figure 6-38 shows how a dowel can be used to secure a fingerlap joint so it will never come apart. Drill the hole for the dowel after the parts have been assembled.

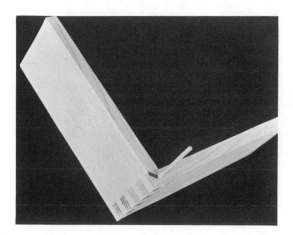

Figure 6-38. Use a dowel to provide a lock so the joint will never come apart.

A SWIVEL JOINT

This is also done using a dowel (Figure 6-39). Drill the dowel hole and then shorten the fingers slightly. Dress the corners so the parts can move freely.

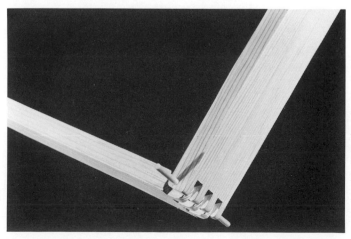

Figure 6-39. A dowel is also used when you design the fingerlap as a swivel joint.

A fingerlap jig can be used to form the notches required for the kind of work shown in Figure 6-40. Opposite frame pieces are held together to make both cuts at the same time. This will assure accuracy not only in the size of the notches, but in alignment as well.

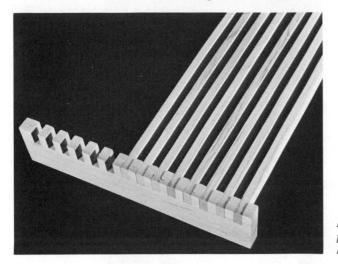

Figure 6-40. Notches are used in frame pieces of grid constructions. They may be cut with the fingerlap jig.

Chapter 7

MORTISE-TENON JOINTS

The mortise-tenon joint ranks with the dovetail in terms of good, quality construction. It's a craftsman's joint that can be used on doors, leg-stretcher or leg-rail assemblies for tables, cabinet assemblies, and so on. It's a joint that can hold up under racking or twisting stresses from any direction.

Too often, a doweled joint is used as a substitute. Not to downgrade a good dowel joint, but if used in place of a mortise-tenon in, for example, a rail to leg assembly, it is nothing more than a butt joint that is reinforced with dowels. The mating surfaces are end grain to surface grain and this does not provide the strongest glue bond. Strongest joints occur when the glue bonds long grain to long grain. The dowel doesn't contribute much to this, but a tenon in a mortise does. So, in addition to the interlock feature of the joint, you get an optimum glue bond on interior contact surfaces.

There are many variations of the mortise-tenon joint, some of which are shown in Figure 7-1, but as you will see, the general design involves an integral projection of one part that suits a cavity formed in the mating piece. The cavity is the mortise, the projection is the tenon. Knowledge of how to form the two parts is required to construct any type of mortise-tenon joint.

Often a mortise is used alone. A common example is the seat required for the leaf of a butt hinge. While this is not a wood-to-wood joint, the cutting procedure will be shown because the operation is an important one on any project that has hinged doors.

THE BASIC MORTISE-TENON

The parts of the joint are shown in Figure 7-2. The mortise may be blind or through and, of course, this determines how long the tenon must be. When the tenon passes through the mating piece, it is a good idea to form it longer than necessary so the projecting end can be sanded flush after the glue dries.

When the parts are joined you don't see more joint line than would be present if the joint was a simple butt. Exterior surfaces are flush if the pieces are

145

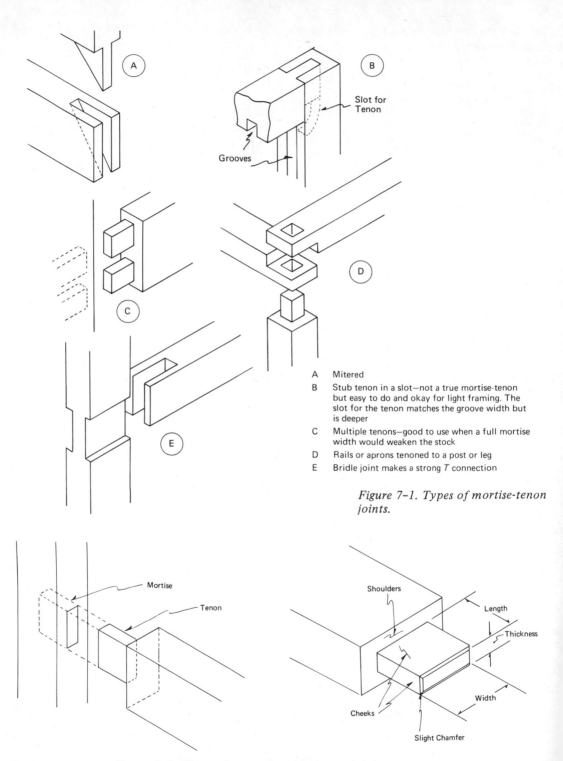

A   Mitered

B   Stub tenon in a slot—not a true mortise-tenon but easy to do and okay for light framing. The slot for the tenon matches the groove width but is deeper

C   Multiple tenons—good to use when a full mortise width would weaken the stock

D   Rails or aprons tenoned to a post or leg

E   Bridle joint makes a strong *T* connection

Figure 7-1. Types of mortise-tenon joints.

Figure 7-2. Nomenclature of mortise-tenon joints.

equal in thickness. When this is not the case, a typical example being the connection between legs and rails (or aprons), the rails should be set back, on the visible side at least, so there will be a small shoulder where the two parts meet (Figure 7-3). This is done so that a hairline crack that might in time develop along the joint line will not be so visible.

A good rule to follow when deciding on the thickness of the tenon is that it should not be more than one-third to one-half the thickness of the part it enters. There can be much variation in the length and width of the tenon. Its length depends on two factors: the width of the mating piece, and whether the mortise is blind or through.

The maximum width of a tenon should be about five inches. This is determined in relation to the mortise that must receive it. An oversize mortise can weaken the part it is cut in. The best way to handle situations in which a very wide tenon is needed is to form two or more tenons with ample space between them, as shown in Figure 7-1C.

Tenons should be cut a bit shorter than the depth of a blind mortise. Round off or chamfer the end of the tenon to provide some room for excess glue. The tenon should not fit the mortise loosely, nor should excessive force be necessary to seat it. A slip fit, one you can accomplish with only hand pressure, is best.

A good procedure to follow when shaping the parts for the joint is to form the mortise first and then cut the tenon to fit. Overall, this is a good way to achieve accuracy, especially when you are forming the cavities with mortising bits and chisels on a drill press. The cutters are not adjustable, but you can always cut the tenon a bit thicker or thinner.

MAKING A HINGE MORTISE

This requires as much care as any joint part if doors are to fit nicely and open smoothly. Start by using the hinge itself as a template to mark the outline of the mortise, as shown in Figure 7-4. Use a hard, sharp pencil and be sure the

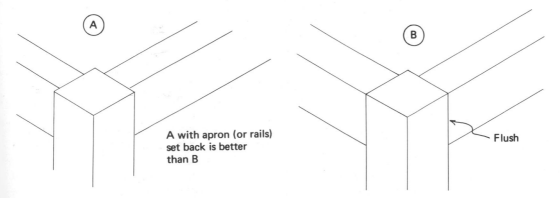

Figure 7-3. Parts set back as in A are less likely to show separation than parts set flush.

Figure 7–4. Use the leaf of the hinge as a template for marking the work.

hinge is held parallel to the work. Incise the lines with a sharp knife using a square as a guide (Figure 7–5) and favoring the hinge side of the pencil lines. Score several times, using more pressure each time to sever the surface fibers. If the mortise is very shallow you can score to the full depth of the cut. If you can't work this way, or if the wood is very hard, go over the scored lines with a chisel.

Figure 7–5. Score the lines with a sharp knife deeply enough to sever the surface fibers.

Use a chisel and mallet to make cuts across the mortise as shown in Figure 7–6, to make waste removal easier. This step is not always included. Often, a chisel is used immediately after the lines are scored (Figure 7–7). Remove the bulk of the stock by working with a mallet and keeping the bevel of the chisel down. Finish the job with only hand pressure, taking light, shaving cuts with the chisel's bevel up.

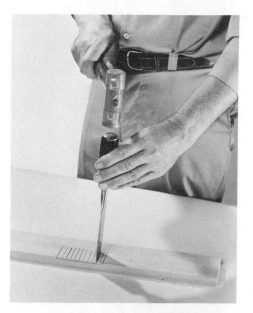

Figure 7-6. Make crosscuts with a chisel so removing the waste will be easier.

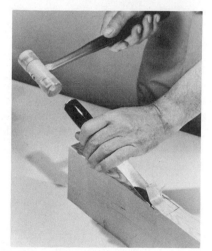

Figure 7-7. You can work without the crosscuts if you prefer but be careful not to cut too deeply.

FORMING A TRUE MORTISE WITH HAND TOOLS

The steps to follow when using hand tools are shown in Figure 7-8. First make a layout of the mortise using a marking gauge for the lines that are parallel to edges and a square for the others. Work with a sharp knife to score the lines deeply enough to sever surface fibers. Use a brace and bit to form overlapping holes that will remove the bulk of the waste. Work with a stop on the bit to control hole depth if the mortise is blind. If you drill through, use a piece of scrap under the work to minimize the splintering and feathering that will occur where the bit breaks out.

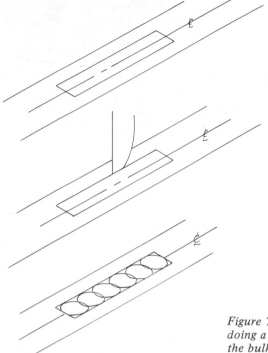

Figure 7-8. The steps to take when doing a full mortise and removing the bulk of the waste by drilling.

Clean out the mortise with chisels as shown in Figure 7-9. It isn't necessary to square off the ends of the mortise since the tenon can be rounded off to fit, as shown in the same illustration.

When working this way, plan the width of the mortise so the waste holes can be done with a standard bit. This does not impose serious limitations since bit sizes change by 1/16 inch.

Figure 7-9. Finish the job by working with a chisel. The edges of the tenon are rounded off to fit.

To cut a mortise working only with chisels, start the job as shown in Figure 7-10, removing the surface material after you have scored the layout lines with a knife. The idea is to make the entrance as clean as possible. Complete the job by following the steps shown in Figure 7-11. Make angle cuts in series, placing pressure on the chisel toward the center of the cavity. Do the final cleaning of the sides by using the chisel vertically.

Jobs like this will be easier to do with an assortment of chisels so you can choose the most appropriate width for the cut you are making. Removing a little material at a time is better than chewing out big chunks. The chisels must be *sharp.*

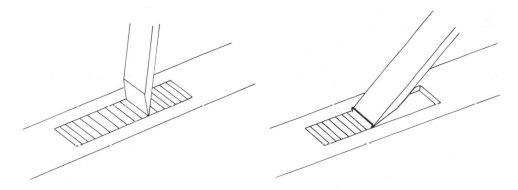

Figure 7-10. Start a full mortise this way when you are doing the job entirely with chisels.

Figure 7-11. Always make diagonal cuts toward the center of the cavity. Finish with vertical, shearing cuts.

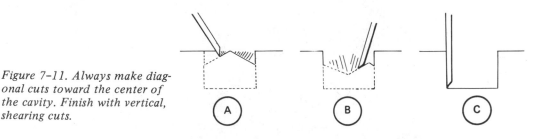

MORTISING ON A DRILL PRESS

The drill press must be equipped with a special mortising attachment which includes a fence and hold-down, and a device that mounts on the spindle and holds the mortising chisels (Figure 7-12). The mortising bit, which is encased in the chisel, works much like a regular drill bit to remove stock, but the chisel moves with it to clean out the corners that remain, the result being a square hole. The slot in the chisel allows waste to escape. Standard chisel sizes are 1/4 inch, 5/16 inch, 3/8 inch, and 1/2 inch, so size mortises accordingly.

The larger the chisel, the slower the drill speed you should use, especially on hardwoods. A general rule for chisels up to 1/2 inch is to use a speed range of 1800 to 2800 rpms for softwoods and 800 to 1500 rpms for hardwoods.

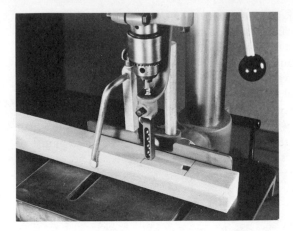

Figure 7-12. A drill press set up with a mortising attachment. Do the end cuts first.

Judge the *best* speed to use by the pressure of the cut. Excessive feed pressure should not be necessary, but a light touch won't do either. Remember that the chisel cuts under quill-feed pressure only. Be sure the chisel is organized so it is square to the fence.

The best way to operate is to mark lines on the work that tell where the mortise starts and ends. Make the end cuts first, as shown in Figure 7-12, and then remove remaining waste by making successive overlapping cuts (Figure 7-13). This procedure fights the tendency of the chisel and the work to move (Figure 7-14).

Figure 7-13. Remove the remainder of the waste by making overlapping cuts.

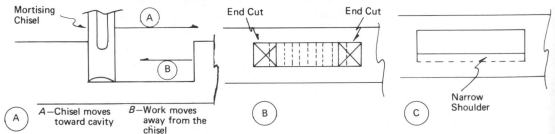

Figure 7-14. Guard against chisel and work movement when doing drill-press mortising.

Ideally, the overlap cuts should be about three-fourths of the chisel width. This can't always be done but stay as close to it as you can. Don't leave narrow shoulders if the mortise you need is wider than the largest chisel you have (Figure 7-14). It's better to work with a smaller chisel, overlapping the cuts across the stock as well as along the length of the mortise.

Mortising can be done on shaped stock like the table leg shown in Figure 7-15. Be sure, however, that the component is positioned so the mortise will be parallel to edges and perpendicular to the surface.

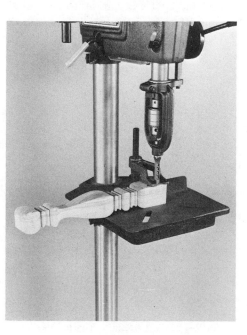

Figure 7-15. Preshaped parts can be mortised but be sure they have ample bearing surface so cuts will be square.

MORTISING ROUND STOCK

The mortise and tenon joint does not have to be restricted to square stock. By following a special procedure you can form joints like the samples shown in Figure 7-16. You can mortise rails or stretchers to round legs or even form radial mortises so corners of shelves can be inserted in round posts.

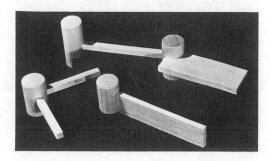

Figure 7-16. Mortises can be formed in round components if you make the jig shown in the next illustration.

For this, you must make the jig shown in Figure 7–17. While this is used in place of the regular mortising attachment, it doesn't cause any changes in the speed or feed pressure that you normally use. The purpose of the jig, basically, is to provide a holding device for round stock (Figure 7–18). You must be very careful when marking the stock since this is the layout you will follow when cutting. Be sure that the spindle and the *V* in the jig are on the same centerline and that the side of the chisel is square to the long line of the *V*. An alternate layout method you can use is to mark a longitudinal line on the work after you have formed the first end cut. Alignment of the following cuts will then just be a question of keeping the front edge of the chisel on the line.

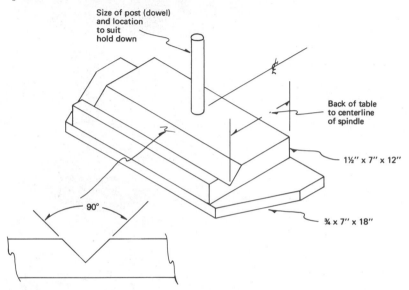

Figure 7–17. This jig, which you make, is used on the drill press in place of the regular mortising attachment.

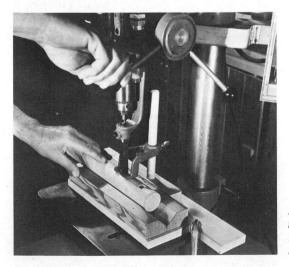

Figure 7–18. Round work nestles in the V-block. Mortises are cut without changing basic procedures.

Work as shown in Figure 7-19 to do radial mortises. You can do the end cuts first and then clean out the stock between them, or make successive overlapping cuts as you rotate the stock. Tack-nail a stop block across the jig as shown in the illustration in order to have a gauge with which to control work position. Figure 7-20 shows how you can use the same jig to form mortises in a corner of square stock.

Figure 7-19. A radial mortise is done by rotating the stock. A tack-nailed stop block gauges work position.

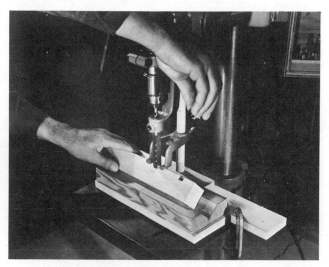

Figure 7-20. The same jig can be used to form mortises in the corners of square stock.

A little imagination will lead you to many off beat but practical additional uses for mortising bits and chisels. For example, consider the multitenon joint shown in Figure 7-21. This makes a strong connection and it can also add a design element if you allow the tenons to project as shown.

Figure 7-21. This is a special joint that is made by forming square holes with a mortising bit and chisel.

A portable router will cut clean, smooth mortises, but the operation must be organized so the tool will have adequate bearing on the work. One way is to broaden the work edge by clamping blocks on each side of it and using an edge gauge to guide the tool. A second method is shown in Figure 7-22. Here, an L-shaped guide that you make is secured to the base of the router to provide extra support and to guide the cut. If you cut slots in the guide for the attachment screws you can then adjust it in relation to the thickness of the stock.

Don't try to form deep mortises in one pass. It's better to make repeated cuts, adjusting for a deeper bite after each. Mortises formed this way have round ends so the tenon must be shaped to match.

Figure 7-22. How to cut a mortise by working with a portable router equipped with a homemade guide.

The Electrichisel® will form a mortise if used as shown in Figure 7-23. Note that the clamped guide block controls the depth of the cut and its alignment. Here too, the finished mortise calls for a rounded tenon.

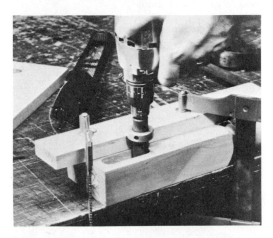

Figure 7-23. The Electrichisel® will form mortises but be sure the guide and the work are clamped securely.

156

An open mortise is a slot cut in one component to receive the tenon that is on the mating part (Figure 7-24). These are much easier to form than the mortises already discussed, but they must be done just as accurately. If you work with hand tools, do outline cuts first with a backsaw and then clean out the waste with a chisel. The job will go faster if you use a coping saw to remove the bulk of the waste and then a chisel to clean out the bottom of the slot.

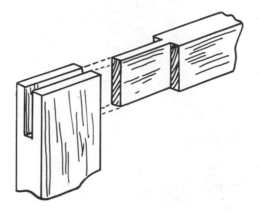

*Figure 7–24. Example of an
open mortise-tenon joint.*

Use a tenoning jig if you work with a table saw (Figure 7-25). Usually, the slot is centered. The best way to do this accurately is to make one outline cut and then do a second one after you have changed the position of the stock so the opposite face is against the jig. Clean out any waste that remains between the two cuts by making repeat passes.

*Figure 7-25. Using a tenoning jig to
form an open mortise. It's safer
than hand-holding the work against
a rip fence.*

157

The job can be done on a radial arm saw by using a height table (Figure 7-26). Here too, make outline cuts first, flipping the stock for the second one. Then clean out the waste with repeat passes.

A dado set can be used on either tool if you can get sufficient projection for the depth of cut you need. Remember that a dado set removes a lot of material, so passes must be made very slowly and carefully. Working with a dado isn't a bad idea even if you can't get enough projection. The cut you do form will be a good guide for finishing the job with hand tools.

Figure 7-26. A height table will position the work so you can cut open mortises on a radial arm saw.

CUTTING TENONS

The most common tenon designs are shown in Figure 7-27. All of them can be either blind or through (Figure 7-28). Good practice calls for doing an accurate layout on the wood of the shape you need, regardless of the tools you work with. Having scrap pieces on hand will let you do test cuts that you can check against the mortise before you cut into good stock.

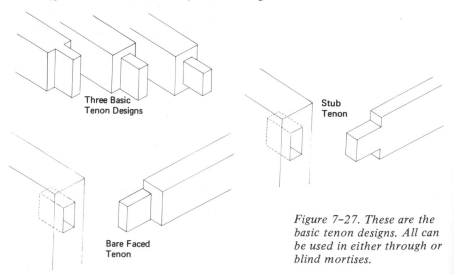

Three Basic
Tenon Designs

Stub
Tenon

Bare Faced
Tenon

Figure 7-27. These are the basic tenon designs. All can be used in either through or blind mortises.

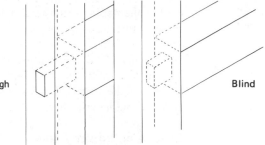

Through   Blind

Figure 7-28. A through tenon is exposed on one side of the joint. A blind tenon is completely concealed.

Figure 7-29. Use a marking gauge to mark parallel lines. Work with a square for the others.

Use a marking gauge to mark the lines that are parallel to edges (Figure 7-29). Do the other lines on *all* edges and surfaces by working with a square.

Cutting by Hand

When cutting by hand, work with a backsaw to do the shoulder cuts first (Figure 7-30). When the parts are narrow enough, you can gang them to make the saw cut across several at the same time. Clamp a stop block to the saw to

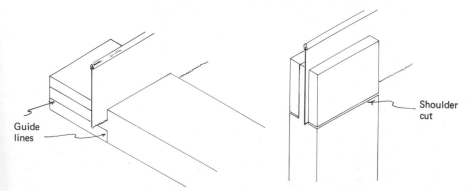

Guide lines

Shoulder cut

Figure 7-30. Use a backsaw to do the shoulder cuts first. Then saw the cheek cuts.

159

control the depth of the cut. An alternate method would be to clamp a block of suitable thickness to the work. This would control depth of cut and would also serve to keep the saw perpendicular. Finish the job by making the cheek cuts as shown in the same illustration.

If the tenon requires four shoulders, the operation described above is repeated on the edges of the stock. In this case you can clamp pieces together and do shoulder and cheek cuts on all of them at the same time.

Cutting on Power Tools

On a table saw, do the shoulder cuts first, using the setup shown in Figure 7-31A. The distance from the rip fence to the *outside* of the blade equals the length of the tenon; the projection of the saw blade will determine the tenon's thickness. Work like this must always be advanced with the miter gauge unless the stock is wide enough to provide adequate bearing against the fence.

If the tenon has four shoulders, repeat the cuts described above but with the stock on edge, and with the projection of the saw blade adjusted if necessary. The edge cuts *must* be done with a miter gauge regardless of the width of the stock.

The cheek cuts are made with the stock on edge (Figure 7-31B). Using a tenoning jig will help you work safely and more accurately than you could if you tried to handhold the work. The commercial units we have already shown can be used, or you can make your own by following the design shown in Figure 7-32. The fit of the jig over the rip fence must be precise, but not so tight

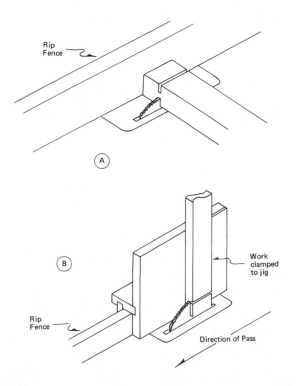

Rip
Fence

A

B

Work
clamped
to jig

Rip
Fence

Direction of Pass

Figure 7-31. Procedure to follow when forming tenons on a table saw.

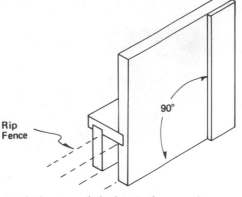

Rip
Fence

90°

Figure 7–32. A tenoning jig you can make.
Size it to slide on the rip fence without
wobbling.

that you must use force to move it. It's a good idea to polish the rip fence and
the contact surfaces of the jig with a hard, paste wax. Establish the position of
the 90-degree guide by using a square while the jig is in place over the fence.

Tenons can also be cut by using a dado set as shown in Figure 7–33. This
is an especially useful procedure for square tenons on square stock since the
tenon can be formed by making four passes, each time with the stock turned to
an adjacent surface. Notice that miter gauge stop rods are used to position the
work.

Tenons can be cut on a radial arm saw by using the height table as you did
to form an open mortise (Figure 7–34). The illustration shows repeated passes
being done to do the job, but if you made shoulder cuts first with the machine
in crosscut position, the waste could be removed by making single cheek cuts.

Figure 7–33. Cutting a four-
side tenon by using a dado
assembly on a table saw.

Figure 7–34. The height table can
be used when forming tenons on
the radial arm saw.

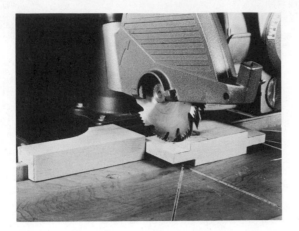

Figure 7–35. Similar tenons can be cut on many pieces when you use a setup like this.

Figure 7-35 shows how a dado set can be used. A stop block is used to gauge the length of the tenon; repeat passes are done to remove the waste. Notice that cuts can be made on opposite sides of the work merely by flipping the stock. Matching cuts are made on ends without changing the setup by turning the stock end for end.

Tenons that must fit round-end mortises are dressed as shown in Figure 7-36. The best procedure is to form the tenon in normal fashion with square edges, rounding them off by working with a file and then sandpaper.

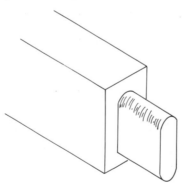

Figure 7–36. Tenons to fit round-end mortises are shaped this way. Use a file and sandpaper.

INTEGRAL ROUND TENONS

These can be formed on round or square stock by hand by following the procedures shown in Figure 7-37. Shoulder cuts to determine the length of the tenon are first done with a backsaw. The depth of the cut can be controlled with a clamped-on stop block regardless of whether the work is round or square.

The second step is to make a series of tangent cuts to remove the bulk of the waste. Finish the job by working with a file and then sandpaper. The more tangent cuts you make, the less material there will be to remove. The final smoothing should be done by using a narrow strip of fine sandpaper, buffing as you would a shoe with a polishing rag.

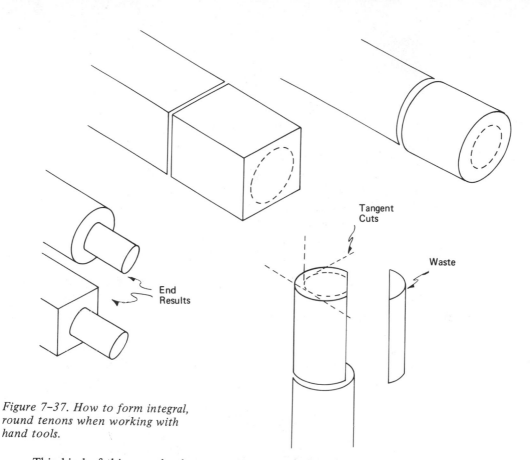

End
Results

Tangent
Cuts

Waste

*Figure 7-37. How to form integral,
round tenons when working with
hand tools.*

This kind of thing can be done on a power tool if you work with a plug cutter. The first step is to cut the kerfs that form the shoulders and determine the length of the tenon (Figure 7-38). The next step is to organize the power tool so the plug cutter can remove the waste. Figure 7-39 shows how this can be accomplished on a multipurpose tool that is set up for horizontal drilling. The same job can be done on a vertical drill press if the table is tilted 90 degrees and blocks are clamped to the table so the work will be positioned correctly under the spindle.

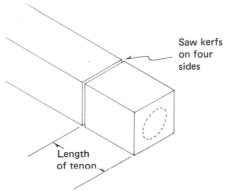

Saw kerfs
on four
sides

Length
of tenon

*Figure 7-38. The job can also
be done with a plug cutter on
a power tool. Make the shoulder cuts first.*

163

Figure 7–39. The plug cutter finishes the job by removing the waste stock. Accurate setups are critical.

HOW TO LOCK A TENON

The easiest way to lock the joint is to drill a hole and insert a dowel as shown in Figure 7–40. Do this while the parts are under clamp pressure.

A variation of the idea is shown in Figure 7–41. Here, the holes are drilled before assembly with one of them offset from 1/32 to 1/16 inch so that driving the dowel will force the joint parts tightly together. Notice that the dowel pin has one end rounded off so it will be easier to drive through the misaligned holes. In both cases, the dowel should be longer than necessary so it can be sanded flush later.

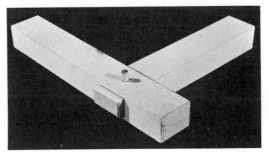

Figure 7–40. You can lock a mortise-tenon joint by driving a dowel this way.

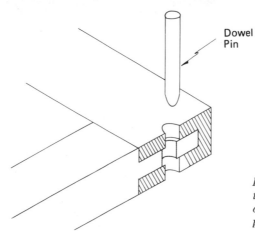

Dowel
Pin

Figure 7–41. If the holes in the mortise and the tenon are offset, the dowel will pull the parts tightly together.

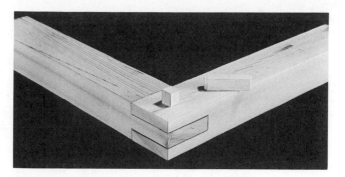

Figure 7-42. A square peg can be used to lock a mortise-tenon joint. Form the cavity with a mortising bit and chisel.

Figure 7-42 shows how a square peg can be used the same way. The square hole is formed with a mortising bit and chisel. The peg can be sanded flush or it can be precut to the exact length with chamfered ends so it can project as a decorative detail.

Tenons can be locked with wedges if they are slotted before assembly as shown in Figure 7-43. The best procedure is to assemble the parts and hold them under clamp pressure when you drive the wedges. Don't overdo the thickness of the wedges. They must expand the tenon to fill the mortise tightly but not to the point where they create a strain of their own.

Tusked tenons are shown in Figure 7-44. In both cases, the cavity through the tenon is located so that driving the tusk or the half-dowel will pull the parts of the joint tightly together. The square or rectangular tusk should have a slight

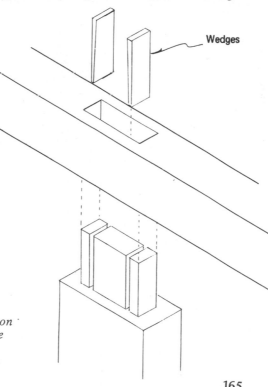

Wedges

Figure 7-43. A wedged mortise-tenon joint. Wedges can also be used if the tenon is not through. Just cut the wedges a bit shorter than the depth of the mortise.

165

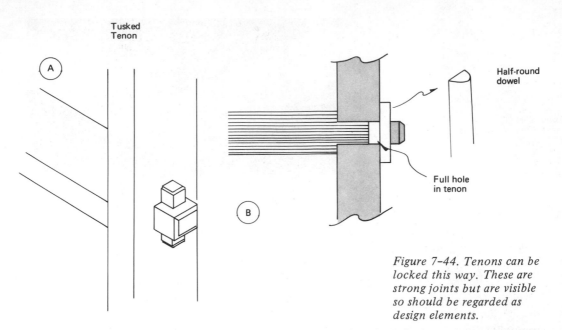

Tusked
Tenon

A

B

Half-round
dowel

Full hole
in tenon

Figure 7–44. Tenons can be locked this way. These are strong joints but are visible so should be regarded as design elements.

taper to make driving it home easier. Notice that the hole shown in Figure 7–44B can match the diameter of the lock dowel. Its position in the tenon is critical. If your accuracy in locating the hole is less than perfect, you can always shave off a dowel so its cross-section is more than half a diameter.

ANGLED JOINTS

The connection between stretchers or rails and slanted legs can be designed as shown in Figure 7–45. The mortise is formed so it is 90 degrees to the contact surface. The tenon and its shoulders are angle cut to conform.

Another way to make angled joints is to form the mortise so its sides remain on a horizontal plane. This can be done on a drill press (Figure 7–46) if

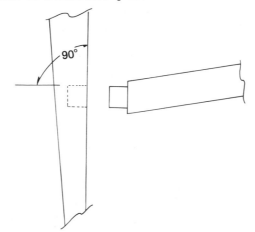

90°

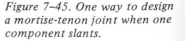

Figure 7–45. One way to design a mortise-tenon joint when one component slants.

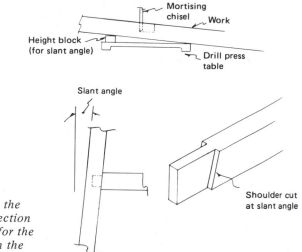

Figure 7–46. If you do the job this way, the connection will be normal except for the slanted shoulder cut on the tenon.

you use a height block under the work as shown. The thickness of the height block establishes the slant angle, but it must be attached to the work *not* the table in order for the mortise to have a flat bottom.

In this situation, the end of the tenon can be square; only the shoulders have to be angle cut to suit the slant on the mating piece.

MITERED TENONS

Mortise-tenon joints are often used to attach aprons or rails to legs. In some situations, especially when the rail or apron is flush with the leg, a standard tenon will not be as long and, therefore, not as strong as one which is mitered to fit, as shown in Figure 7–47. The cutting procedures remain the same. The only modification is the miter cut on the end of the tenon. The joint can be designed this way for both open and closed mortises.

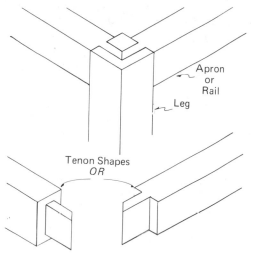

Figure 7–47. Tenons with mitered ends are often used when a regular tenon, being shorter, would not supply enough strength.

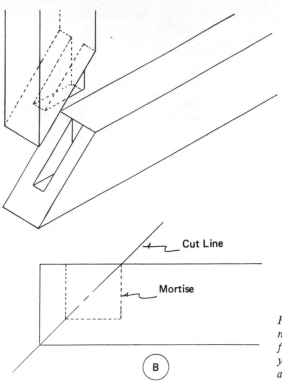

Cut Line

Mortise

Figure 7–48. A mitered mortise-tenon is good for frame constructions where you want strength and good appearance.

It doesn't matter if the joint shown in Figure 7–48 is a mitered mortise-tenon or a miter joint that is reinforced with a tenon. What is important is that the joint provides good strength and good appearance on frame constructions. Cutting the tenon is a matter of making angled shoulder cuts first and then cheek cuts which remove triangular-shaped waste pieces. Shorten the tenon by making a saw cut down through the edge of the stock and then finishing with a chisel.

Figure 7–48B shows an easy way to make the mortise. Form a regular blind mortise as shown and then make a miter cut to finish the job.

The joint shown in Figure 7–49 is something like a lap miter that includes a tenon. The design provides for a considerable amount of glue area. One side has the appearance of a frame half-lap; the other, more attractive side, appears as a miter.

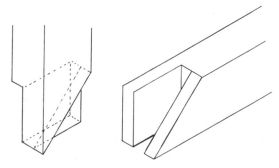

Figure 7–49. This type of joint provides a lot of area for glue. It looks like a half-lap on one side, a miter on the other.

Haunched tenons are often used in the corner joints of frame constructions that are grooved to receive panels (Figure 7-50). Here, the principal purpose of the haunch is to fill the gap that is left visible by the full length groove in the frame members. Note that the width of the mortise and the frame grooves, and the thickness of the tenon are similar. This makes for much easier construction procedures.

Haunched tenons are often used on plain frame constructions because they contribute strength in the joint. Many times, the haunch is sloped as shown in Figure 7-51, so there will be no visible increase in joint lines.

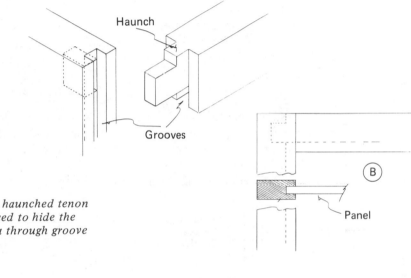

Figure 7-50. A haunched tenon is frequently used to hide the gap caused by a through groove in framework.

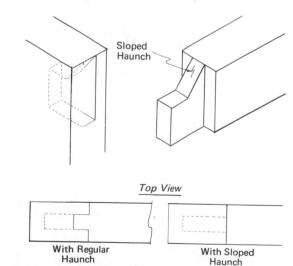

Figure 7-51. A haunch will also provide some extra strength. If it is sloped, it will not contribute any visible joint lines.

169

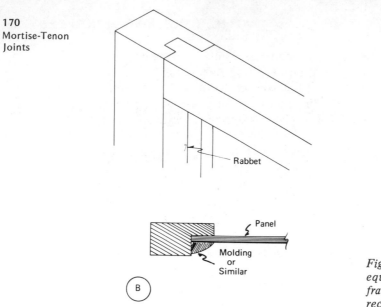

B

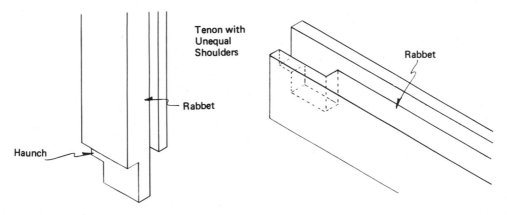

*Figure 7-52. A tenon with un-
equal shoulders is required on
frame work that is rabbeted to
receive a panel.*

Tenons with unequal shoulders are used with a mortise in framework or sash constructions where a rabbet is required (Figure 7-52). The detail B is a cross-section through a frame member to show how the rabbet supplies a seat for a glass or wood panel insert.

Figure 7-53 shows the shapes on the mating pieces.

Figure 7-53. The length of the tenon, on one side, is longer by the depth of the rabbet cut.

Chapter 8

EDGE-TO-EDGE JOINTS

The edge-to-edge joint is important when assembling solid lumber slabs for table and desk tops, chair and bench seats and sides of case goods. It isn't likely that you will find lumber as wide as you need and even if it was available, it might not be wise to use it as is. Unless you decide to use plywood, make up wide slabs by edge joining narrow boards.

Since wide boards can warp badly, it is common practice among crafts-people to rip cut them, say into three pieces, and then reassemble them by edge gluing with the center piece inverted. This alternates the direction of the annual rings from piece to piece, placing stresses opposed to each other instead of work-ing toward a cumulative warp (Figure 8-1).

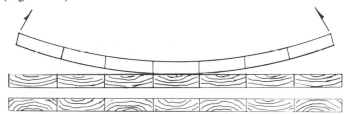

Figure 8-1. One way to join boards is to invert alternate pieces to avoid cumulative warpage.

A reason given for *not* inverting alternate pieces is that distortion in each might result in a rippled or washboard type surface that would be difficult to hold down without a lot of screws. It seems a rather extreme point to make since any "waves" that might occur could be removed easily with a belt sander or a plane. Also, if the parts are joined as shown in Figure 8-2, the arch that could result would certainly require mechanical fasteners to bring the slab to levelness.

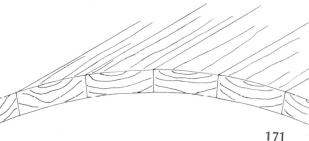

Figure 8-2. Some crafts-people prefer to join boards this way. Reasons are given in the text.

171

Perhaps one of the more important things to consider is a basic characteristic of a tree and how this affects boards that are cut from it. A tree grows by adding cells at its circumference. The old wood (heartwood) is at the center of the tree. The new wood (sapwood) is at exterior areas (Figure 8-3). The new wood, usually more porous than the old, will be more affected by changes in humidity. If you ignore this, different rates of expansion and contraction can result in rough joint surfaces. If you join old wood to old wood and new wood to new wood, as shown in Figure 8-4, you will be doing much to minimize the effects of natural distortions.

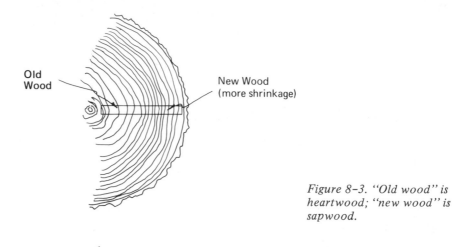

Figure 8-3. "Old wood" is heartwood; "new wood" is sapwood.

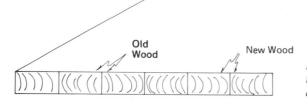

Figure 8-4. Joining wood like this does much to minimize the effects of natural distortions.

Pay some attention to the grain pattern you will have after pieces are joined. Place parts together loosely so you can study the effect. Move them or shift them longitudinally until you get the most attractive results. Draw a light pencil line across the pieces and number them so you will know the position and the order you have established. This can also be important later should you add reinforcements to the joint.

MAKING THE JOINT

Boards have a greater tendency to shrink at their ends where more open pores exist than at middle points. A way to counteract shrinkage or splitting is to use a "spring-type" joint like the one shown in Figure 8-5. This puts the ends of the boards under compression so the shrinkage that can occur there won't result in distortion. A very thin glue line also results with this design. The shaving

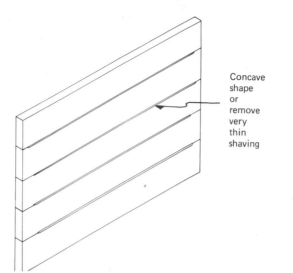

Concave
shape
or
remove
very
thin
shaving

*Figure 8–5. A spring-type joint
requires that the mating edges
have a very slight concave shape.*

that is removed must be very fine and is best done with a hand plane that is set
to remove a see-through shaving (Figure 8-6).

Boards that make up slabs should be tested for fit before the glue is
applied (Figure 8-7). Don't depend on clamp pressure to make up for poor cutting since it will only result in additional stresses that can contribute to failure
or gaps in joint lines.

*Figure 8–6. A hand plane will
enable you to remove a see-
through shaving. The job can
also be done on a jointer.*

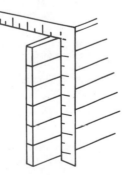

*Figure 8–7. Check to see if the parts for a slab will fit
together nicely before you do assembly work.*

REINFORCEMENTS

A good spring-type, edge-to-edge joint will make a bond as strong as the wood itself. Destruction tests show that adjacent areas may fail before the joint does. So the question is asked, why reinforce it? For one thing, you add a safety factor that helps combat exterior stresses caused by use. Another, possibly more important reason, is that most reinforcement procedures provide a type of interlock so parts will remain in alignment under clamp pressure. Anyone who has ever tried to assemble a considerable number of pieces using only a butt joint will know how helpful an interlock can be.

WORKING WITH DOWELS

Dowels are often used in edge-to-edge joints because the simple lines of what is actually a reinforced butt joint are the least obtrusive. The number of dowels you use is not as critical as the accuracy required to locate them. If the dowel holes are not precisely located the method will do more harm than good.

Some general rules for dowel locations are shown in Figure 8–8. They should not, however, be accepted as bible. Many craftspeople will not use a dowel at the end of the pieces and will increase spacing to as much as 18 or 20 inches. This approach utilizes the dowels more for parts alignment than for reinforcement. Conversely, some people using dowels will go to the opposite extreme and do a layout like the one shown in Figure 8–9 where the dowels are broadcast over the entire slab instead of being in line. This approach may be okay for heavy-duty projects subjected to considerable abuse, but it isn't necessary for components like desk or table tops. When it is done, considerable attention should be given to the grain relationship of adjacent pieces.

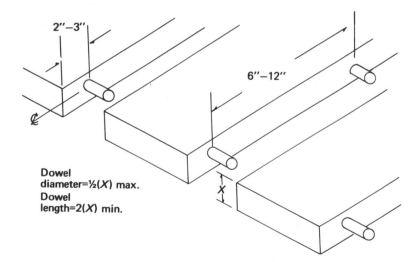

Figure 8–8. Guide rules for dowel placement. The text explains why these rules are often ignored.

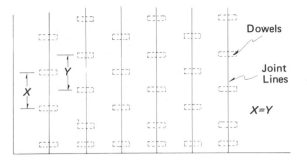

Figure 8-9. Dowels are often broadcast when the slab is for heavy-duty use.

MARKING AND DRILLING

Centerlines should be established by marking from the same surface of each piece. This way, a slight error will be consistent. The lines may not be exactly centered but since the edge distance will be the same on all pieces, the dowel holes will still be aligned.

The distance between holes can be marked with a compass or dividers (Figure 8-10). Here too, a slight error will not cause problems as long as the first piece is used as the gauge to mark others.

A common method is to work with a square, as shown in Figure 8-11, to carry the lines across other edges. If the dowel holes are going to be formed on a drill press, centerlines are not required. The location of a fence, clamped to the drill press table to position the work under the spindle, will control edge distance if the same surface of each piece is placed against the fence.

A good way to work when drilling the holes with a brace is shown in Figure 8-12. After spotting the hole centers on one piece, tap in small, short brads and then snip off the heads. Pressing the next piece in place will mark it for

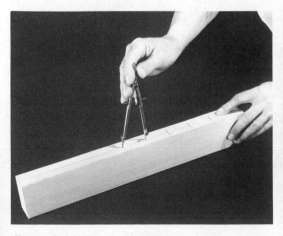

Figure 8-10. Use a compass or dividers to lay out the spacing between dowel holes.

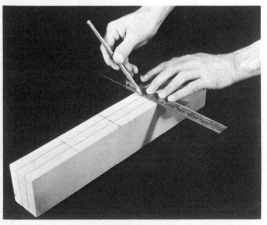

Figure 8-11. Carry the lines across the slab parts by using a square as a guide.

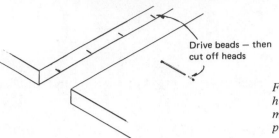

Figure 8–12. Brads, with heads cut off, make good markers for locating hole positions on mating pieces.

accurate drilling. You must be sure the parts are aligned when pressing them together. An accurate way to do the job is shown in Figure 8–13. Tack-nail guide strips to the workbench so they form a 90-degree angle. The guide piece is placed as shown and the mating part is moved against it.

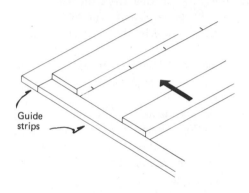

Figure 8–13. Set up temporary guide strips so parts will be aligned when you press them together.

A similar way to work is to locate and bore the holes in the pattern piece by working with a brace and a doweling jig (Figure 8–14). For each hole be sure to place the solid side of the jig against the face side of the stock to keep edge distances the same. Dowel centers can then be used (Figure 8–15) to locate hole centers on the mating piece.

Figure 8–14. Drill dowel holes by working with a doweling jig. Be sure the solid side of the jig is against the same side of the stock for each hole.

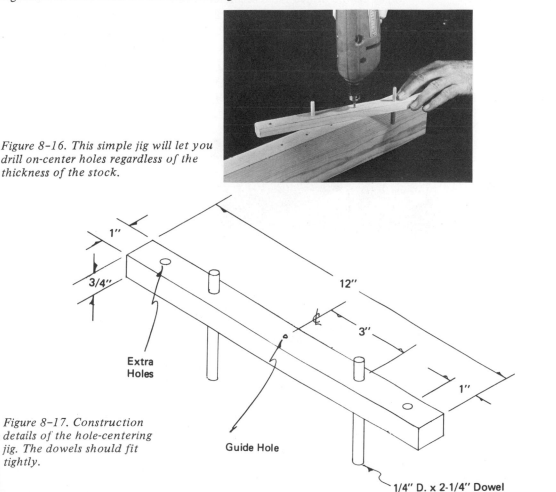

Figure 8-15. Dowel centers can be used in drilled holes so the pattern piece can be used to mark others.

The jig shown in use in Figure 8-16 is easy to make and handy to have since it will automatically locate holes in the center of edges regardless of the stock's thickness. The construction details are shown in Figure 8-17. When you use the jig, work with a 1/16-inch drill point or twist drill and form the holes only as deep as the dowel will penetrate. Form a hole so that the screw point on a brace can still be gripped. Use a stop on the bit (Figure 8-18) to control hole depth when you open the holes to full size. The jig, of course, can be used regardless of what tools do the final drilling.

Figure 8-16. This simple jig will let you drill on-center holes regardless of the thickness of the stock.

Figure 8-17. Construction details of the hole-centering jig. The dowels should fit tightly.

1"

3/4"

12"

3"

1"

Extra
Holes

Guide Hole

1/4" D. x 2-1/4" Dowel

Figure 8–18. Use a stop on the bit so the hole depths will be uniform.

Holes can be drilled more accurately and with less fuss if the job is done on a drill press (Figure 8-19). A fence is clamped to the drill press table behind the work to keep the part vertical and to control edge distance of the holes. A second block is clamped as shown to guard against tilting the work as the drilling is done. The mark indicated by the arrow is a guide for positioning work correctly for each hole. In this case, hole locations are marked on the surface of the pieces. A centerline on the edge of the stock is not needed if the same surface of each piece is placed against the fence.

Figure 8–19. Drilling dowel holes on a drill press. The clamped fence is set to control edge distance.

Figure 8-20 shows how the job can be done on a horizontal boring machine, which in this case is a multipurpose tool set up for horizontal drilling. Here, hole locations are marked on the edges of the pieces. It's just as important to place pieces so the same surface of each will be either up or down. The depth of the holes is controlled by using the built-in stops on the machine. The hold-down is actually a mortising attachment accessory, which serves a practical function when used this way.

Figure 8-20. This is a multi-purpose tool set up as a horizontal boring machine to drill dowel holes.

SPLINES

Edge-to-edge joints can be splined as shown in Figure 8-21. The parts in the photograph are offset only so the cuts can be seen. Note that the ends as well as the edges of the pieces are grooved. This may be done when an end strip is added to the slab to conceal the splines. General rules for sizing grooves and splines are shown in Figure 8-22. The width of the spline may be a fraction less than the combined depth of the grooves, but it must never be more. If it is, the joint edges will not come together.

Figure 8-21. Use of splines in an edge-to-edge joint.

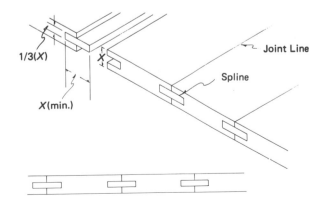

Figure 8-22. Guide rules to follow when sizing splines.

End strips serve a double purpose. They hide the splines and they cover the end grain of the slab components. Cut these end pieces so they will be slightly concave on the edge that mates with the slab. This will cause the ends of the piece to exert extra pressure when the parts are clamped together. Many woodworkers will use glue only at the center area of the end piece regardless of how the joint is designed. The logic is that the length of the end boards will remain fairly stable while the pieces in the slab might change in width because of moisture variations. If parts can move a bit, they won't split. If the job is done this way, it is recommended that a dowel pin be used at the center area in place of or in addition to glue.

End boards that are attached with splines, or with a tongue and groove arrangement, will still reveal objectionable joint lines as indicated in Figure 8-23. To get away from this you can use a blind spline to attach the end board or you can design the slab for a perimeter frame as shown in Figure 8-24.

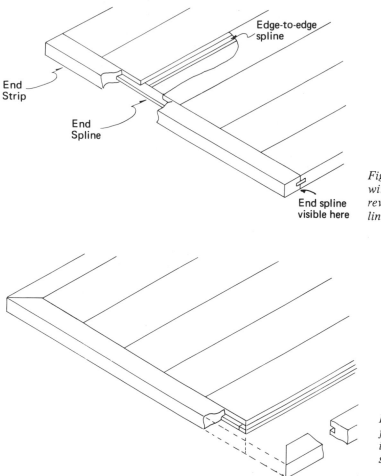

End Strip

Edge-to-edge spline

End Spline

End spline visible here

Figure 8-23. An end board with a through spline will still reveal some unattractive joint lines.

Figure 8-24. A perimeter frame with mitered corners is attractive and conceals all splines.

Grooves for splines, or for tongue and groove joints, can be cut on a table saw by making repeat passes (Figure 8-25). An easy way to be sure the groove will be centered is to establish edge distance by measuring from the fence to the inside surface of the blade. Then make two passes, each with an opposite surface of the stock against the fence. Clean out between the first cuts by making repeat passes.

Figure 8-25. Spline grooves can be cut by making repeat passes with a regular saw blade.

The job can be done in a single pass if you work with a dado set. In this case, make all the cuts so the same surface of each piece will be against the fence.

Splined joints can be done without exposing the splines if the grooves are stopped, as shown in Figure 8-26. The radius left at the ends of the grooves is not objectionable since the splines can be shaped to fit.

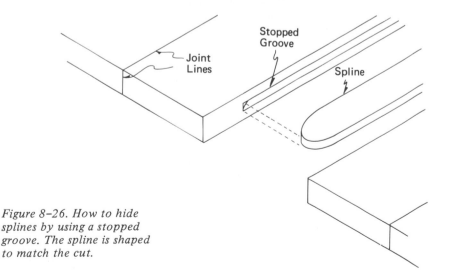

Joint Lines

Stopped Groove

Spline

Figure 8-26. How to hide splines by using a stopped groove. The spline is shaped to match the cut.

DECORATIVE SPLINES

Splines can be designed as shown in Figure 8-27 to serve as parts of the joint and to provide an attractive inlay effect. The results are more beautiful when the splines are cut from a contrasting wood. The grooves are cut in routine fashion, but the best way to form the splines is to preshape a board as shown in Figure 8-28. A careful layout and a precise machine setup are required. Remember that the splines must be separated and that the width of the saw kerf must be considered. A molding head fitted with a blank blade is being used in the illustration, but a dado set could be used as well.

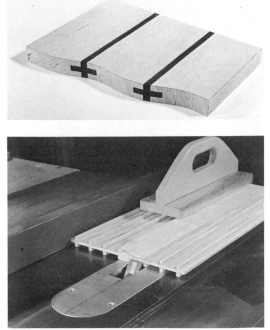

Figure 8-27. Special splines can be used to add an inlay effect to the project.

Figure 8-28. The special splines may be shaped with a blank knife in a molding head.

The splines may be separated by working as shown in Figure 8-29. The cuts must be made very carefully, especially when the width of the vertical part of the cross-form does not provide much bearing surface on the table. Work with a hollow ground blade to get a smooth cut, and be sure to use a pusher stick to feed the stock.

The height of the vertical part of the spline can be greater than the thickness of the slab pieces. This will allow you to sand them flush after the glue dries.

TONGUE AND GROOVE JOINT

This is much like a spline joint except that the parts are integral. General rules for dimensioning are given in Figure 8-30. Both the tongue and the groove can be formed in conventional ways by working with a regular saw blade on a

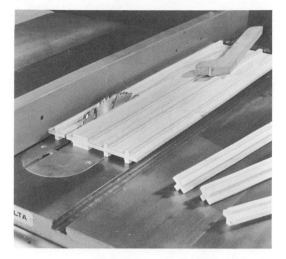

Figure 8-29. Separate the splines by making rip cuts. Use a push stick. Be careful so the cut-off won't tilt.

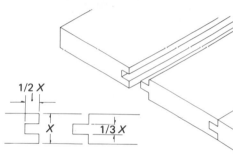

Figure 8-30. Guide rules for sizing tongue and groove joints.

table saw or radial arm saw. The tongue is formed by doing a two pass rabbeting operation on opposite edges of the stock, and the groove by making repeat passes. Faster production is possible if you work with shaped cutters. These come in matched sets for use with a molding head that can be mounted on a table saw or radial arm saw or, as three-lip shaper cutters for use on a shaper. Figure 8-31 shows a groove being formed by a molding head operation.

Figure 8-31. Cutting a groove by using a special cutter in a molding head. A matching tongue cutter is also available.

An important point to remember when making tongue and groove joints is that the width of the tongue must be considered when determining the true width of the pieces on assembly (Figure 8-32). Note that even though the two parts are 2 inches wide, the total width is reduced by 1/4 inch when the pieces are joined.

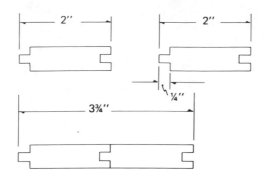

Figure 8-32. The total width of two pieces joined with a tongue and groove is reduced by the width of the tongue.

RABBET JOINT

The best way to plan the rabbet joint is to size cuts as shown in Figure 8-33 so cuts can be made on opposite edges of the stock without having to change a tool setting. The fastest way to cut the rabbets is to use a dado assembly on a saw or to work on a jointer. The width considerations we discussed in relation to the tongue and groove joint also apply to the rabbet joint, as shown in Figure 8-34.

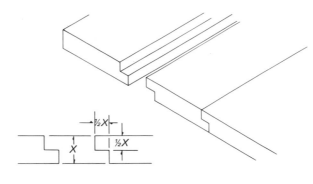

Figure 8-33. Guide lines for sizing edge-to-edge rabbet joints.

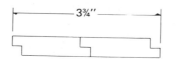

Figure 8-34. The width reduction that happens with a tongue and groove joint also happens with a rabbet joint.

This is the popular name for a milled joint that is easy to accomplish with a molding head on a saw or with a three-lip cutter on a shaper (Figure 8-35). The cutter is designed so the shaped edges will fit perfectly if the second piece of stock is flipped for the mating cut. It's one way to use only one cutter where two might otherwise be needed.

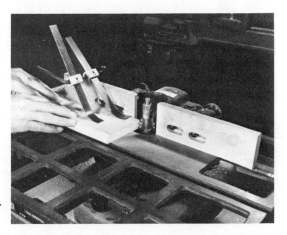

Figure 8-35. The glue, or milled joint is easy to form when you use a special cutter on a shaper.

The joint provides extra glue area and also provides an interlock so pieces will not move during assembly. The joint is neat and unobjectionable should you decide to leave end grain exposed.

The mating edges of the stock must be dressed for a tight fit before they are shaped. Irregularities will merely be duplicated by the cutter. Organize the shaper fences to be in line with the smallest diameter of the cutter. Make a test cut with a scrap piece of material so you can adjust the depth of the cut and the height of the spindle. If test pieces do not go together so that surfaces are flush, you know that further adjustment is necessary.

Once the setup is correct, proceed to make cuts as shown in Figure 8-36.

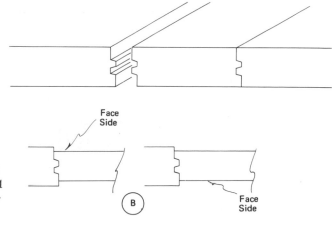

Figure 8-36. The one cutter will form the shape on both pieces. A careful setup is required so make test cuts first.

The *V*-joint can be accomplished with a regular saw blade but the joint will be neater and tighter if the *V* is milled with a shaper cutter and the point is sawed to fit (Figure 8–37). Notice in detail B of the same illustration that the *V*'s can point in opposite directions. This affords an opportunity to add a decorative detail to the ends of slabs, especially if alternate pieces are a contrasting wood.

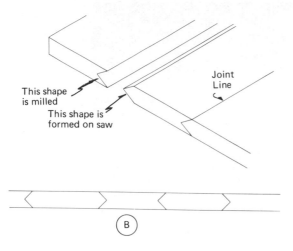

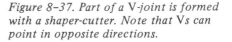

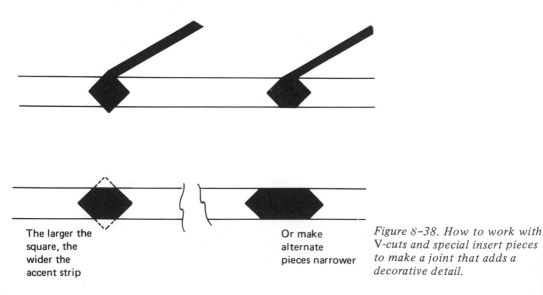

Figure 8–37. Part of a V-joint is formed with a shaper-cutter. Note that Vs can point in opposite directions.

This can be carried further for the effect shown in Figure 8–38. Here, the main pieces of the slab are *V*-cut and then joined with square pieces of contrasting wood between. When the projection of the square pieces is sanded flush after the glue dries, you have accent strips on the surface of the slab and diamond shapes at the ends.

The larger the square, the wider the accent strip

Or make alternate pieces narrower

Figure 8–38. How to work with V-cuts and special insert pieces to make a joint that adds a decorative detail.

End boards are usually used to hide end grain but, as shown in Figure 8–39, they can be shaped to provide lips and make the slab look thicker. One of the sketches shows how the end of the slab can be made more attractive *without* adding an end board. A bevel will put the joint lines below the line of sight. This should be cut or planed off after the slab has been assembled.

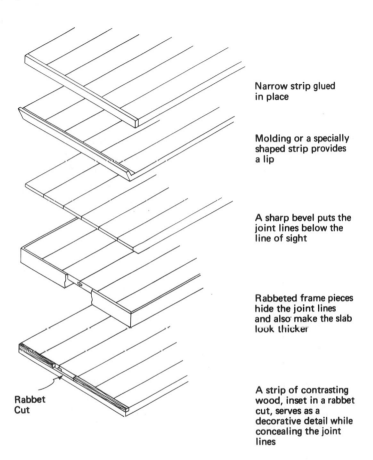

Narrow strip glued in place

Molding or a specially shaped strip provides a lip

A sharp bevel puts the joint lines below the line of sight

Rabbeted frame pieces hide the joint lines and also make the slab look thicker

Rabbet Cut

A strip of contrasting wood, inset in a rabbet cut, serves as a decorative detail while concealing the joint lines

Figure 8–39. Various methods used to finish the ends of a slab.

Chapter 9

DOVETAIL JOINTS

Dovetails have been synonymous with quality construction even though today they can be found on poorly made furniture simply because they can be spewed out by machine like so much spaghetti. This brings up a debatable point. Are handmade dovetails better than those produced by machines? The dovetail concept is there regardless of how they are made. The individual doing hand toolwork can produce more exclusive designs, since the machine must shape the interlocking components in an assembly-line fashion (Figure 9-1).

If design originality is the criterion of quality then the hand toolworker would win hands down, but being exclusive, while it might be an asset, doesn't guarantee quality work or stronger results. As in all phases of joinery it is how the job is done that counts, not the fact that it's original.

MULTIPLE DOVETAILS

The basic designs for multiple dovetails are shown in Figure 9-2. Those that are used most often are the through dovetail and the half-blind dovetail. When assembled, the blind dovetail looks like a simple miter joint. Since it doesn't permit an inspection of how the parts fit and calls for an exceptional amount of labor, the blind dovetail is seldom used and then only on very special work. Most woodworkers feel that since there is no stigma attached to exposed dovetails, there isn't much point in going through the extra chore of hiding them.

The nomenclature of the dovetail joint can be confusing unless you study the shapes of the interlocking parts. As you can see in Figure 9-3, the dovetail shape appears everywhere even though in construction procedures it is the pins and sockets that are referred to. Quite often, the solid piece between the sockets is simply called a tail.

The half-pins are so named only because they are sloped on one side. It is not required that they be half the size of the whole pins. This can be important if you design the joint with very narrow pins since then a half-pin, taken literally,

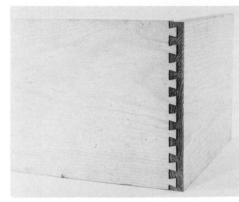

Figure 9–1. Example of a half-blind dovetail joint that you can accomplish quickly with a portable router or on a drill press.

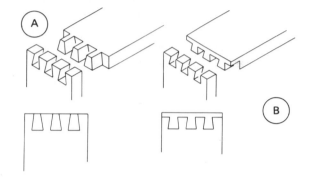

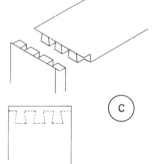

A   Through dovetail
B   Half-blind or
      French dovetail
C   Blind or mitered
      dovetail

Figure 9–2. Types of dovetail joints. The through dovetail and the half-blind dovetail are the ones used most often.

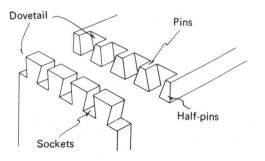
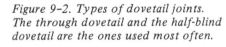

Dovetail   Pins

Half-pins

Figure 9–3. Nomenclature of the mating parts of the dovetail joint.

Sockets

would be quite weak and could easily be chipped off. However, all dovetail joints should start and end with half-pins as opposed to half-tails. Tails get their strength because they are glued to pins. They don't gain much by the connection they make to end grain.

DESIGN AND LAYOUT

The slope of the dovetail to the pin can be from a one-to-five to one-to-eight proportion. Greater angles are required more on softwoods than hardwoods but many craftspeople use the 1-to-8 proportion because they feel it is more appealing visually.

Figure 9–4 shows how to do a layout so you can pick up the slope angle for use on the work. Assuming a 1-to-8 proportion, draw a parallel line eight inches away from the edge of a board and then use a square to mark a perpendicular line. Mark one inch away from the intersection of the parallel and perpendicular lines and then draw the diagonal line. Set a *T*-bevel to match the diagonal line and you will be set to mark the work. Later we'll show how to make and use a template to mark the work faster and with less chance of human error.

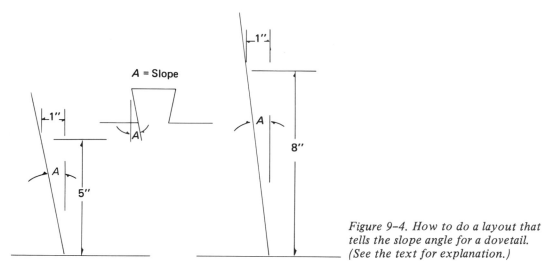

Figure 9–4. How to do a layout that tells the slope angle for a dovetail. (See the text for explanation.)

There is much variation in the sizing and spacing of dovetails when the joint is formed with hand tools. Some workers prefer a uniformity that is achieved by following the general rules shown in Figure 9–5. The thickness of the stock determines the depth of the sockets.

Uniformity in size and spacing is also the rule when dovetails are formed by machine. Many woodworkers prefer a design where the pins vary in relation to the spacing. There are many examples of this found in older pieces of furniture and some of today's craftspeople are doing similar work, using just a couple of pins, even on wide boards (Figure 9–6). In a sense, this is a way of interpreting

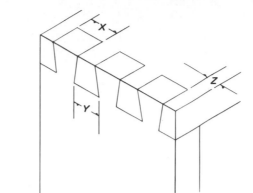

$X = Y$
$Z = \frac{1}{2}X$

Figure 9-5. General rules you can follow for multiple, uniform dovetails.

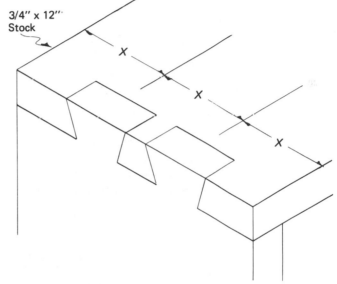

3/4" x 12" Stock

Figure 9-6. Small, uniform dovetails are not a hard and fast rule. Sometimes just a few dovetails are used, even on wide stock.

the concept of the joint and applying the individual's preferences and sense of style to the project.

Woodworkers also like to debate whether to make the pins or the tails first. Either way, the first piece that is formed serves as a pattern for marking the mating part. There do seem to be more votes on the side of doing the pins first but, regardless of the sequence, what counts is how carefully the first step is taken and how accurately the part is used as a pattern. How you work is personal, but the results are what count.

Doing the layout is a matter of dividing the board into X number of spaces in relation to the number of tails and sockets you plan to cut (Figure 9-7). If you are thinking of one wide, centered dovetail, then you would need one line. For two dovetails, you need two lines, and so on. The lines you draw become centerlines for mating parts of the joint.

The initial layout can be done in full size on paper if you wish to preview how the joint will look. It's easier and neater to erase lines on paper than on wood.

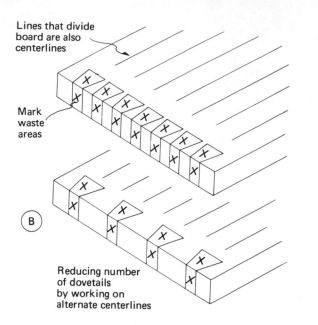

Lines that divide
board are also
centerlines

Mark
waste
areas

B

Reducing number
of dovetails
by working on
alternate centerlines

Figure 9-7. A good way to start a lay-out for dovetails is to divide the board into equal spaces.

The layout on the first part you cut should look like the one shown in Figure 9-8A. All slopes are marked, the waste parts are indicated, and depth-of-cut lines are formed on both surfaces and both edges. When the first part is shaped, it is used as a pattern to mark the mating piece as shown in Figure

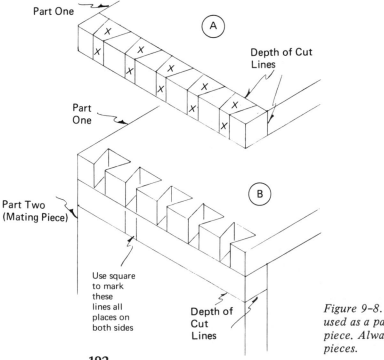

Part One

A

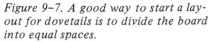
Depth of Cut
Lines

Part
One

Part Two
(Mating Piece)

B

Use square
to mark
these
lines all
places on
both sides

Depth of
Cut
Lines

Figure 9-8. After one part is cut, it is used as a pattern to mark the mating piece. Always indicate the waste pieces.

9–8B. Make the marks with a hard, sharp pencil or a knife. Here too, depth-of-cut lines are indicated and vertical cut lines are carried down from the edge with a square.

Once you have decided on the slope of the dovetails you can easily make a marking template that is sized to suit the design of the joint. Figure 9–9 shows how, by cutting a groove through a length of wood, you can make base stock for cutting dovetail templates of different sizes, and with a particular slope angle. Figure 9–9B shows examples of templates made by cutting at an angle through the grooved piece.

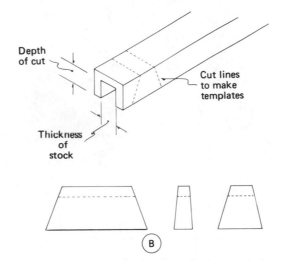

Figure 9–9. A piece of grooved base stock can be angle cut to form dovetail templates of various sizes.

Figure 9–10 shows a template you can make by first shaping and then bending a piece of thin sheet metal. Although the template is a specific size you still have size options since the spacing between the layouts made with the template is variable.

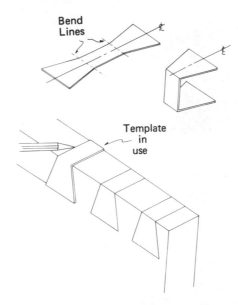

Figure 9–10. Another way to make a template is to shape and then bend up a piece of thin sheet metal.

Both the templates discussed so far are made for a particular stock thickness. If you wish to have more flexibility, make a template like the example shown in Figure 9-11. Here, the wood from which the template was cut was rabbeted rather than grooved, so the guide can be used on different stock thicknesses.

Figure 9-11. A rabbeted template can be used to mark guide lines regardless of the thickness of the stock.

Finally, Figure 9-12 shows a rabbeted, clamped-on block that provides the slope angle and is also a guide for the saw. If the block is designed correctly, it can even serve as a depth gauge since the spine on the dovetail saw will act as a stop when it hits the top edge of the guide.

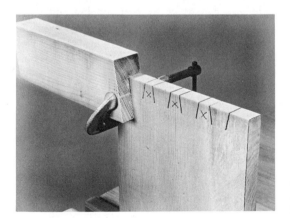

Figure 9-12. A rabbeted template made this way, also acts as a guide for the saw.

CUTTING

Hold the part securely in a vise and do the first cuts with a good dovetail saw (Figure 9-13). Be sure to cut on the waste side of the line. You will be less likely to make a mistake if you mark the waste pieces. Don't rush the job. Even a fine-tooth dovetail saw can cause unnecessary feathering and splintering at cut edges if it is forced. Also, it's easier to be accurate when you work slowly.

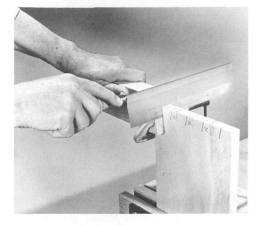

Figure 9–13. If the guide is sized correctly it can also act as a stop to control the depth of the cuts.

Many craftspeople will work only with chisels to clean out between the saw cuts but there doesn't seem to be any good reason why the bulk of the waste can't be removed by using a coping saw as shown in Figure 9–14. Don't, however, attempt to finish the job with the coping saw. The joint lines will be much neater and tighter if the final dressing is done with sharp chisels (Figure 9–15).

Figure 9–14. The bulk of the waste can be removed by using a coping saw like this.

Figure 9–15. Clean out by using sharp chisels. Work from both sides of the stock.

Do the first cut on *both* sides by holding the chisel vertically and rapping it smartly with a mallet to sever surface grain. After this, you can probably work with only hand pressure but do alternate cuts from both sides of the stock and do remove material a little bit at a time. Be sure the bottom of the waste area is flat and that corners are sharp. Choose chisel sizes that are most suitable for the area you are working in.

Often, the area between the pins is slightly undercut so parts will fit together tightly. The undercutting results in a very slight concave form and is accomplished by tilting the chisel just a couple of degrees when the waste is being cut away.

When the first part is complete, use it as a pattern to mark the mating piece. Be sure the parts are related correctly and that they are held firmly in position while the marking is done. Identify the waste areas and then follow the same sawing and cutting procedures that were used to do the first part.

HALF-BLIND DOVETAILS

Half-blind dovetails are often used as the joint between a drawer front and the drawer sides. The strength of the joint is there, but it isn't revealed until the drawer is pulled out. A tested procedure is shown in Figure 9–16.

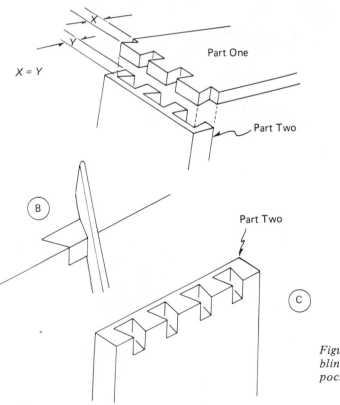

Figure 9–16. Procedure for doing half-blind dovetails. The saw cuts for the pockets are made at an angle.

Lay out tails on the side of the drawer working as you would if you were doing through dovetails. After the shapes are complete on part one, use it as a template to mark the front of the drawer. Be sure you have identified the inside surfaces of each piece. Draw a line with a marking gauge or by other means on the end of the drawer to know the alignment point of the tails on the drawer side. It is important to maintain this alignment while you do the marking.

One way to maintain alignment is to grip the drawer front in the vise so the edge to be marked will be flush with the bench top. Place the side, which you have cut and are using as a pattern, in position and clamp it or weight it down. Work with a hard, very sharp pencil or a knife to transfer the cut lines to the drawer front. The depth of the pocket cuts you must make will equal the thickness of the drawer side *unless* the drawer front will have a lip. If so, the lip can be formed first by making a rabbet cut and then doing the layout on the base of the rabbet cut, or by making the pocket cuts deeper than necessary and then cutting off the excess to form the lip.

Start cleaning out the waste by making saw cuts as shown in Figure 9-16B. Remember to cut on the waste side of the line and not to go past the terminal points. If you wish, you can make several saw cuts between the first two so it will be easier to remove the bulk of the waste. The chiseling is done by working alternately from opposite edges of the pockets. The inside corners will not be outlined by the saw cuts so be sure to work carefully with sharp chisels to avoid splintering when cleaning out. Work so that you remove small chips.

The finished parts should fit together snugly. Some light taps with a mallet are okay but the tails should not be so tight that they must be forced. Test the assembly without glue before you do the final clamping.

With most dovetail work it's a good idea to plan cuts so that pins and tails project a bit after they are assembled. A little sanding, after the glue is dry, will even them out so the corner will be perfect.

MACHINED DOVETAILS

A quick and accurate way to make multiple dovetail joints is to work with a portable router and a special accessory that provides a clamp fixture to hold the work and a finger template to guide the tool (Figure 9-17). The mating

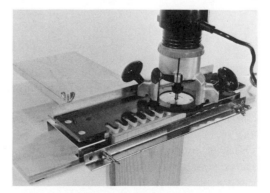

Figure 9-17. A portable router is used with a special dovetail accessory. Dovetails are accurate but must be uniform as dictated by the template.

shapes on both parts are formed in one operation, making it critical to place the pieces correctly in the fixture. It is also important never to move the router on or off the template while the motor is running. Any misalignment while the cutter is turning can damage the template, the work, and even the cutter. Precise joints will result if you follow the detailed instructions that are supplied with the dovetail accessory.

A similar accessory is available for use on a drill press (Figure 9-18). Here, an extension that you make supports the attachment on the drill-press table and you feed the work into the cutter. As with the portable router fixture, both parts of the joint are clamped in the attachment and shaped at the same time so alignment of the pieces is a critical step in the operation. Set the drill press at its highest speed. Work slowly, and be sure the shank on the cutter is in firm contact with the finger template at all times.

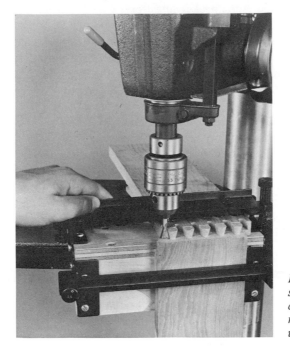

Figure 9-18. A similar accessory is available for use on a drill press. Here, the work is moved into the cutter. Always use top drill-press speed.

DOVETAILED *T* JOINTS

A single through dovetail makes a mechanically strong joint that can be used on frame assemblies and furniture rails (Figure 9-19). The pin can be made with only saw cuts, doing the shoulders first and then sawing down the slopes. The finished pin is then used as a pattern to mark the outline of the socket. Do the socket by sawing outline cuts first and then removing the waste with a chisel. Intermediate saw cuts can be done to make waste removal easier, or you can remove the bulk of the waste by using a coping saw.

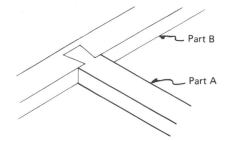

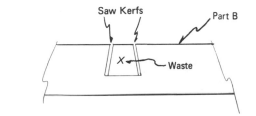

Figure 9-19. Single, through dovetails can be used to make strong frame connections.

Some woodworkers prefer to do the socket first and then use it as a template to mark the pin (Figure 9-20). The pin is formed by doing shoulder cuts and then sawing down the slopes. Stay away from the line so final cleaning can be done with a chisel (Figure 9-21). Working this way lets you test for fit as you shave with the chisel to be sure of a snug joint.

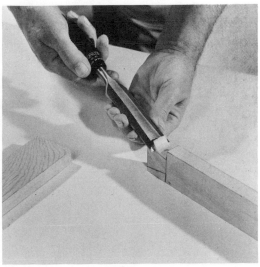

Figure 9-20. Using a formed socket as a template to mark the mating piece.

Figure 9-21. The tail can be finished by making light shaving cuts with a chisel. Test for fit as you go.

Figure 9-22 shows variations of the basic joint. Many of the cuts for these joints can be made on power saws if you plan the setups very carefully and work so parts are firmly supported while you cut. Tails can be cut with the saw blade tilted at the slope angle and with the work secured to a tenoning jig. Do the shoulder cuts by advancing the work with the miter gauge. The saw blade is in perpendicular position, with projection set to meet the base of the slope cut. This can leave a slight imperfection where the slope and shoulder cuts meet, but is not significant unless appearance is very critical. Otherwise, do the shoulder cut so it does not meet the slope cut and then clean out the corner with a chisel.

Sockets can be formed in similar fashion, by doing slope cuts first and then cleaning out the waste by making repeat passes. Use a tenoning jig since the stock stays on edge for the entire operation.

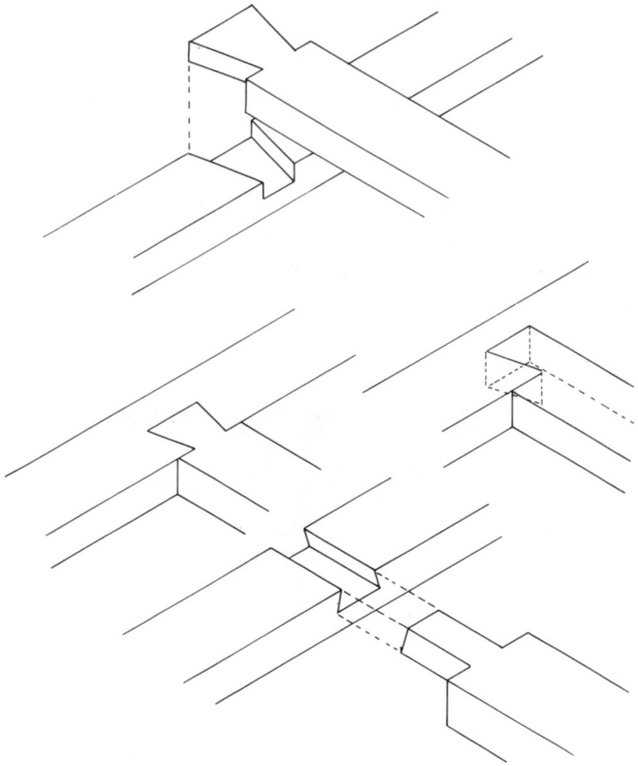

Figure 9-22. Various types of dove-tailed T connections.

DOVETAIL SLOTS

There are many situations where a dovetail slot provides better construction than a simple dado or groove. The sample frame corner shown in Figure 9-23 shows this clearly. The joint forms an interlock that will hold regardless of glue conditions. It may seem like a lot of work but the amount of work is rela-

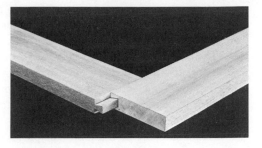

Figure 9–23. Dovetail slots and matching pins are good joints to use in many areas of woodworking.

tive. Other joints often used involve dowels or a mortise-tenon and these also take time and care when done correctly.

Another situation where a dovetail groove can be an asset is when joining shelves to case sides (Figure 9–24). When done this way, the union doesn't have to be strengthened with glue or mechanical fasteners. This permits the shelves to expand or contract without harm to themselves or other components.

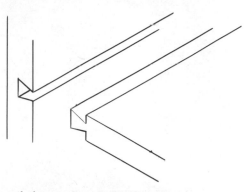

Figure 9–24. Shelves done this way do not have to be reinforced with glue or mechanical fasteners.

A good way to form the dovetail slots and to make the matching pins is to work with a portable router. Dovetail cutters (Figure 9–25) for use in the router come in various sizes. The most frequently used are either 1/4 inch or 1/2 inch. The most common shank size is 1/4 inch, allowing the cutters to be used in all portable routers that are available to the individual craftsperson.

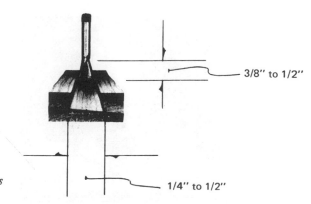

3/8″ to 1/2″

1/4″ to 1/2″

Figure 9–25. The most common sizes of dovetail bits are shown here.

A setup for doing a dovetail groove in the edge of a board is shown in Figure 9-26. The support blocks, which merely provide more surface for the router to ride on, are clamped to the work, or the three pieces can be held in a vise. The edge guide is locked in place so the bit will travel down the center of the board. If forming the groove in one pass proves too difficult, work as follows. Use the same setup but make a first pass by using a straight bit to remove the bulk of the waste stock. Then change to a dovetail bit and make a second pass to complete the shape.

The male part of the joint (the pin) is done the same way except that two cuts are required, one on each side of the stock. Each of these cuts is made so that the bit is biting into the support block as well as the work.

The width of the dovetails made is not limited by the size of the bit. If you work carefully, you can make several passes so the dovetail slot can be widened.

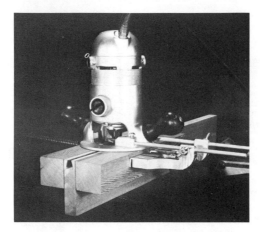

Figure 9-26. How to set up a portable router for cutting a dovetail groove in the edge of a board.

Slots that are not in the end or edge of a board can be handled as shown in Figure 9-27. The guide strips are either clamped or tack-nailed to the work. Actually, one guide strip would be enough but using two provides additional security.

Figure 9-27. This is a very accurate setup to use when a dovetail groove is required on a surface.

Dovetail slots may be cut on a drill press as shown in Figure 9–28. If the tool you work on does not have a rip fence, clamp a straight piece of wood in place to serve the same purpose. Be sure to feed against the direction of rotation of the cutter so the action of the bit will tend to keep the work against the fence. If the grooves are stopped, clamp a piece of wood to the fence so it will act as a gauge for the length of the cut. This is especially important if you are doing the same cut on many pieces.

Figure 9–28. This is one way to do dovetail slots on a drill press. Feed against the direction of rotation of the cutter.

A dovetail is an excellent connection between rails and square legs (Figure 9–29). Both the stopped dovetail slots and the pins can be formed with a router by following the procedures already described, or they can be done on a drill press. A good setup to follow for forming the slots is shown in Figure 9–30. Note that a straight shank router bit is used first to remove the bulk of the waste. A second pass is made to complete the form with a dovetail bit. When work is done this way, the first pass is done on all the pieces involved before the cutters are changed. Be sure that the parts are marked so you will be making the cuts on correct surfaces.

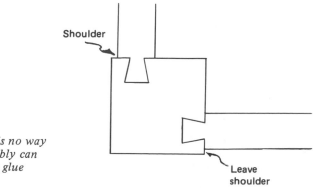

Figure 9–29. There is no way this rail-to-leg assembly can fall apart even if the glue quits.

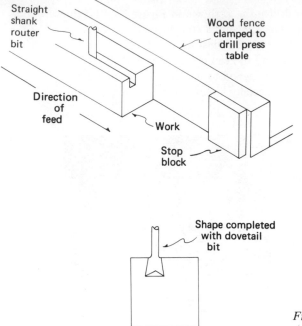

Figure 9-30. How to work on a drill
press to form stopped dovetail grooves.

Dovetail slots can also be cut in round parts; for example, a pedestal for a table. Figure 9-31 shows two ways you can work to fit the pinned part against the circumference of the other. The flats are formed before the dovetail slots are cut. The best way to shape shoulders so they will conform to a curve is on a bandsaw. If such a tool is not available, the job can be done by cutting very carefully with a dovetail saw and then finishing with a file.

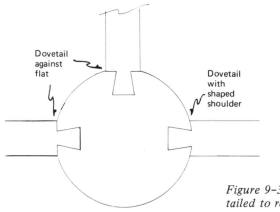

Figure 9-31. Rails or legs can be dovetailed to round pedestals in one of the two ways shown here.

A method you can use to do the slots on a drill press is shown in Figure 9-32. The cutting procedure to follow doesn't vary from that you would use if the stock was square. The holder shown in the illustration grips the round piece securely and makes it possible to use a fence in routine fashion as a guide.

204

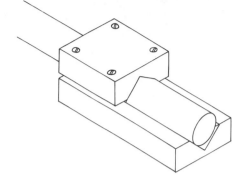

Figure 9-32. This special holder makes it possible to do stopped dovetail grooves in round stock on a drill press.

POCKET DOVETAILS ON CASE GOODS

This type of joinery, which is really just a single, half-blind dovetail, is often used in quality construction to join top rails to legs or to panels in cabinets (Figure 9-33). The pocket isn't difficult to do on a drill press or with a portable router. Work first with a straight router bit to clean out the waste and then flare the sides by using a dovetail bit. The pin can be cut by hand with a dovetail saw. In this situation it is usually best to form the pocket first and then size the pin to match.

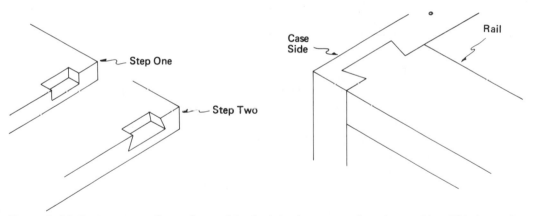

Figure 9-33. Pocket dovetails can be used in the joint between rails and case sides. This is good, quality construction.

DOVETAIL SPLICES

A single, through dovetail, sometimes called a face dovetail, is an effective method of splicing two pieces of lumber end to end (Figure 9-34). A way to make the necessary cuts on a table saw is shown in Figure 9-35. The slope cuts for the tail are made first by tilting the blade to the angle required and making

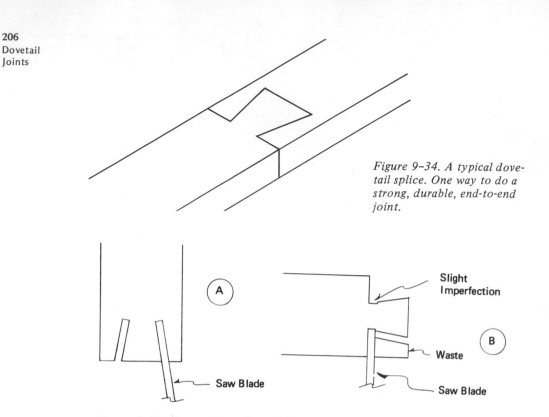

Figure 9–34. A typical dovetail splice. One way to do a
strong, durable, end-to-end
joint.

Figure 9–35. How to form the tail for an end-to-end dovetail joint by working
on a table saw.

the passes with the work secured to a tenoning jig. Make the shoulder cuts (Figure 9–35B) by advancing the work with the miter gauge. Note that a slight imperfection results if the blade projection is set to remove all the waste stock and
leave a sharp corner. To avoid this, keep blade projection lower than necessary
and clean out the corner with a chisel.

A similar type of connection has the dovetail passing through the edge of
the stock instead of down through the surface. The cuts can be made on a table
saw following the procedures outlined above. On a radial arm saw, the job is
done by using a height table. The first step is to make slope cuts that will outline
the socket (Figure 9–36). Most of the waste can be removed by making repeat
passes with the blade set parallel to the table. The remaining corners can be
cleaned out with a chisel.

The slope cuts for the pin are cut the same way; the only difference is
that the blade is raised so the kerf is on the *outside* of the tail. The final step is
shown in Figure 9–37. The machine is set in crosscut position and the blade is
elevated so it will meet with the bottom of the slope cut. Here too, a slight imperfection that results is acceptable, or you can get a more perfect corner by
finishing the job with chisels.

Figure 9–36. Using a height table on a radial arm saw to do the slope cuts for a dove-tail socket. Use the same setup to make the slope cuts for the pin.

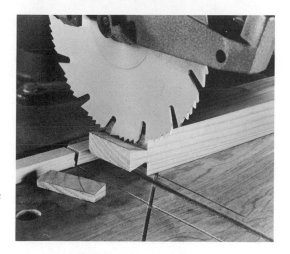

Figure 9–37. Finish the pin by making crosscuts as shown here. Adjust the blade height so the corners can be cleaned out with a chisel.

DOVETAIL KEYS AND SPLINES

These are integral, back-to-back pins, or tails, that may be used as decorative reinforcements in any of the ways shown in Figure 9–38. Note in each case that if the keys or splines are correctly sized, they not only provide an interlock but can pull parts tightly together. They can be made of material that matches or contrasts with the parts they join.

Regardless of whether you want keys or splines, the procedure to follow to form the base stock is shown in Figure 9–39. First, square the stock you are going to use so its thickness is equal to the widest part of the dovetail and its width equals twice the depth of the dovetail slot.

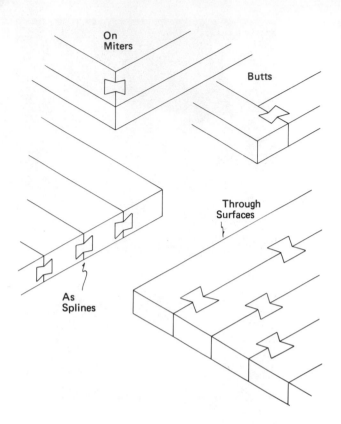

*Figure 9-38. Various ways that you can use dovetail keys
or splines. The reinforcements can match the project
material or they can contrast to add a decorative detail.*

Step One: Angle the saw blade to match the slope of the dovetail and set
its projection so the kerf will end exactly on the stock's centerline. Adjust the
rip fence so the blade will just barely touch the corner of the work. Make the
first pass as shown.

Step Two: Flip the stock and turn it end for end and make the second
pass.

Step Three: Repeat the procedure to make the third cut.

Step Four: Repeat the procedure once more to finish the job.

Cut the splines, or keys, to the length you want by crosscutting through
the shaped piece.

Accurate sizing of the base stock and precise adjustment of the saw blade
and rip fence are critical. As always, where precision is paramount, have scrap
pieces on hand for making test cuts before shaping the good material.

Don't work on jobs like this without using a push stick to get the work
past the saw blade.

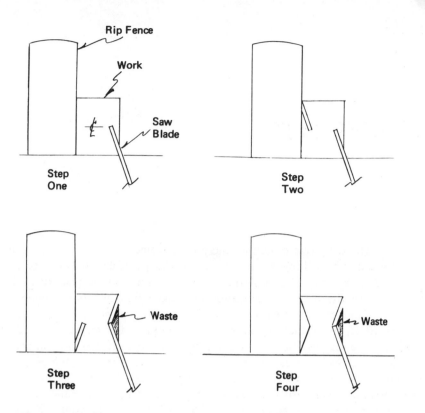

Figure 9–39. Steps to follow when cutting the dovetail key or spline stock. The shaped pieces are then crosscut to necessary lengths.

Chapter 10

SEGMENTS

The technique of cutting and joining segments can be used in many areas of woodworking. Projects can range from table pedestals and lamp bases to posts for a porch. Sometimes, a segmented construction used in place of a solid component results in savings on material costs and definitely cuts down on weight.

Other times, especially on projects like the tub storage seat shown in Figure 10-1, this is the only method that is feasible to use. We've already talked about the mathematics involved but, to summarize: If you saw flat boards into strips that have a wedge-shaped cross section and then join the pieces edge to edge they will form a circle. The only critical factor is that the total of the cut angles must equal 360 degrees. The width of each segment is immaterial. In fact, some interesting variations are possible when you design along the lines of the example shown in Figure 10-2. The fluted pieces are narrower than the segments, and are not bevel cut. This kind of work does call for careful planning on paper especially in relation to the width of the pieces if the assembly is to have the necessary diameter.

Figure 10-1. The tub storage seat is an example of how segments come together to form a circular project.

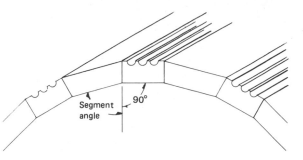

Figure 10-2. Pieces with square edges can be inserted between angle-cut segments without destroying the circle-forming concept.

Figure 10-3 shows how you can change the direction of the curve, do half-round shapes, or form round corners. Ideas like this can be put to use on aprons, rails, curved backs or arms for chairs and seat frames. Often, the technique makes it possible to produce a component that would otherwise require an intricate bending procedure.

The more segments you use, the closer to a true circle you get, but the circumference will always be a series of flats. However, it doesn't take much work to change a segmented assembly to a full round one, especially if you work with a portable belt sander. The job can also be done by hand with a plane or spokeshave, or even with a scraper.

The segments are easiest to cut on a power saw. The idea is to bevel cut one edge of the stock and then work as shown in Figure 10-4. Invert the stock

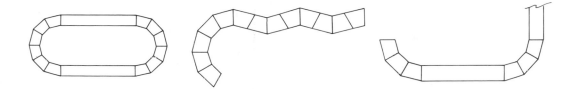

Figure 10-3. Segments can be placed to change the direction of the curve or they can be used to form half-round shapes or to turn corners.

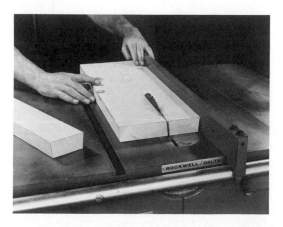

Figure 10-4. Cutting beveled segments on a table saw. The edge that is already beveled rides against the rip fence.

211

and turn it end for end for each cut. The bevel that is already formed rides against the rip fence. The segments can be formed from pieces of stock that have been cut to correct length or you can bevel long pieces and then crosscut them into the number of segments required. An advantage of working with pieces that have been precut to exact length is that it offers the opportunity to use up odd lengths of lumber.

Many segmented assemblies are joined with only glue. Since glue forms the strongest bond when parts mate long grain to long grain, this works best when the grain of wood runs parallel to the beveled edges.

Splines can be incorporated to add strength or to make assembly procedures easier. As shown in Figure 10-5, form the spline grooves so they are at right angles to the bevel cut. The grooves in both edges of each segment can be cut without changing the setup. Be sure, especially if the parts are small, that you feed the work through by using a push stick. If you need a groove that is wider than the saw kerf, make a second pass on each piece after adjusting the rip fence.

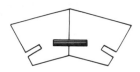

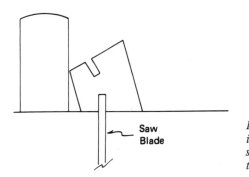

Saw
Blade

Figure 10-5. How to cut spline grooves in beveled segments. Be sure to use a push stick so your hands won't come too close to the blade.

When the size of the project permits, segmented assemblies can be organized as shown in Figure 10-6, ready to be mounted in a lathe as you would solid stock. The assembly can then be turned to full round, shaped along its entire length, or in particular areas.

A type of segmented work, often called staved construction, is shown in Figure 10-7 as a built-up block that will be mounted in a lathe and shaped as a lamp base. Some of the advantages of working this way are as follows. The weight of the project is lightened because of the hollow center. The hollow center, in this case, is a ready-made groove for electrical wiring. Checks, splits and shrinkage are less likely to occur since flat boards can be seasoned with greater success than large, solid squares. The segments can all be cut from flat grained lumber, and if you work with material that is quartered or has a vertical grain, any shrinkage will be uniform. Finally, you can produce projects with inlayed effects by making segments of contrasting woods.

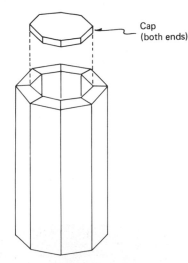

Cap
(both ends)

Figure 10-6. Segmented constructions that
are sealed at both ends can be mounted in a
lathe for turning to full round or for shaping.

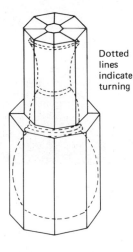

Dotted
lines
indicate
turning

Figure 10-7. A staved construction done to
provide stock for a turned lamp base. The
openings at the ends are plugged so the
piece can be mounted in the lathe.

FLAT SEGMENTS

Segmented pieces can form flat structures as well as columns (Figure
10-8). The cut-angle factor does not differ from what we have already discussed,
regardless of whether the pieces are to form a full circle, half circle, or just part
of an arc. The advantage here is that each of the segments can be preshaped to
contribute to an overall effect that might otherwise require intricate carving procedures. There is also the opportunity to do things with contrasting woods or
to create spectacular effects simply by the grain relationships of adjacent pieces.

Flat segments can be cut using routine sawing procedures but when you
need many similar pieces, it will pay to make a special cutting jig like the one
shown in Figure 10-9. After the first angle cut is made, the stock is flipped for
each of the cuts that follow. This will assure the accuracy of the cut angle and of
the length of each piece.

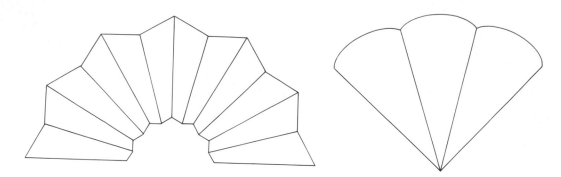

Figure 10-8. Flat segments can be preshaped and then assembled for use as surface decorations, pediments, and so on.

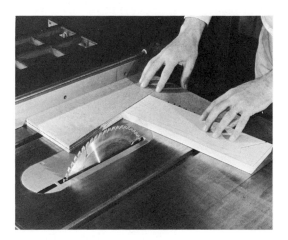

Figure 10-9. A special jig can be made so any number of pieces can be cut to the same angle and length.

FOUR-SIDED COLUMNS

This type of construction is often used for table pedestals and is considered segmented work even though the number of pieces required is minimal. A common joint used is the miter, regardless of whether the cross-section of the column is square or rectangular. Reinforcement of the miter with a spline is an optional consideration. As with any segments, a glue bond between edges that are long grain to long grain can be fairly strong in itself as long as the mating edges are accurately cut.

Figure 10-10 shows some other joint designs. Both the tongue and groove and the rabbeted joints are strong enough for use, so the major consideration is how much visible joint line you can tolerate. Figure 10-10B shows how you can get an elaborate effect without complicated cuts. On jobs like this it's best to attach the molding to opposite sides of the column first, and then do a final assembly treating all sides as if they were one piece units. The drawing shows glue blocks only at the end of the assembly but in practice they should be situated along the entire length of the project. The visual effect of the assembly will

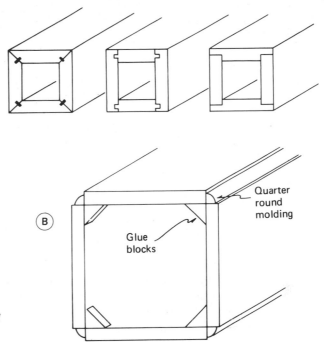

Figure 10-10. Several methods of assembly you can use on four-sided columns.

be there regardless of how you design it. Its strength will depend on how carefully you put the parts together.

Figure 10-11 shows two other methods you can use to provide decorative effects at the corners. The joint in detail A is a combination rabbet-dado. The decorative reeds are formed on the parts on a shaper or a table-saw molding head before the pieces are joined. If the size of the finished project permits, the reeds or similar details, can be added after the assembly is completed.

In Figure 10-11B, one side of the column has square edges. The mating piece is shaped with the same shaper-cutter or molding head knife you would use to form a cabinet-door lip.

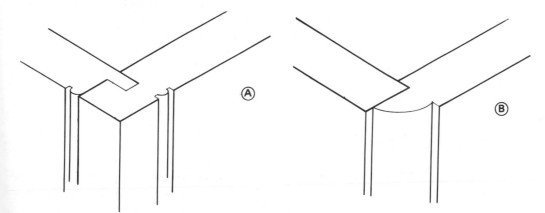

Figure 10-11. Joint areas can be made more decorative by using one of the ideas shown here.

215

Chapter 11

JOINTS FOR MOLDING

Ready-made moldings are available in many shapes and sizes (Figure 11-1). Generally, they can be classified as structural (architectural) or decorative. The terms relate more to how the moldings are used than to individual designs. A molding might be architectural when used in house constructions to cover the gap that exists between a door frame and the adjacent walls but the same molding can be used to decorate the side of a cabinet or the front of a drawer. In some cases, a "decorative" molding, like the scalloped design shown on the project in Figure 11-2, might be used in an architectural capacity.

There may be a limited number of wood species that architectural moldings are available in, especially in a local lumberyard. Typically, these would be available in pine, spruce, or fir. Some do-it-yourself centers carry a line of hardwood or composition-type moldings that fall in the decorative category. Craftsman mail-order supply houses will often list architectural and decorative moldings made of walnut, cherry, or oak. Sometimes they are pointed out as being moldings for clock cases and fine furniture.

Manufacturers of cabinets and furniture often make special moldings that will be found only on their products. The individual worker can adopt the same policy and do exclusive designs by forming molding on a shaper or by using a molding head on a table saw. The moldings can be made from scratch if the proper equipment is available or, as was done on the project in Figure 11-3, a standard molding can be treated so it is more than a product that can be purchased by anyone, anywhere.

TYPICAL MOLDING APPLICATIONS

Figure 11-4 shows a basic chest which becomes a more exciting project because of the added molding details. The moldings on the drawer front can be preassembled as a frame which is then added to the project, or they can be attached one piece at a time. The best bet for the base is to do the front piece

216

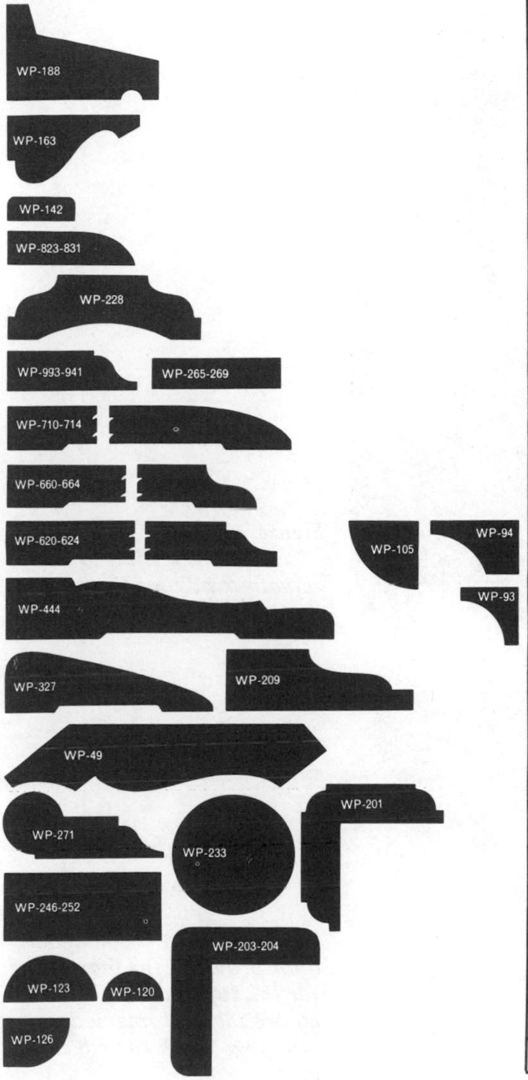

KEY	
NUMBER	NAME
188	Drip cap
163	Cap & brick
142	Screen
823-831	Stop
941	
228	Batten
265-269	Lattice
710-714	
660-664	Casing
620-624	&
444	base
327	
209	Shingle
49	Crown
271	Picture
233	Rounds
201	Corner guard
203-204	
246-252	Screen stock
123	Half round
120	
126	Base shoe
105	Quarter round
94	Cove
93	

Figure 11-1. These are structural or architectural moldings but many can be used for decorative or practical purposes on cabinets and furniture.

first, mitering the ends so the inside of the cut is exactly in line with the corner of the chest. Cut the side moldings a bit longer than necessary so you can trim them to exact length after you have cut the miter and are sure it is right.

Figure 11-5 shows a similar chest which takes on a Spanish motif simply because of the different types of molding which are used. The moldings on the drawer fronts can be attached as described for the first chest. The base treatment is different because of the crown molding that is called for. Because of the slope

217

Figure 11–2. The scalloped edges on this project are actually ready-made moldings that were glued and nailed in place.

Figure 11–3. A secondhand door provided the material for the top and shelf of this coffee table. Homemade moldings finish the edges very nicely.

at which the molding sits, the corner joint becomes a compound angle. The easiest way to cut it is to situate the molding in a miter box at the same slope it will have on the project and then to do a simple 45-degree miter cut. Cut the front piece first. Do the two sides by starting with stock that is longer than you need. Trim to length after you are sure the miter joint is exact.

A stronger way to do the base is shown in Figure 11–6. Since it is not possible to add the glue blocks *after* assembly, the base structure must be completely preassembled and then added to the chest. Careful work is required to be sure the fit will be perfect but the actual joint cutting procedure does not differ from what was described above.

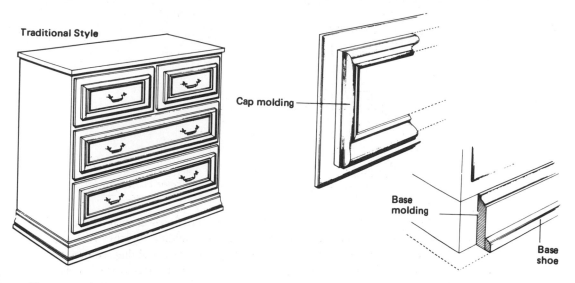

Figure 11–4. The architectural moldings used on this basic chest transform it into a much fancier piece.

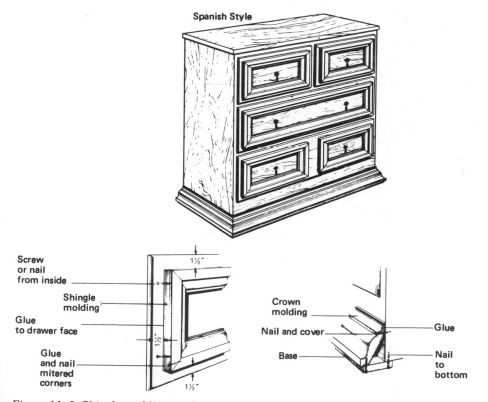

Figure 11–5. Shingle moldings and crown moldings were used on this project. Ready-made moldings are good to use, especially when you don't have the equipment to form your own designs.

219

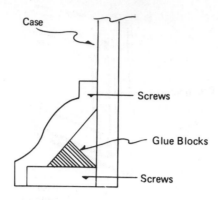

Figure 11-6. Another way to use cornice or crown molding at the base of a chest.

Figure 11-7 shows how moldings can be functional as well as decorative. If you use this idea, glue the two pieces of cove molding together first so they can be attached to the drawer fronts as a unit. The base molding requires simple miter cuts but follow the usual procedure. Do the front piece first, then add the sides.

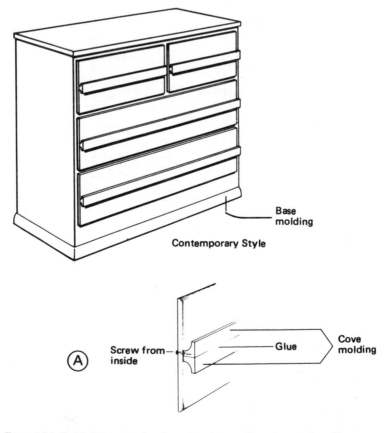

Figure 11-7. Molding can be functional as well as decorative. Here, cove molding is used to form drawer pulls.

Another typical, practical application for ready-made moldings is shown in Figure 11-8. The molding hides the unattractive edges of the plywood and adds a decorative touch of its own. The shingle molding that is shown is not the only design that can be used this way. Various types of stops, or quarter-rounds, or base shoes, for example, can be used as well. If the molding you would like to use is too thick for the panel, attach it so only the top surfaces are flush, or shave the molding with a plane to reduce its bulk.

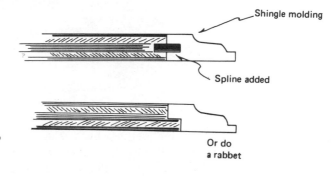

Shingle molding

Spline added

Or do
a rabbet

Figure 11-8. An example of how ready-made moldings can be used to finish plywood edges.

JOINTS

Moldings that are flat on one side and which will be surface mounted, like those used on the drawer fronts of the projects we have shown, can be joined with mitered corners like any flat material used in a frame (Figure 11-9). The cutting can be done on a radial arm saw, a table saw, or by hand with a backsaw. If you work with a handsaw, it will be much easier to do an accurate job if you use some type of miter box (Figure 11-10). Accuracy on each of the cuts is vital. A small error on each cut can accumulate to a total disaster. Nothing is more apparent than a bad miter joint, whether it is the union between two project components or a molding frame overlay.

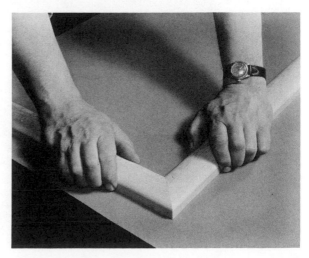

Figure 11-9. Mitered corners must fit together tightly and must make a 90-degree turn.

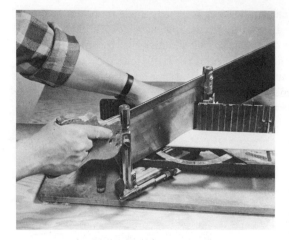

Figure 11-10. The miter cuts will be more accurate if you use a mechanical guide that helps eliminate human error.

Test tool settings by making test cuts on scrap stock. Work with fine blades that will not splinter or produce feathered edges. Many workers will make the cuts a fraction oversize and then bring the stock to exact size by working on a disk or belt sander. If you use the latter method, be sure to set up a guide so the work can be advanced against the abrasive paper at the same angle used to make the saw cut.

Some moldings, like cornice or crown designs, must be cut at a compound angle. The best way to do this is to make a simple 45-degree miter cut but with the work supported at the correct slope angle. A typical procedure with a miter box is shown in Figure 11-11. The strip of wood that is clamped to the bed of the tool is a stop that assures each piece of work will be held at the correct angle. The stop will also keep the work firm while the sawing is done. Don't rush the cut. The weight of the saw will supply sufficient feed pressure. Just concentrate on making smooth, steady strokes.

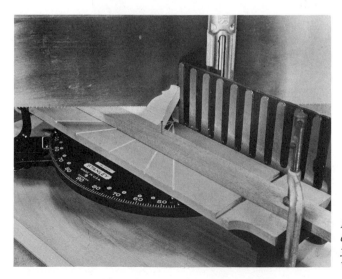

Figure 11-11. Situating the molding at the correct slope angle will let you produce a compound angle while doing a simple miter cut.

A miter joint occurs when both pieces are cut at the same angle. A coped joint (Figure 11-12) is made by cutting a reverse profile of one piece in the end of the mating part. Visually, the joint will still be a miter, but its advantage is that any separation that might be caused by shrinkage of parts after installation will not be visible. The coped joint is more common on trim work in house constructions but it can be useful on furniture and cabinetwork also. It is used only where moldings meet at an inside corner.

There are two ways you can form a coped joint. The simplest method is to transfer the profile of one piece to the end of the mating piece by using a compass and then to make the cut with a coping saw. This works best on flat molding and where the pattern design is not extreme.

The first step in the second method is to cut a routine 45-degree miter in the part that will be coped. Be sure you have fixed in your mind how the molding will be placed. Know which will be the back and which will be the base of the molding and make the miter cut accordingly.

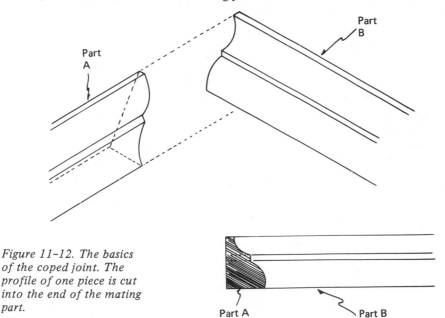

Figure 11-12. The basics of the coped joint. The profile of one piece is cut into the end of the mating part.

Part A   Part B

The cope cut is made by following the line of the miter cut with a coping saw (Figure 11-13). Make the cut so it is perpendicular to the back surface of the molding, or undercut it just a bit to be sure of a tight fit where the moldings meet at the front edge of the joint (Figure 11-14). Be very careful to follow the line of the miter cut precisely. Use a fine-toothed blade in the coping saw since it will be easier to control and will make a smoother cut. The edge will be easier to follow if you darken it a bit with a pencil after having made the initial miter cut.

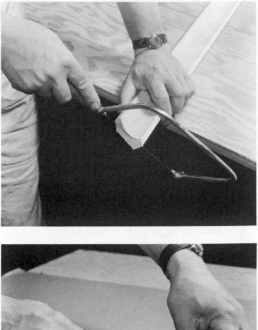

Figure 11–13. The coping saw follows the line of the miter cut. The waste removed resembles a 45-degree angle wedge.

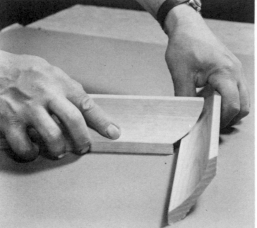

Figure 11–14. An accurate miter cut followed by careful work with the coping saw results in parts that fit correctly.

INTERSECTIONS

Moldings that are symmetrical can be easily blended if you make two 45-degree miter cuts in one to form a point, and then use it as a pattern to trace the cutout required in the mating piece (Figure 11-15). Saw out the *V* by cutting carefully with a backsaw or dovetail saw. Stay on the waste side of the line just a fraction so you can work with sandpaper or a file to finish the cuts for fitting the parts together snugly (Figure 11-16). If the top surfaces are not even—there might be some irregularity in the moldings—blend them by working very carefully with fine sandpaper.

Figure 11-17 shows another joint you can use when similar or symmetrical moldings intersect or cross. Note that one piece is continuous and the others are coped. The cope cut on the half-round molding shown in the illustration will be very precise if first cut with a coping saw and then smoothed with a small drum sander or sandpaper wrapped around a suitable dowel.

Figure 11–15. The point on the molding that intersects is formed by making two 45-degree cuts. Use it as a pattern to mark the mating piece.

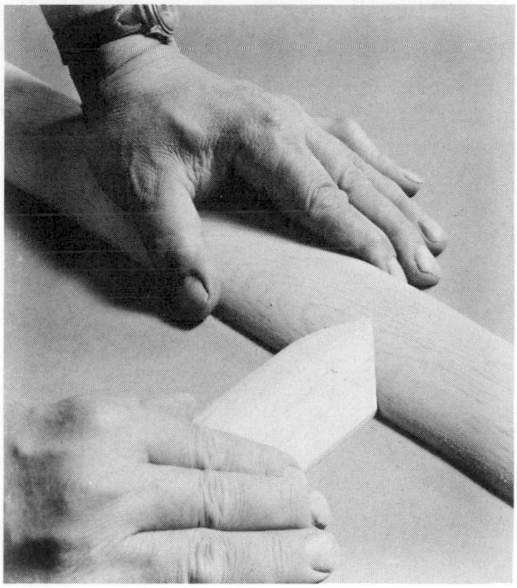

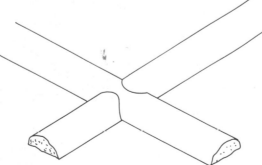

Figure 11–16. Careful work will result in a professionally made joint. Any sharp edges that remain can be removed with fine sandpaper.

Figure 11–17. Plan for one piece to be continuous where moldings cross. Coped joints were used here.

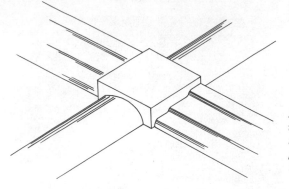

Figure 11–18. A butt block is used when intersecting moldings do not have symmetrical patterns. The block itself can be carved or embossed.

A transition piece, often called a butt block, (Figure 11-18) can be used where dissimilar moldings meet or cross. The block itself can be a decorative detail, especially if it is carved or embossed in some fashion.

SPLICES

Preferably, molding should be one-piece, but if you must join pieces to continue a run, use the "scarf" joint shown in Figure 11-19. Each piece is cut at a 45-degree angle and mated as shown. This type of joint, as opposed to a simple butt, is less likely ever to show a gap. A slight undercut is desirable if the project permits since this will assure that the visible line of the joint will be tight.

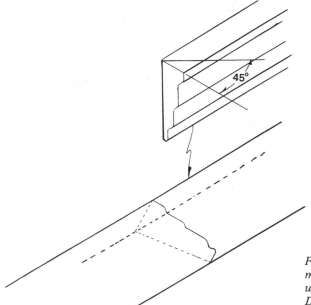

Figure 11–19. Lengths of molding can be spliced but use the scarf joint shown here. Do not use a butt joint.

Most moldings are attached with glue and reinforced with small finishing nails. Drive the nails into corners of profiles whenever possible for easier concealment (Figure 11-20). Nails driven this way are set below the surface of the wood and then covered with a wood dough.

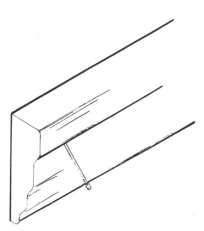

Figure 11-20. Drive finishing nails into corners of profiles whenever possible. They will be easier to conceal.

To do the nailing job in a very professional manner follow the technique shown in Figure 11-21. Use a small, very sharp chisel to lift a slim sliver of wood from the area where the nail will be driven. Drive the nail into the depression and set it so its head is flush. Then glue the sliver back into place using a small piece of tape as a clamp. Smooth the area with sandpaper after the glue is dry and no one will ever know how the job was done. This method is especially useful when you intend to use a clear finish on the project.

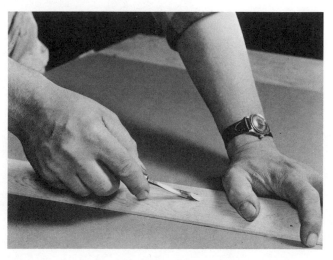

Figure 11-21. This is a clever trick used by many experts. Lift a thin sliver of wood and drive the nail in that area. Glue the sliver back in place for complete concealment.

A JIG FOR PREASSEMBLING

Moldings are often put together as a frame before they are attached to the project. The best way to handle this, especially when you need many similar constructions, is to make an assembly jig like the one shown in Figure 11-22. Be sure that the jig has square corners and that its inside dimensions are exactly right. If the corner joints of the frame are nailed as well as glued, the assembly can be removed from the jig immediately. You can then attach it to the project or let it sit until the glue is dry.

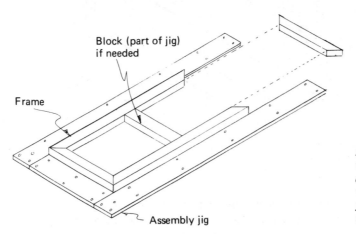

Block (part of jig)
if needed

Frame

Assembly jig

Figure 11-22. Frames you wish to put together before attaching them to the project will be easier to assemble if you make a temporary holding jig.

Chapter 12

JIGSAW BEVEL JOINTS

This type of joinery involves a very special woodworking technique that will enable you to make deep projects like the bowl shown in Figure 12-1. This is made from a single, flat, square board with sides that are not longer than the bowl's largest diameter. The method becomes clear when you study the illustrations in Figure 12-2.

Figure 12-1. The techniques described in this section will enable you to make deep bowls from single, flat boards.

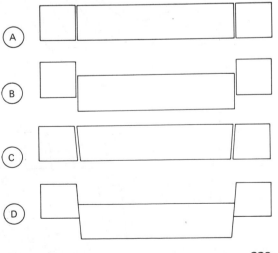

Figure 12-2. Internal disks cut normally will fall through the part they are cut from. If the cut is a bevel, the parts will jam tightly.

If you jigsaw a disk in the center of a board with the tool's blade set 90 degrees to the table (A), the disk (B) will fall through. If, however, you tilt the table so you are cutting a bevel (C) the disk will jam tightly in the part it was cut from (D). If you cut a series of concentric rings instead of a single disk, each ring will fit tightly inside its neighbor and the result will be a cone shape like the one shown in Figure 12-3. The more rings cut, the deeper the cone will be. How much each ring will project depends on the bevel angle, the thickness of the stock, and the width of the kerf made by the saw blade.

The bevel angle must be chosen in relation to the kerf width and the stock's thickness. The smallest bevel angle will result in the greatest projection but the least amount of contact area between rings. Extreme bevel angles will provide a lot of contact area but little projection. A bevel of from two to five degrees will work pretty well in materials that are from 1/4-inch to 3/4-inch thick but don't use a large blade that makes a heavy kerf.

A jigsaw blade that is .020-inches thick by .110-inches wide and has 15 teeth to the inch works well on many jobs, but heavier blades can be used on thick stock and lighter ones on thin material. Don't make a decision without first making a couple of test cuts on scrap material. Be aware that the amount of projection should not be the prime factor. It's also important to have enough contact surface between rings so the joint will be strong. The amount of contact area also determines the cross-sectional thickness of the project through the

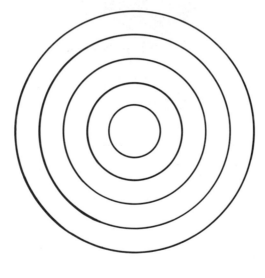

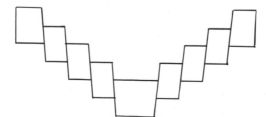

Figure 12-3. The more rings you cut, the deeper the project will be. Ideally, the bevel angle will provide good projection and sufficient contact area between rings.

joint areas. This is very important when the procedure is used to form a base material for further treatment.

TYPICAL APPLICATIONS

Figure 12-4 shows a bowl being lathe turned from a blank that was built up using the bevel joint technique. This is one situation where the thickness of the pieces at the joint-contact area is very critical. Since several factors determine the wall thickness, it's best to make a full-size, cross-sectional plan on paper before you do the bevel cutting.

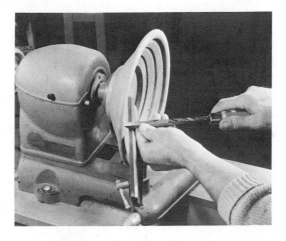

Figure 12-4. A built up blank made by doing bevel joints makes good stock for lathe turnings. Wall thickness of the blank is critical on jobs like this.

Deep shapes are not the only application. Trays and plates with raised lips (Figure 12-5) are simple to make with a single bevel joint cut. The project can be finished by hand with files and sandpaper or it can be mounted on a faceplate for more shaping in a lathe.

Figure 12-5. A single bevel-joint cut provides a lip for tray and plate projects. The same technique can be used if the project is square or rectangular.

The model boat hull shown in Figure 12-6 serves as an example of what you can do by varying the contour of the cut. On projects like this it makes sense to first draw a profile and top view of what you have in mind before marking the stock for the cuts.

The assembly of bevel joint components does not require clamping. The contact areas fit tightly enough when the pieces are jammed together. Be sure to use plenty of glue and remove the excess immediately with a damp cloth. If the appearance of the inside of the assembly is not important, as inside the model boat hull, don't bother to clean up there.

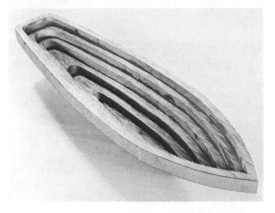

Figure 12-6. Projects like this hollow boat model hull can be formed by changing the contour of the cut.

CUTTING ON THE JIGSAW

Lay out the cuts you must make on the surface of the stock and drill a blade insertion hole for each cut. The starting holes are a drawback to using the technique but they will not be too detrimental if you drill the smallest holes possible.

When you cut, always be sure to keep the work on one side of the blade (Figure 12-7). If you were to swing the work to the opposite side of the blade,

Figure 12-7. Blade insertion holes are required for each cut but make them as small as possible. Always keep the inside ring on the down side of the table.

you would change the direction of the bevel and the parts would not fit. Bear in mind the direction of the bevel as you cut. Usually, it's best to work so the piece which will fit inside is on the lower side of the table.

Remember that the cut edges cannot be sanded. Work slowly and use the blade that will produce the smoothest cuts.

CUTTING ON A BANDSAW

Bevel joints can be accomplished on a bandsaw with a major change in the technique. One-pass cuts can be made on a jigsaw because you can insert the blade through a hole in the stock before you do the cutting. A bandsaw blade is a continuous loop so you can't insert it through a starting hole unless you are organized so you can break the blade and then reweld it. The best way to work is to saw the stock in half and then do the bevel cutting on the half sections. Reassemble them with staggered joints as shown in Figure 12–8.

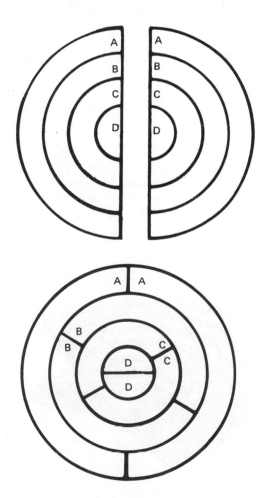

Figure 12–8. Circular work on the bandsaw is done by making the cuts on half sections. Note how the parts are assembled so the joints will be staggered.

Figure 12-9 is an example of how to work on the bandsaw when the project is not a circle. Make the sections longer than necessary and then cut them to length so they can be assembled with staggered joints.

Figure 12-10 shows half of a project that was bevel cut on a bandsaw. In practice, the joints should be staggered as explained above.

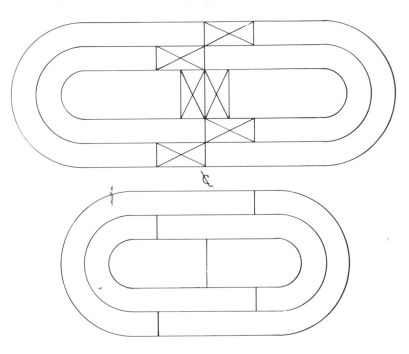

Figure 12-9. Bandsaw work that is not circular can be handled in similar fashion, but make the parts longer than necessary so they can be trimmed as shown to provide staggered joints.

Figure 12-10. A half section of a project that was cut on a bandsaw to provide bevel joints. Staples were used here only to hold the parts together for the picture.

Figures 12-11 and 12-12 demonstrate a variation of the bevel joint technique which can be done on either a jigsaw or bandsaw. The cut is continuous, following a spiral line and providing the same kind of projection you get with concentric rings. An advantage is that starting holes for the blade are not needed if you are working on a jigsaw, and you don't have to work in half-part fashion if you are cutting on a bandsaw. A disadvantage is that the gluing procedure might be a little more difficult to do. Slim brads, however, can be used to hold the project in its projected form until the glue dries.

Figure 12-11. One continuous spiral cut can be used in place of concentric rings. This will work on either a bandsaw or jigsaw.

Figure 12-12. A project cut spirally will project like one cut concentrically. The spiral effect on the exterior will not be too noticeable unless your design emphasizes it.

235

MISCELLANEOUS JOINTS AND TREATMENTS

DROP LEAF TABLE JOINT

A drop leaf can be installed by leaving square edges on both the table and the leaf, and using plain butt hinges or a full-length piano hinge as the pivot mechanism. The true drop leaf joint or "rule joint" as it is often called (Figure 13-1) is neater in appearance. It's also a design feature on many pieces of traditional and modern furniture.

The shapes required can be formed on a shaper or by using a molding head on a table or radial arm saw. Figure 13-1B shows how standard cutters can be used to form both the table edge and the leaf. The cutter used on the table edge is a quarter-round cutter. The mating cut on the leaf is done with a combination quarter-round and cove cutter. The radius of the cutters must match and the set-up must be made so the parts have equal shoulders. It's also possible to get sets of cutters that are specifically designed to form the drop leaf joint (Figure 13-1C). Their use, however, is not limited to this one application. If you view them as individual tools you will see that they are basically quarter-round and cove cutters which can be used to shape any edge or to form moldings.

A common hinge used on the drop leaf joint is called a back flap and is installed so the knuckle seats in a shallow groove cut into the wood. The center of the knuckle and the center of the cut's radius must be the same. A similar hinge comes with one leaf slightly bent, to be installed without a groove for the knuckle. Ordinary hasp hinges will also work. Whatever you use, be sure to provide some clearance between the shaped edges so they will not rub together. A good way to provide this clearance is to put a piece of heavy paper between the edges of the table and the leaf when you are assembling.

LOCK CORNER JOINT

A lock corner joint is often used in drawer and box constructions and can be found at corners of chest projects. It is a strong joint with a good interlock, (Figure 13-2) and is not difficult to make even though it calls for very careful cutting.

236

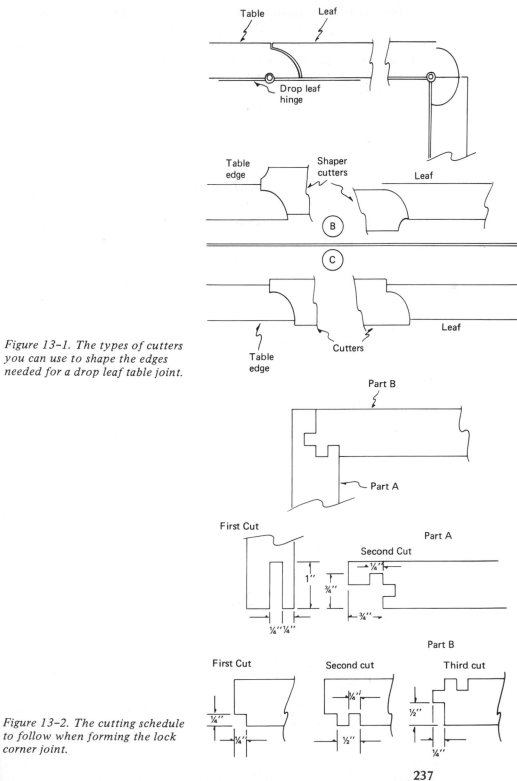

Figure 13-1. The types of cutters you can use to shape the edges needed for a drop leaf table joint.

Figure 13-2. The cutting schedule to follow when forming the lock corner joint.

237

On a table saw, organize a dado for cutting a 1/4-inch groove and then start cuts on one part as shown in Figure 13-2A. Make the first cut with the stock on edge and with the dado projecting 1 inch (for 1-inch thick stock). Make the second cut by using the miter gauge and with the stock flat on the table.

The cuts on the mating piece are shown in Figure 13-2B. Notice that only the dado's projection is changed; the width of cut remains the same. Accuracy is all important, so be sure the work is positioned correctly for each cut.

COMBINATION DADO RABBET

A combination dado rabbet (Figure 13-3) is similar to the lock corner joint. It does not have the same degree of interlock, but it makes a strong joint that has general applications. It is used extensively in connecting a drawer front with the drawer sides.

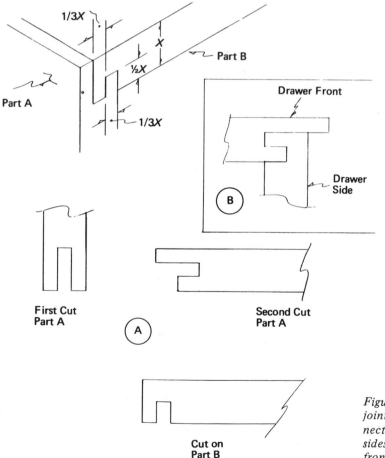

Figure 13-3. A dado-rabbet joint is often used to connect a drawer front to its sides. Note that the drawer front can have a lip.

The cuts required in both pieces are shown in Figure 13-3A. All the cuts can be made with a dado assembly that is set to provide the correct cut width. The second cut on part A can be made with the dado set, but you can switch to a regular saw blade (Figure 13-4) to remove the waste *after* all dado cuts are formed. Work as shown in Figure 13-3B if the drawer front must have a lip. The only modification in the procedure occurs on the first cut of part A. The groove must be deeper to provide the lip on the front of the drawer.

The dado rabbet joint can be used on corners of boxes and case constructions. If the visible end grain is objectionable and the design of the project permits, you can add corner guards as shown in Figure 13-5.

Figure 13-4. The shape in the drawer front can be finished by making this cut after the groove is formed.

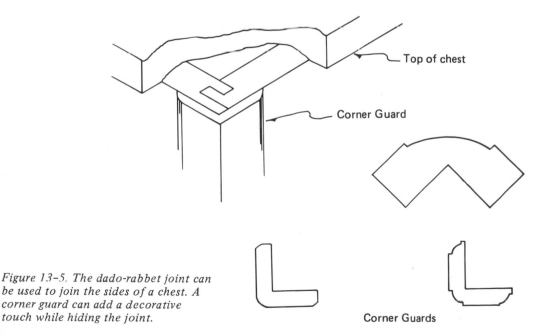

Top of chest

Corner Guard

Corner Guards

Figure 13-5. The dado-rabbet joint can be used to join the sides of a chest. A corner guard can add a decorative touch while hiding the joint.

MAKING THE WATERFALL JOINT

This joint, as we have said before, is an exceptionally good joint to use on plywood (Figure 13-6) since it hides objectionable edges and allows the surface grain pattern to flow neatly over the edge. There is no reason, however, why it can't also be used on solid stock.

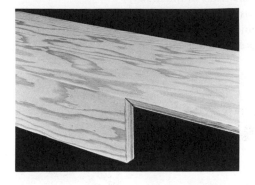

Figure 13-6. The waterfall joint lets the grain of the wood flow neatly over the edge.

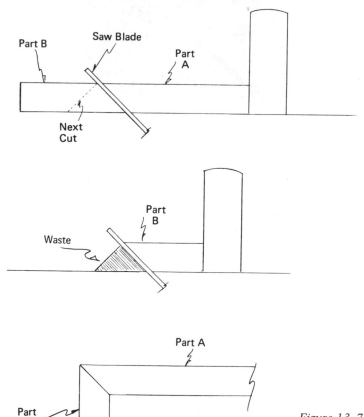

Figure 13-7. Work this way to make the cuts that are needed for the waterfall joint.

The cutting procedures, as they would be done on a table saw, are shown in Figure 13-7. To make this joint, you actually remove a wedge of material, allowing one part to fold down against the other with minimum disruption to the surface grain pattern. Be especially careful when you make the second cut so the kerf will meet exactly with the top corner of the part. Something will be lost simply because the saw kerf has width, but it looks better than matching two strange pieces of wood. Do the sawing with a fine, smooth-cutting blade.

MILLED DRAWER JOINT

The same cutter used to make the milled edge-to-edge joint, or glue joint, can be used as shown in Figure 13-8 to make a good connection between a drawer front and its sides. The drawer front can be flush with the sides or it can have a lip. In either case, you can make the shaping operation easier if you first form a conventional rabbet to remove the bulk of the waste stock.

Be very careful, regardless of whether you work on a shaper or with a molding head, to be sure the relationship between work and cutter is correct. Do test cuts first on scrap pieces.

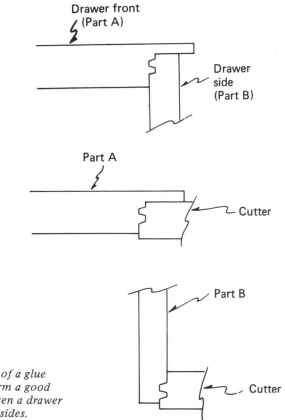

Figure 13-8. Use of a glue joint cutter to form a good connection between a drawer front and drawer sides.

Door assemblies on quality furniture and good cabinets often consist of panels that are framed with solid wood. The frame is usually four pieces: two vertical stiles and two horizontal rails. If a third member is introduced either vertically or horizontally, it is called a cross-rail or a cross-stile.

Sticking is a term used to describe the treatment of the inside edges of the frame members. As shown in Figure 13-9, the sticking can be square or have a shape. The ovolo, ogee, and cove and bead are the standard molding forms used when the sticking is shaped, but other treatments are possible. For example, edges can be beveled or chamfered. Commercially made frames are formed on a machine called a sticker, but the same work can be done in a small shop with a shaper or a router and sometimes with a molding head used on a table or radial arm saw.

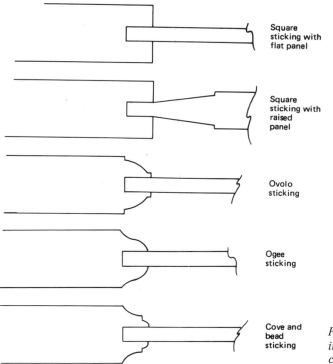

Square sticking with flat panel

Square sticking with raised panel

Ovolo sticking

Ogee sticking

Cove and bead sticking

Figure 13-9. Some standard "sticking" that is used on frame-panel constructions.

A very basic square stuck frame is shown in Figure 13-10. Inside edges are flat so the panel is held in place with frames made of molding used on both the back and the front side. The appearance is of shaped sticking, but no elaborate equipment is required to do the job. The corner joint does not have to be tenoned as shown. It can be a splined or doweled miter, or even a doweled butt joint.

In Figure 13-11 the basic idea is taken a step further by including the panel groove that is shown in detail A. In this case, the length and thickness of

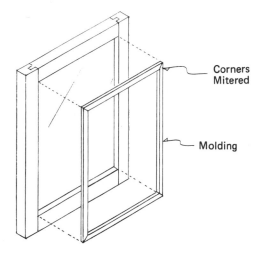

Figure 13-10. A simple frame will look like sticking if molding is used to hold the panel.

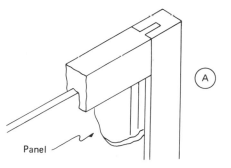

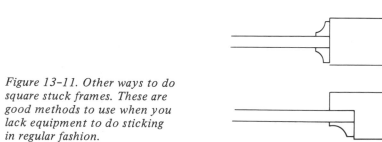

Figure 13-11. Other ways to do square stuck frames. These are good methods to use when you lack equipment to do sticking in regular fashion.

the tenon on the rails matches the dimensions of the groove. The detail B is a cross-section view of square sticking without a groove. The panel is held with add-on frames made with moldings. Detail C shows a section through rabbeted rails and stiles so the panel may be secured with an add-on frame on only one side. In this case the corner joints can be simple half-laps.

Rabbeted frames can also be handled as shown in Figure 13-12. A good procedure to follow is to shape the edges of the frame stock first, working with a router, a shaper, or with a molding head, and then do the rabbet cut. If a miter joint is used at the corners, then the frame parts require no further attention.

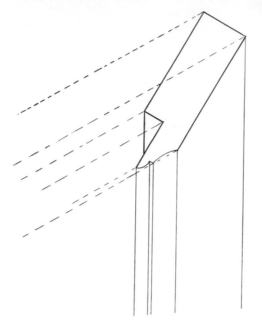

Figure 13-12. Frame stock can be edge shaped and then rabbeted. A miter joint lets you get by without doing a cope cut.

If, however, the corner joints are doweled butts or involve a tenon design, then the ends of the rails must be coped so the shaped edges will mate (Figure 13-13).

The cope cuts required are no different from those described when joining moldings. In this application the cope cuts are formed by machine instead of by hand using a cutter whose profile is the reverse of the shape on the stile (Figure 13-14). Standard cutters may be used in routine fashion in many situations but often, especially when the corner joint involves a tenon, the cope cutter must

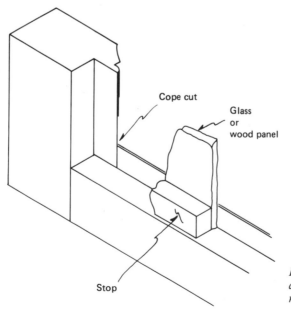

Cope cut

Glass
or
wood panel

Stop

Figure 13-13. Frame parts that are butt jointed must have coped rails.

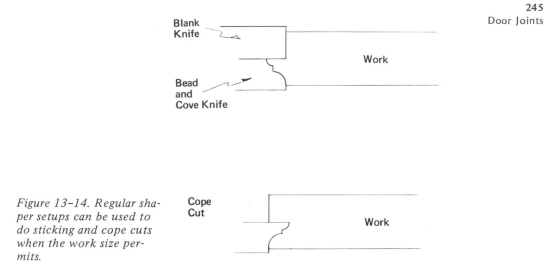

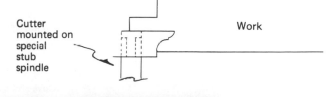

*Figure 13-14. Regular sha-
per setups can be used to
do sticking and cope cuts
when the work size per-
mits.*

be mounted in the shaper on a special stub spindle (Figure 13-15). This permits
the cut to be made regardless of how far over the spindle the work extends.

A common joint between rails and stiles that involves a cope cut is shown
in Figure 13-16. With the correct shaper setup, the parts can be formed in a
single pass. In addition to the shaped edges and the necessary cope cuts, the
stiles and rails will then have a groove for the panel and the rails will have a
tongue or tenon (Figure 13-17).

*Figure 13-15. Cope cuts on tenoned
joints are done by mounting the
cutter on a special stub spindle.*

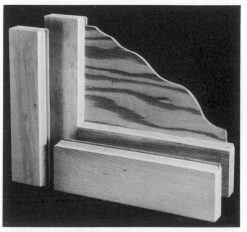

*Figure 13-16. A fairly common
cabinet door assembly that involves sticking and cope cuts.*

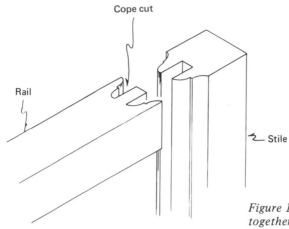

Cope cut

Rail

Stile

Figure 13–17. How stiles and rails fit together. The cope cut is just a reverse profile of the shape on the stile.

The shaper arrangement is shown in Figure 13-18. For the edge shaping, mount the cutters with a blank knife between them as shown in detail A. The result, in this case, will be cove and bead sticking with a groove for the panel. The setup for the cope cut is shown in detail B. Reverse cove and bead cutters are used, separated by a collar whose thickness and diameter produces a tenon that fits the groove formed in the first operation.

Other types of coped joints used on door frames are shown in Figures 13-19 and 13-20.

Figure 13-21 shows a setup you can use on a radial arm saw or a drill press. Here, a cove and bead cutter is combined with a blank knife to produce a shaped edge and a groove for a panel. This operation can be done on one piece of stock which can then be cut into lengths suitable for the frame. Use a miter joint at the corners.

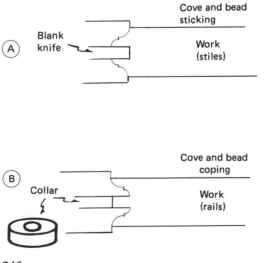

Cove and bead sticking

Blank knife

(A)

Work (stiles)

Cove and bead coping

(B)

Collar

Work (rails)

Figure 13–18. Setups to use to form the joint parts that were shown in Figure 13–17.

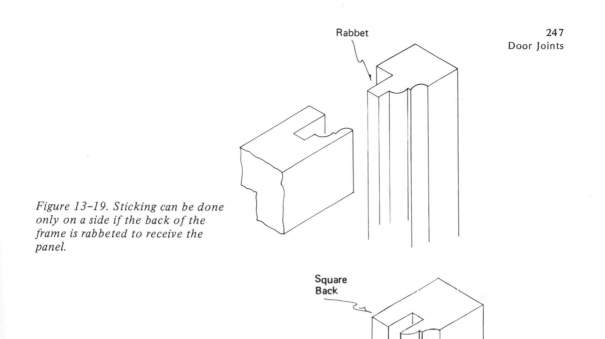

Figure 13-19. Sticking can be done only on a side if the back of the frame is rabbeted to receive the panel.

Figure 13-20. The same thought applies here but with a groove added to receive the panel.

Figure 13-21. A radial arm saw setup to do sticking. Frame parts like this do not have to be coped if miter joints are used.

COGGED JOINT

A cogged joint makes a good connection between an on-edge piece and the surface of the part it crosses (Figure 13-22). Do the stopped sockets first. If only a few are needed, form them by making cuts with a backsaw, as you would for blind dovetail sockets. Clean out the waste with a chisel. If many are needed, parts can be clamped together and the sockets formed by working with mortising bits and chisels on a drill press. The notch in the crossing pieces can be formed by working with a dado set or by using a backsaw for the shoulder cuts and a chisel to remove the waste.

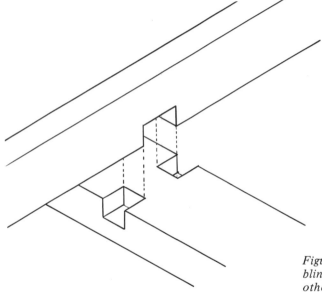

Figure 13-22. A cogged joint. Do the blind sockets first, then notch the other part to fit.

ROUND CORNER JOINTS

These are suggestions for joints when a frame for a padded seat or a rail or apron assembly that should have a round corner is needed. Figure 13-23 shows a solid corner block attached to rails with a mortise-tenon joint. Shape the block after the glue is dry.

Figure 13-24 shows two other ideas for blocked corners and a special technique (detail B) that does the job without visible joint lines. The corner section can be thinned out by cutting on a bandsaw, or on a jigsaw, or by making a series of overlapping cuts with a dado set. Be sure the section is thinned only enough so the wood can be bent without cracking. Soaking the wood in hot water or steaming it over a kettle will make it more pliable. Do some test work first since some wood species bend more easily than others. Cut the filler block after the bend is made so it will fit exactly.

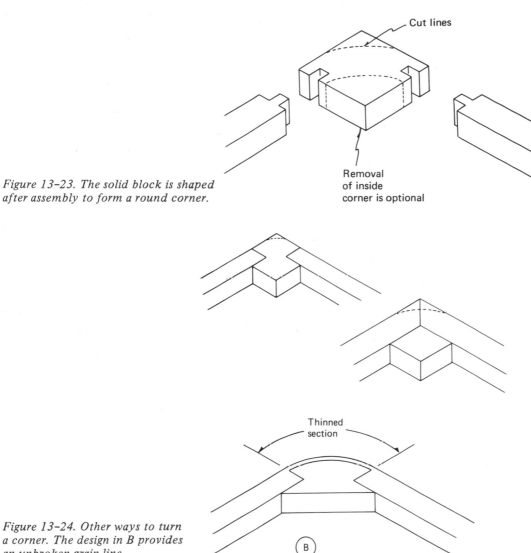

Figure 13-23. The solid block is shaped
after assembly to form a round corner.

Cut lines

Removal
of inside
corner is optional

Thinned
section

B

*Figure 13-24. Other ways to turn
a corner. The design in B provides
an unbroken grain line.*

SQUARE RAIL TO ROUND LEG

The major consideration with a square rail to round leg joint is in shaping
the rail to fit the contour of the leg. This consideration applies no matter what
the connection.

Figure 13-25 shows a dowel joint being used. When this joint is used the
concave shape on the rail can be formed by working with drum sanders chucked
in either a portable drill or a drill press. If a tenon is involved, the shoulders can
be shaped on a bandsaw or by hand with files.

249

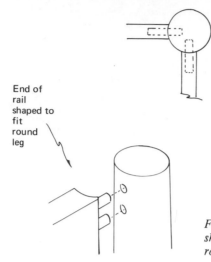

End of
rail
shaped to
fit
round
leg

Figure 13-25. Square-end rails should be shaped as shown when they connect to a round component.

ROUNDS TO FLATS

Methods you can use for round to flat connections are shown in Figure 13-26. It's important that the hole formed for the round member permits a slip fit. Too often the worker feels that having to force the parts together contributes to a better joint. Actually, it just adds stresses the project can do without.

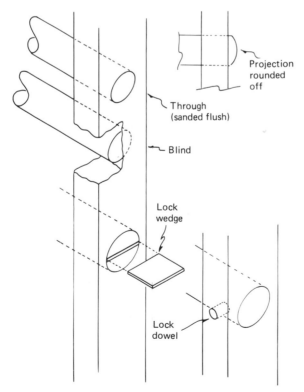

Projection rounded off

Through (sanded flush)

Blind

Lock wedge

Lock dowel

Figure 13-26. Various ways to work when connecting round parts to squares or flats.

A similar thought applies when using a lock wedge. Don't make the wedge so thick that you must smash it home with a hammer. Also, drive the wedge so it is across the grain of the component the round part enters. A tension that might cause a split can be created when a wedge is driven parallel to the grain line.

A wedge may also be used when the round member seats in a blind hole. The wedge must be sized so it will do its job without preventing the round part from bottoming in the hole.

A lock dowel can be used regardless of whether the inserted member is through or blind.

TWO SPECIAL SLAB JOINTS

A locking arrangement that is provided by using long wedges is shown in Figure 13-27. The rectangular openings through the slab pieces can be done by working with mortising bits and chisels on a drill press. Do not cut the wedges until the mortising is done. Then size them to fit, cutting them longer than necessary so they can be trimmed and sanded flush after the assembly is complete. Set the wedges in loosely when assembling. Tap them in gradually with a mallet as you apply clamp pressure to adjacent areas.

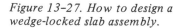

*Figure 13-27. How to design a
wedge-locked slab assembly.*

Figure 13-28 shows how dovetailed pieces may be used. In detail B the additional piece is sized to serve as a rail or apron in addition to reinforcing the slab. In designs like this, the slab pieces should be joined in routine fashion. The addition pieces should only be glued or mechanically attached at the center area. This will permit the pieces in the slab to expand or contract without causing damage.

LOCKING METHODS

Most joints can be locked either by designing the connection in a special way or by adding a component, usually a dowel or a spline.

A doweled butt joint can be locked by using additional dowels as shown in Figure 13-29. Drill the holes for the lock dowels while the joint is under

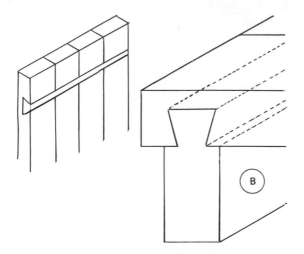

Figure 13-28. Dovetail shapes can be used on slab assemblies. Detail B is an integral rail design.

clamp pressure. The diameter of the lock dowel should not be greater than half the diameter of the joint dowel.

Figure 13-30 shows how you can lock in a part that might ordinarily be set in a simple dado. The cut in one piece can be viewed as twin dadoes with material left between them as a wedge to fit a groove formed in the insert piece. The thickness of the wedge should be just a fraction greater than the width of the groove.

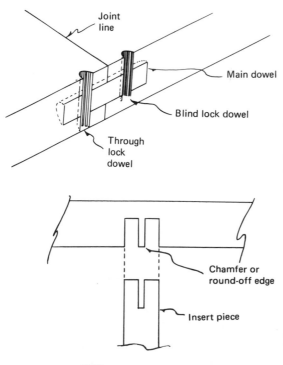

Figure 13-29. Dowels can be used as locks in a doweled butt joint.

Figure 13-30. An integral wedge is formed when twin dadoes are cut like this.

Figure 13–31 shows how to use a spline to lock a part set in a conventional dado. The width of the dado will have some bearing on the cut angle you use for the spline. Note how the spline groove is cut in the insert piece. This is a cut you can make freehand as long as the stock is wide enough to be handled safely. Use a tenoning jig if the work is narrow.

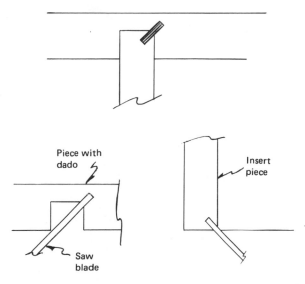

Figure 13–31. How to include a spline in a dado joint.

A spline can be used in a mortise-tenon joint as shown in Figure 13–32. Be careful not to make the spline so thick that it can split the joint parts. Make the spline from a contrasting wood if the joint is exposed and you wish to show it as a decorative detail. A spline used this way locks the joint only in one direction. In Figure 13–33A a lock is supplied in both directions. The design in Figure 13–33B is similar, but dowels are used in place of a spline. Always make the lock piece larger—longer in the case of a dowel—than necessary so it can be sanded flush after the assembly is complete.

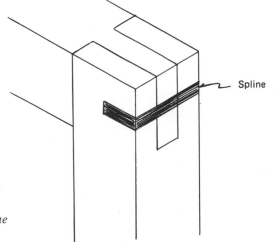

Figure 13–32. A spline used this way in a mortise-tenon locks the joint from only one direction.

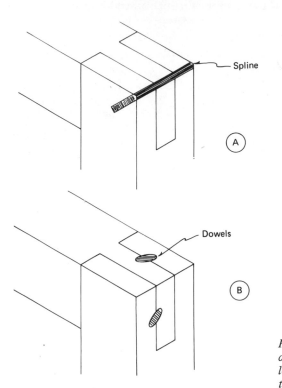

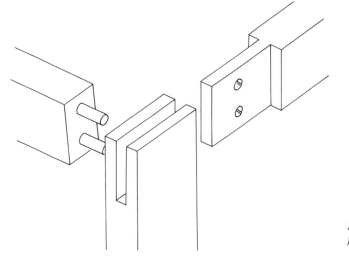

Figure 13–33. Splines or dowels used as shown here lock the joint in either direction.

Joints that involve three members can be designed so they will be strong *and* have an interlock. A basic design that can be adapted for use in many areas is shown in Figure 13-34. The best procedure is to hold the mortise-tenon parts together with clamps while you drill the holes for the dowels. The dowels can be through or blind.

Figure 13–34. A three-way lock joint that has many applications.

A similar procedure is shown in Figure 13-35 in a three-part joint involving the rails and back leg of a chair. Here too, the holes for the dowels should be drilled in the side rail and leg while the parts are held together with clamps.

Figure 13-36 shows a three-way joint that makes a simple but strong design for the understructure of, for example, a table. Figure 13-37 shows a three-way joint that is good to use on open framework or on a skeleton frame that will be sheathed with a panel material. In this case, all three of the parts should be held together in correct position when the dowel hole is drilled.

The joint assembly shown in Figure 13-38 calls for careful cutting. It is, however, the kind of attention that contributes to high quality and long lasting constructions.

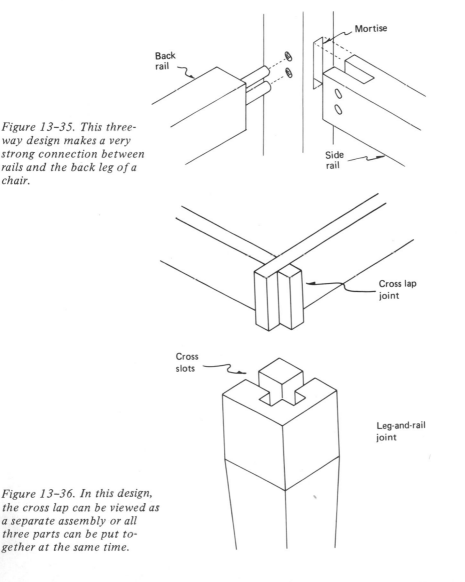

Figure 13-35. This three-way design makes a very strong connection between rails and the back leg of a chair.

Figure 13-36. In this design, the cross lap can be viewed as a separate assembly or all three parts can be put together at the same time.

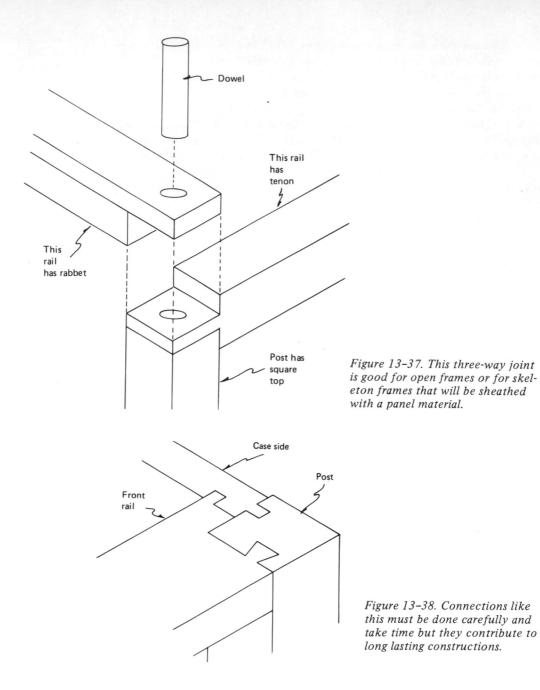

Dowel

This rail
has
tenon

This
rail
has rabbet

Post has
square
top

Figure 13–37. This three-way joint is good for open frames or for skeleton frames that will be sheathed with a panel material.

Case side

Post

Front
rail

Figure 13–38. Connections like this must be done carefully and take time but they contribute to long lasting constructions.

Chapter 14

SCULPTURED JOINTS

A sculptured joint is not a type of connection. It is a design method for treating any joint so lines will flow naturally together instead of meeting at sharp angles (Figure 14-1). Sculpturing is successful when the parts meld to conceal the joint lines. This isn't difficult to accomplish. Since the slight separations that eventually can occur because of shrinkage in connected pieces are even more obvious than they would be on a conventionally made joint, maximum attention to the strength and durability of the joint itself is the first rule when sculpturing.

Any joint should be as strong and stable as possible. Conventional treatments often include features like the slight setback that is recommended where a rail joins a leg, that make joint separation less obvious. This is not done when sculpturing, so whatever you can do to reinforce and lock the joint will work in your favor.

It can be said that sculpturing itself is contrary to the nature of wood—the lines of the joint might flow but the grain pattern will not. This criticism, however, can apply to any joint, so it's a minor argument against the concept.

Figure 14-1. Sculpturing means a melding of parts so there is a smooth flow at the joint lines instead of square corners and edges.

257

Many commercial pieces are often sculptured in limited areas. The joints that connect the arms, rails, and legs of the chair shown in Figure 14-2 are sculptured. Other joints are not sculptured, but it doesn't affect the overall appearance of the project, especially when all components are shaped to flow nicely.

Figure 14-2. Commercial pieces are often sculptured only in limited areas. Other joints are done conventionally but the components are shaped to contribute to the overall feeling.

TRANSITION PIECES

Parts must often be bulked out in the joint area so there will be sufficient material for sculpturing. The most economical way to do this is to add an extra part as shown in Figure 14-3. This will work, but it adds to the number of

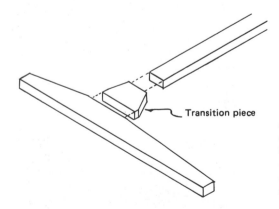

Transition piece

Figure 14-3. Transitions can be done by using extra pieces in the joint. This can save material but can cause problems because of additional joint lines.

glue lines to worry about. You can also work with a piece that is wider than needed so it can be preshaped to provide an integral transition area as shown in Figure 14-4.

This method will also work when components have a circular cross-section (Figure 14-5). It's often possible on this type of work to save some time and effort by using a ready-made part, for example, a large dowel (Figure 14-6). However, the visible joint line between the dowel and the flat area will not be as easy to meld as it would if the parts were square.

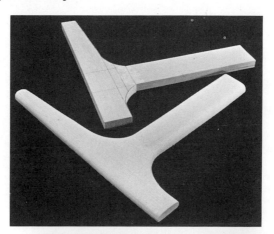

Figure 14-4. A better method is to work with wide stock that can be cut to provide an integral transition area. Joint lines will be minimal.

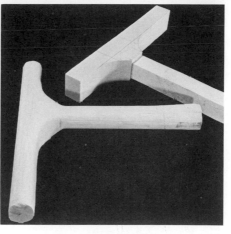

Figure 14-5. Components with round or oval cross-sections can be handled as shown here. The assembly in the foreground is rough shaped; final smoothing has yet to be done.

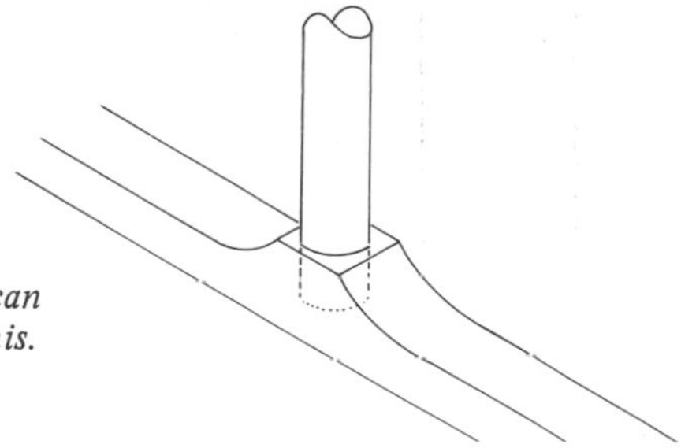

Figure 14-6. A ready-made round can be joined to a square section like this. Square areas are then shaped to blend at the joint line.

Transitions can also be made from round or oval shapes to components which have a basically flat form by making the initial connection as shown in Figure 14-7.

Figure 14-8 shows one way to work when you need to turn a corner. The outside and inside corners of the block can be removed with a saw before you do the shaping.

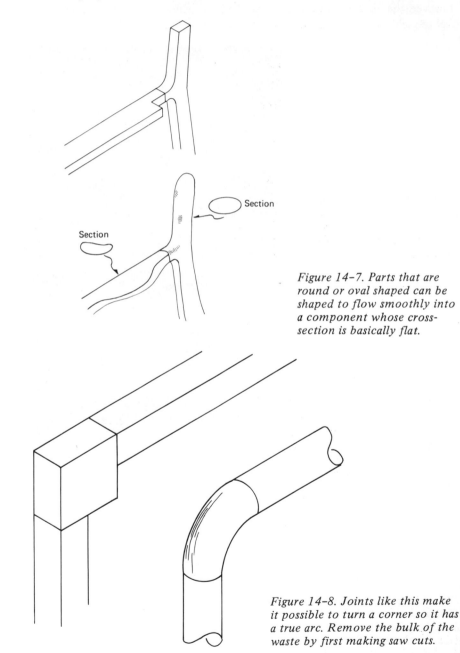

Figure 14-7. Parts that are round or oval shaped can be shaped to flow smoothly into a component whose cross-section is basically flat.

Figure 14-8. Joints like this make it possible to turn a corner so it has a true arc. Remove the bulk of the waste by first making saw cuts.

Legs and similar components that are formed in a lathe can have bulked sections for use as transition pieces when assembling (Figure 14-9). Turnings are done in a conventional manner when the bulked section is on a true longitudinal centerline. Offset turning techniques are used if the bulked area must provide more transition material in a particular direction. In many cases, most of the turning can be done with the work mounted on true centers, with a shift made to off-centers for the bulked areas. Experienced lathe turners know that off-center work will be out of balance. This causes a vibration problem which you should be aware of. Work at reduced speeds, take slight cuts, and be sure the tool rest is clear of the work's greatest projection. If you haven't done this kind of work before, experiment by doing some tests on small scrap pieces of softwood.

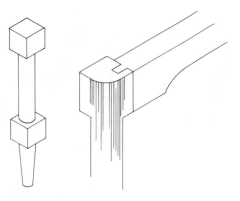

Figure 14-9. Turned parts can be designed so bulked areas can be shaped after assembly to flow into other components.

Sculpturing applies to the edges of components as well as to joint areas. Compatible edges on shelves or table tops are essential to the overall feeling. Most times the job is easiest to do if you remove the bulk of the waste by first making saw cuts like those in Figure 14-10.

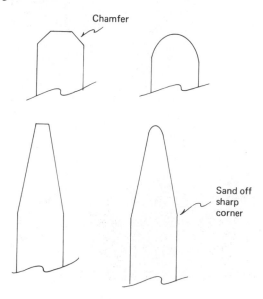

Chamfer

Sand off sharp corner

Figure 14-10. Edges of table tops, seats, or shelves should be shaped to conform to the overall sculptured effect.

Some preshaping of parts on power tools is possible but since the final forms are usually compound contours and fillets, final work is always done with hand tools. A good argument against too much preshaping is presented by the fact that parts do have to be clamped. It's much easier to fit clamps against square edges.

Figures 14-11 through 14-15 show various tools and methods that can be used when sculpturing. The basic procedure is to use a tool that will remove the bulk of the waste stock quickly. To get the necessary smoothness, work with progressively finer grits of sandpaper.

Figure 14-11. A half-round rasp is a good tool to use for initial waste removal chores. Stroking with the grain of the wood will leave the least rough surface. Finish with sandpaper.

Figure 14-12. A spokeshave is another good tool to use. Cuts can be light or heavy depending on how much projection you set on the blade. Work with the grain of the wood.

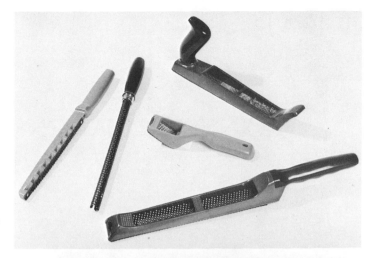

Figure 14-13. "Surform" tools (by Stanley) come in many shapes and sizes and are very useful when doing sculptured joints.

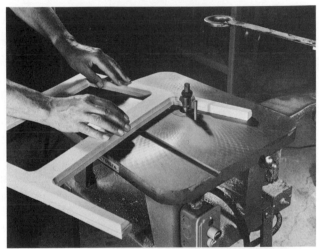

Figure 14-14. Sometimes it's possible to do a lot of preliminary shaping after assembly by using a power tool. Here, corners are rounded off on a shaper but the same job can be done with a portable router. Final melding will be done by hand with sandpaper.

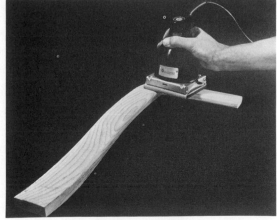

Figure 14-15. A good pad sander is an excellent tool to use for doing the final shaping and smoothing on sculptured joints. This is a critical step and must not be rushed.

Chapter 15

JOINT APPLICATIONS

There are many joint designs and many variations of basic joints. Which one to use to make a particular connection will not be a problem if you study, as we have suggested, the type of stresses imposed on a joint area. Where more than one joint design is applicable, base a choice on the one that is easiest to do or which you can do most efficiently with the tools you have.

There are practical considerations and there are preferences the woodworker will have in selecting a joint design to use. If you intend for the projects that you produce to have permanence, select joints accordingly. If putting things together adequately but as quickly as possible is a prime consideration, avoid making elaborate connections that require time and patience.

Whatever you decide—no matter how complex or simple the joint—remember it will only do its job as efficiently as you do yours. A sloppy dovetail is *not* better than doing without a dovetail. A butt joint will not look as good as it might, or hold as well as it can, if the mating surfaces are not square and do not make maximum contact.

Shown in this section are some typical and some not so typical joint applications. Browse through these illustrations before designing a project to find some ideas you can put to use.

A   Frame assembly
B   Case sides
C   Tenon
D   Groove
E   Dust panels of plywood, hardboard or particleboard
      (dust panel is not required in top frame since it will
      be covered by the top of the case)
F   Tenons (or dowels) into sides
G   Screws can be used to secure the top

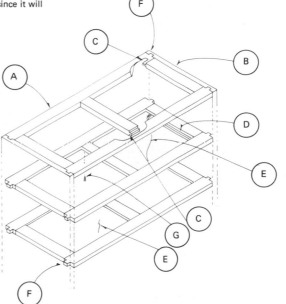

Figure 15–1. This is a type of case construction using solid sides and web frames. Units designed this way have good dimensional stability. Humidity variations will cause minimal changes.

Figure 15–2. The pieces running between the front and back rails of the web frames are drawer guides.

265

Figure 15–3. The sides of the chest shown in the previous illustration are a frame-panel construction. The inserted panels should not be glued in place so they can change dimensionally without splitting.

WEB FRAMES

A	Frame assembly (often called "web frame")
B	Front and back rails
C	End rails
D	Drawer guide
E	Groove (for dust panels)
F	Dust panels
G	Integral tenon fits stopped dado in case side
H	End rails have a groove on one side, tongue (tenon) on the other

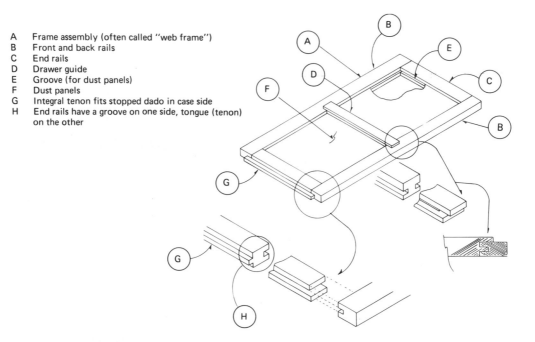

Figure 15–4. The basics of a web frame. Note how the end rails are formed to provide a tenon (or tongue) that will mate with a groove formed in the sides of the case. This is a strong construction but the joints shown are not the only ones that can be used.

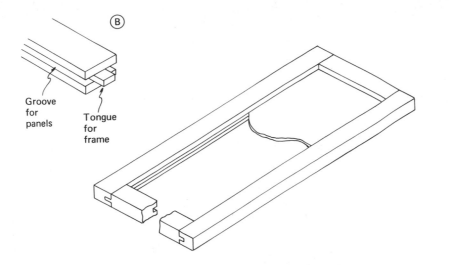

Figure 15-5. This web frame is easier to do and can be installed in dadoes formed in the sides of the case. If you include an intermediate rail, it should be shaped as shown in the detail B.

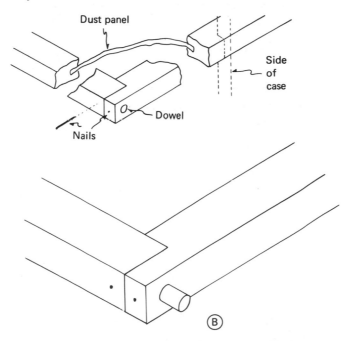

Figure 15-6. This web frame design calls for grooves for the dust panels and simple rabbet joints for the corners. Note, in detail B that the corner can be reinforced with a dowel, which in turn can be locked with nails. Insert the dowel and drive the nails while the frame parts are under clamp pressure.

CABINET BASE

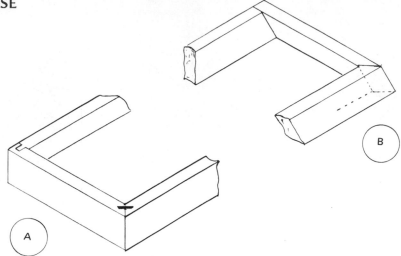

Figure 15–7. Here are several methods to use when making a separate assembly for a cabinet base. If the base slopes, as in B, the front corner requires a compound miter joint. The back corner does not since the rear rail doesn't slope. The joints shown in A do a good job when all base parts are vertical.

BOOKCASE CONSTRUCTION

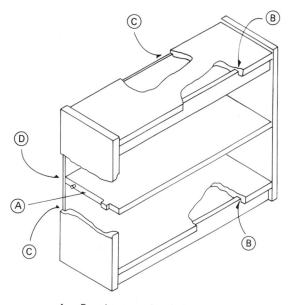

A   Dowel or tenon into sides (all shelves)
B   Dado
C   Back inset in rabbets (sides and top shelf)
D   Butt (bottom and middle shelf)

Figure 15–8. This is a good construction design for projects like open bookcases. A back adds to the appearance of the project and provides strength to resist lateral stresses.

KITCHEN BASE CABINET

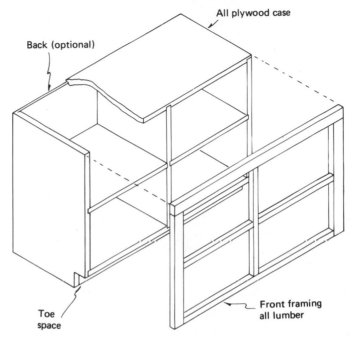

All plywood case

Back (optional)

Front framing
all lumber

Toe
space

Figure 15-9. Box, or all-panel construction is often used on kitchen cabinets. The back is optional because most cabinets of this type are placed against a wall. Doors are hung on the solid face framing. Note the simple joints.

DRAWERS

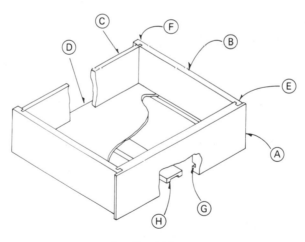

Figure 15-10. Nomenclature of a typical drawer. Bottoms are always let into grooves. Ready-made metal guides are available.

A   Drawer front
B   Drawer sides
C   Drawer back
D   Drawer bottom (let into grooves in front and sides)
E   Combination dado and rabbet joint
F   Dado in sides; rabbet in back
G   Grooves
H   Centered drawer guide

269

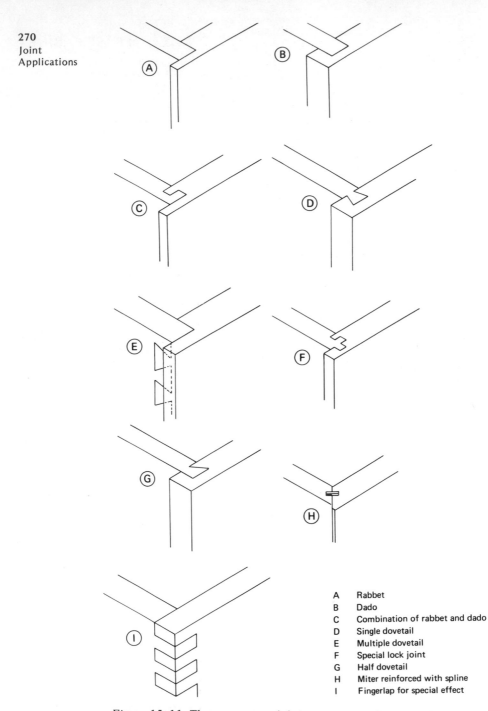

A   Rabbet
B   Dado
C   Combination of rabbet and dado
D   Single dovetail
E   Multiple dovetail
F   Special lock joint
G   Half dovetail
H   Miter reinforced with spline
I   Fingerlap for special effect

Figure 15-11. There are many joints you can use to connect a drawer front to its sides. Factors to consider are: the general design of the project, what the drawer will contain, tools you have to work with, and your personal woodworking preference.

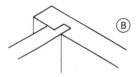

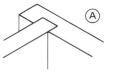

A   Dado
B   Dado in drawer side; rabbet in drawer back
C   Butt
D   Single dovetail or half dovetail
E   Dado in drawer side; tongue in drawer back
F   Double dado in drawer side; single dado in drawer back

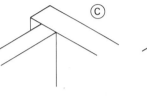

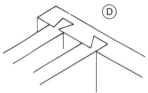

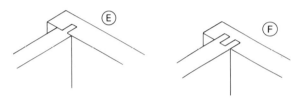

Figure 15-12. Some of the joints you can use to connect the back of the drawer to the sides. Comments made in relation to drawer front joints also apply here.

LEG AND RAIL ASSEMBLY

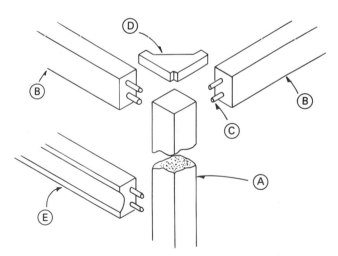

Figure 15-13. A typical leg-rail-stretcher assembly. Two dowels in the joint resist twisting stresses. Fit corner blocks as carefully as you do other components.

A   Leg
B   Rails
C   Minimum of two dowels each place
D   Well fitted corner block
E   Stretcher (also doweled)

271

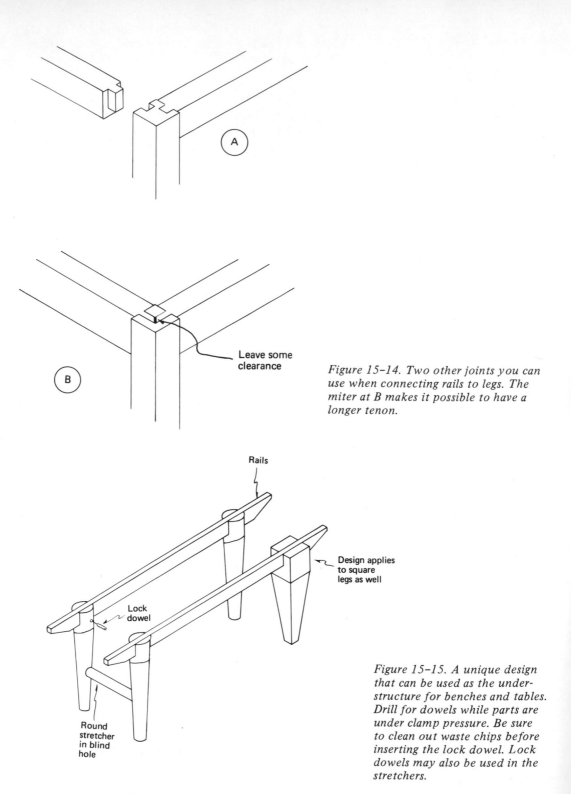

A

B

Leave some
clearance

*Figure 15-14. Two other joints you can
use when connecting rails to legs. The
miter at B makes it possible to have a
longer tenon.*

Rails

Design applies
to square
legs as well

Lock
dowel

Round
stretcher
in blind
hole

*Figure 15-15. A unique design
that can be used as the understructure for benches and tables.
Drill for dowels while parts are
under clamp pressure. Be sure
to clean out waste chips before
inserting the lock dowel. Lock
dowels may also be used in the
stretchers.*

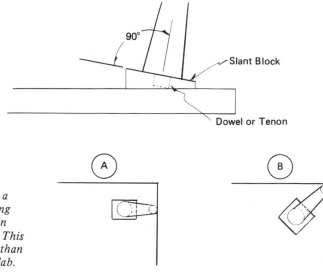

Figure 15-16. How to set a leg at a simple or compound angle by using a slant block. The block is glued in place and reinforced with screws. This makes a strong joint and is easier than attaching the leg directly to the slab.

TRESTLE TABLE

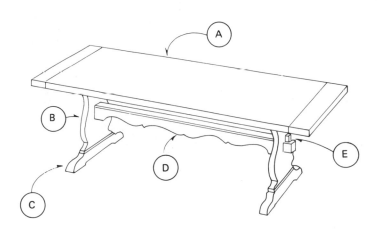

Figure 15-17. A typical trestle table design and suggestions for strong joints that suit the project's style. The same design can be used for coffee, cocktail, dining tables, and even for benches.

A Slab made of narrow boards, edge-joined and with end boards
B Legs also of glued-up boards with wide tenons formed at each end before curves are cut
C Base mortised to receive leg tenon
D Heavy stretcher with tenon at each end to pass through legs
E Tenon is tusked
   Note: Bottom of slab is mortised to receive tenon in top of legs

273

ATTACHING TABLE TOPS

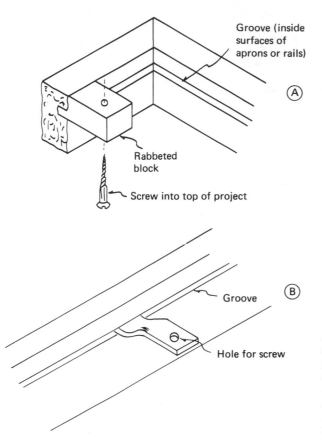

Groove (inside
surfaces of
aprons or rails)

(A)

Rabbeted
block

Screw into top of project

Groove (B)

Hole for screw

*Figure 15–18. Solid lumber tops
should be attached so they can expand and contract without splitting or
separating at a joint. Detail A shows a
type of block you can make yourself.
Detail B illustrates a ready-made table-
top clip. Install the fasteners about 12
inches apart.*

PEDESTAL TABLE

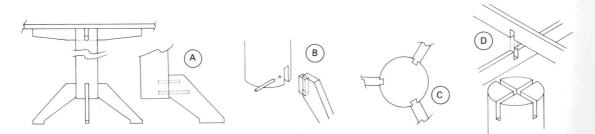

*Figure 15–19. These are joints you can use on a pedestal table: (A) dowels, with a longer one used
at the point of greatest strain; (B) mortise-tenon with a lock dowel; (C) dovetails make a very
strong joint; (D) edge-lapped rails to fit grooves cut in the pedestal.*

A   Frame with mitered joints
B   Reinforcement (Spline shown)
C   Groove
D   Panel
E   Flush panel has a groove in the frame and a rabbet in the panel. This design is often used for the sides of case goods as well as doors

FRAMED PANELS

F   Elevated panel uses grooves in both the frame and the panel
G   Panel raised on one side but with square shoulders
H   Panel raised on one side but with beveled shoulders
I   Rabbeted frame for a thin panel or glass insert. Wood stops are used to secure the panel

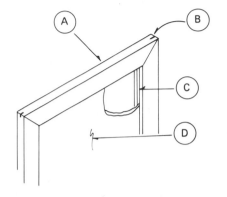

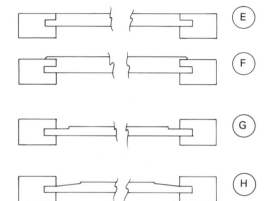

Figure 15–20. These are various ways to insert a panel in a frame. All the ideas can be used for doors and for sides of cabinets.

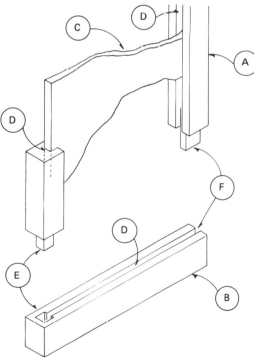

A   Stile
B   Rail
C   Panel
D   Grooves
E   Blind mortise-tenon
F   Open or stub mortise-tenon

Figure 15–21. This is a basic frame-panel construction with parts identified and suggestions for two corner-joint designs.

275

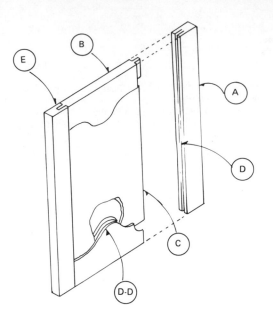

A	Stile
B	Shaped rail
C	Panel cut to fit
D	Groove
D-D	Groove in shaped rails done on a shaper
E	Tenon

Figure 15–22. Frames can be made fancier if you work along the lines shown here. Square sticking is shown but edges can also be shaped.

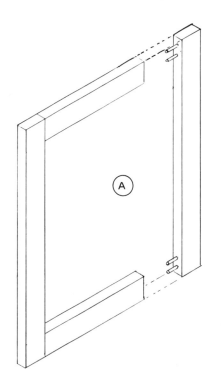

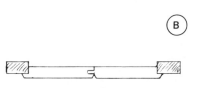

Figure 15–23. Frame-panel construction used on the doors of the project shown in Figure 15–24. The center tongue and groove joint should not be glued. This will permit the boards to move without causing damage.

Figure 15–24.

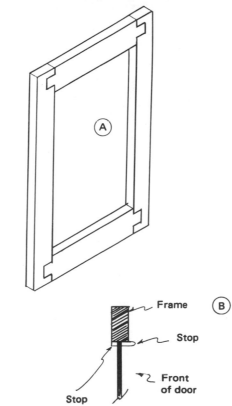

Figure 15–25. A different type of frame-panel assembly that adds styling to the project shown in Figure 15–26. Note how the stops (detail B) project to add a detail. The same design was used for both the glass and solid panel doors.

Figure 15–26.

CHAIRS

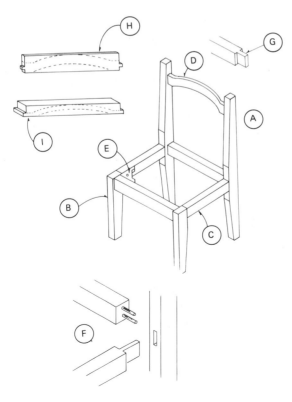

A   Back legs
B   Front legs
C   Rails
D   Back (one or more pieces)
E   Corner blocks (to reinforce frame and for attachment
      of padded seat
F   Leg to rail joint (dowels penetrate tenon on rails.
      Dowels may be through leg or blind)
G   Back-to-leg joint is mortise tenon (may be pegged)
H   How to do back if curve is vertical
I   How to do back if curve is horizontal
      Note that both back shapes have tenons formed
      before curves (dotted lines) are cut

Figure 15–27. A basic approach to chair construction. Chairs take a lot of use and abuse so connections should get maximum attention.

Figure 15–28. Chairs like this rocker rate among the toughest to do projects because of the amount of turning required and the limitations imposed on joint designs. All should be integral tenons, preferably locked in place with blind wedges.

CHAIR SEAT-FRAMES

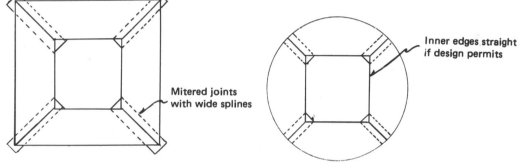

Mitered joints
with wide splines

Inner edges straight
if design permits

Figure 15–29. One way to make a chair-seat frame that will support an added pad. The same idea can be used for any project that requires a circular component you can't cut from one piece of material. Assemblies like this can actually be stronger than a one-piece part.

PLYWOOD EDGES

Figure 15–30. Pieces of plywood used as slab material can be framed to conceal the unattractive ply lines. Here, rabbeted strips are used to make the slab look thicker.

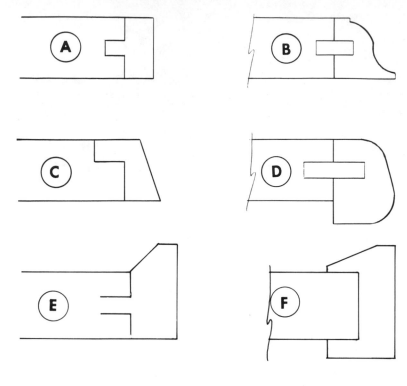

A   Plain wood strip with integral tongue; groove
     in plywood
B   Molding with spline
C   Rabbet cuts in both the plywood and the banding
D   Bulk edge with spline
E   Wood strip shaped to provide a lip; integral
     tongue; groove in plywood
F   Strip is grooved for the full thickness of the
     plywood; provides bulk as well as a lip

Figure 15-31. Other methods you can use to hide plywood edges.

Chapter 16

CLAMPS AND CLAMP USE

Once you have formed the parts of a joint, the pieces must be held together in correct alignment until the glue is dry. This is done with various types of clamping devices except in those cases where the joint design involves mechanical fasteners. Even then, it is often a good idea to hold parts together under clamp pressure while you drive the nail or screw.

In order to do a variety of gluing operations efficiently, it is necessary to have an assortment of clamps. Some types are more useful than others, but there is no such thing as one clamp for all work. All woodworking shops should have a basic assortment. The number of clamp types needed will depend on the type and scope of the work. Some assemblies require few clamps; others are less frustrating to do correctly when the clamp supply and assortment is not too limited. The logical way to start a collection of clamps is to purchase the types that are needed for the work on hand. Chances are you will need a variety, like C-clamps and handscrews for small assemblies, and a type of bar clamp for larger work on slabs and frames.

This chapter will show the clamps that are available. Some basic uses for each will be demonstrated to enable the woodworker to make good clamp choices, whether he is starting or adding to a collection.

HANDSCREWS

Handscrews are very popular with woodworkers because they can be easily adjusted to apply pressure evenly over a broad surface. Since the jaws can be set unparallel without interfering with the tool's function handscrews can also be used to clamp odd-shaped pieces of work (Figure 16-1). These are referred to as standard handscrews. Some workers prefer, or have as part of their collection, handscrews that are "non-adjustable." The jaws of these are always parallel and can't be set at an angle.

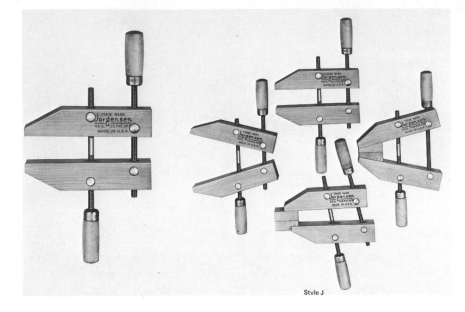

Figure 16-1. Standard handscrews have jaws which may be adjusted to angles.
Other types have jaws that remain constantly parallel.

Handscrews can be set quickly if you practice the habit of grasping the end spindle with your right hand and the middle spindle with your left hand (Figure 16-2).

When the clamp is held this way, use your hands as if they were on the pedals of a bicycle and adjust the jaws until the opening is approximately correct. Be sure to hold the handles firmly, with your arms extended, so the clamp is well away from your face. A wrist action is sufficient to cause the jaws to revolve around the spindles.

Place the handscrew on the work so the end spindle is either on your right or in an upper position and with the middle spindle as close to the work as possible. Adjust one or both of the handles so the jaws are gripping easily but so they are open a bit more at the end. Then turn the end spindle to close the jaws and grip the work firmly.

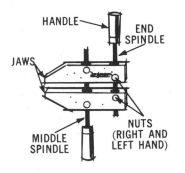

Figure 16-2. Identification of the parts of a handscrew.

Ideally, final pressure is applied only by turning the end spindle so the middle spindle acts as a fulcrum. In any event, be sure that pressure is not applied only at one end of the work, but evenly along the full length of the jaws. Since handscrews have smooth, wooden jaws, it isn't necessary to use a pad, or *caul,* to protect the work. Sizes of handscrews are shown in Figure 16-3.

SIZES OF HANDSCREWS		
OVERALL LENGTH OF JAWS inches	MAXIMUM OPENING BETWEEN JAWS inches	REACH – FROM MIDDLE SPINDLE TO END OF JAWS inches
4	2	2
5	2½	2½
6	3	3
7	3½	3½
8	4½	4
10	6	5
12	8½	6
14	10	7
16	12	8
18	14	9
20	14	10
24	17	12

Figure 16-3. Handscrews are available in all the sizes shown on this chart.

In addition to routine clamping uses, handscrews can serve in many auxiliary capacities. Figure 16-4 shows how to use one on a slab assembly so the pieces won't buckle under bar-clamp pressure. When the clamps are used in this fashion it's a good idea to place strips of wax paper between the work and the jaws of the clamp. This prevents excess glue from messing the clamp jaws.

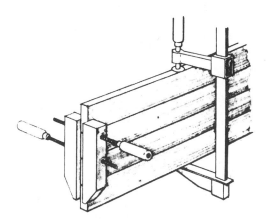

Figure 16-4. How to use a handscrew on a slab assembly so the parts won't buckle under clamp pressure.

The arrangement shown in Figure 16-5 is actually a repair job, but it does demonstrate the versatility of handscrews. A small handscrew is used on each side of a crack that has developed in the chair component. A larger handscrew puts pressure on the small ones to bring the broken edges together until the glue dries. This would be a rather difficult job to do without such special clamp use.

Figure 16–5. This shows handscrews in use on a repair job, but the application points up the flexibility of the tools.

Figure 16-6 shows how a handscrew can provide a bearing surface for another type of clamp. In this case a leg is being glued to a round pedestal. A C-clamp is being used, but a bar clamp could do the same job if required because of the size of the work. If the pedestal has four legs, opposite ones would be in line so you can use a handscrew on each and glue two legs in place in one operation.

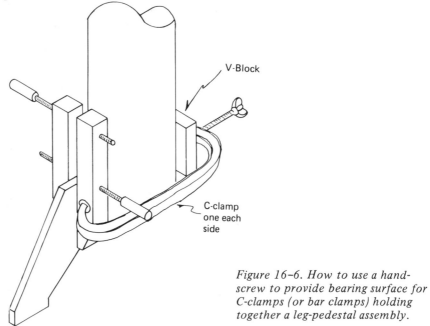

V-Block

C-clamp
one each
side

Figure 16–6. How to use a handscrew to provide bearing surface for C-clamps (or bar clamps) holding together a leg-pedestal assembly.

Figure 16-7 shows an offbeat but practical application of handscrews that allows gripping of round or square stock for, among other things, concentric drilling. The matching *V*-notches that must be cut into the jaws of the clamp will not interfere with the tool's primary function. Be sure the *V*s are cut so they are square to the sides of the clamp jaws.

Figure 16–7. Cut matching V-notches in the jaws of a handscrew and it becomes an excellent holding device for jobs like this.

BAR CLAMPS

Bar clamps, often called cabinet or furniture clamps, are indispensable for jobs like gluing up slabs (Figure 16-8), assembling frames (Figure 16-9), and similar chores that require clamping over relatively long lengths. Either the tail stop or the head of the clamp is movable so a quick adjustment can be made to suit the size of the work. The movable part has a built-in friction clutch or catch so it will not move wherever it is located on the bar.

In use, it is a good idea to unwind the screw completely and then set the clutch so the gripping length of the clamp is a bit more than the length of the work. Final pressure is applied by turning the screw. When more than one clamp is used the pressure should be equally distributed by tightening each clamp a bit at a time.

If you are clamping finished stock you must protect the wood by using wooden pads against the clamp jaws. Such protection isn't needed if the affected edges will be sawed off or jointed. Special non-marring pads that can be slipped on the jaws of bar clamps to protect the work are available. The pads are easily

Figure 16–8. Bar clamps are fine tools for slab assemblies. Placing them on alternate sides of the work will equalize the clamp pressure.

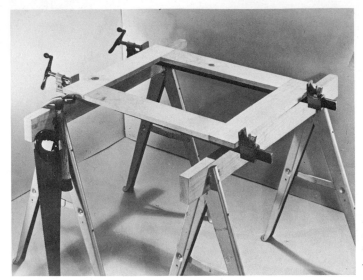

Figure 16-9. Using bar clamps to hold a frame assembly. Be sure to check the corners of the frame with a square as you apply the pressure.

slipped on or off the clamp jaws and eliminate the need for makeshift blocks that are often a nuisance to keep in correct position.

Figure 16-10 shows a practical bar clamp setup to use when gluing a slab. The cross pieces will keep the slab parts from buckling when the main clamp pressure is applied. Use strips of wax paper between wood surfaces that must not adhere.

Figure 16-11 shows typical bar clamps and the average sizes in which they are available.

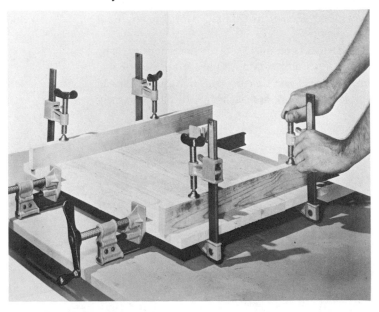

Figure 16-10. A well organized slab assembly clamping procedure. The cross pieces will keep the slab part from buckling.

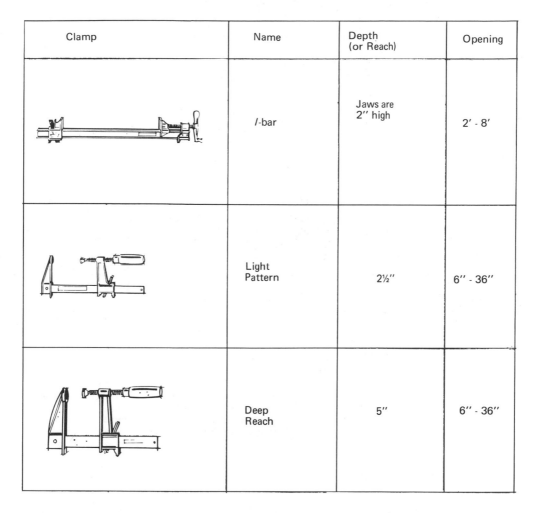

Clamp	Name	Depth (or Reach)	Opening
	I-bar	Jaws are 2" high	2' - 8'
	Light Pattern	2½"	6" - 36"
	Deep Reach	5"	6" - 36"

16–11. Types and sizes of bar clamps. These are typical. Other designs are also available.

HINGED BAR CLAMPS

Hinged bar clamps, when attached to a bench as shown in Figure 16–12, will swing to a clamping position when needed and out of the way when not in use. A typical in-use application is shown in Figure 16–13. This setup is ideal for use as a jig or fixture to perform repeat-production operations. The clamp's swivel plate can be mounted on any flat surface so use is not limited to bench work. Actually, the clamp can be used like any bar clamp and, because of the swivel plate, it is especially useful when a component being glued has an angled shape.

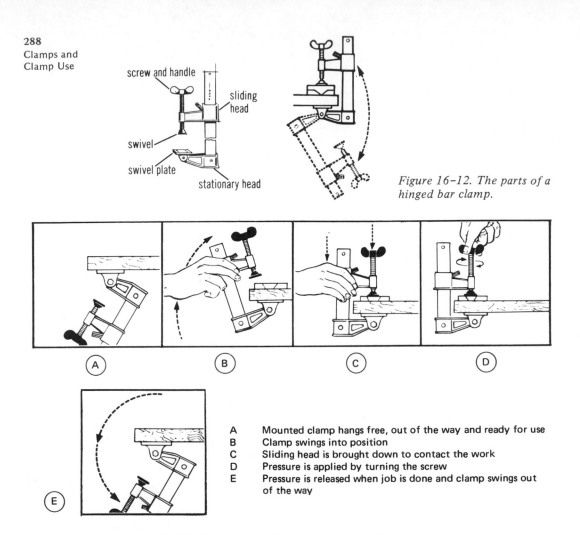

Figure 16-12. The parts of a hinged bar clamp.

A   Mounted clamp hangs free, out of the way and ready for use
B   Clamp swings into position
C   Sliding head is brought down to contact the work
D   Pressure is applied by turning the screw
E   Pressure is released when job is done and clamp swings out
     of the way

Figure 16-13. A typical application for a hinged bar clamp.

Special steel tracks are available for mounting the hinged bar clamps, as shown in Figure 16-14. This does not interfere with the swivel action and makes it possible to easily remove the clamp for use elsewhere.

CLAMP FIXTURES

Clamp fixtures are actually a kit that includes an unmounted tail stop and clamp head that can be used on any length of readily available pipe. Thus, a single set of fixtures can be used to make any number of different length bar clamps merely by stocking different lengths of pipe.

The pipe must be threaded at each end. The tail stop or the clamp head, depending on the fixture's design, attaches at one end; a coil-spring stop is used at the other end. Once assembled, the units are used like any standard bar clamp.

Clamp fixtures are available in all the styles shown in Figure 16-15. The

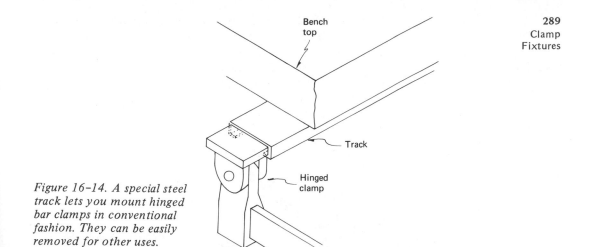

Figure 16-14. A special steel track lets you mount hinged bar clamps in conventional fashion. They can be easily removed for other uses.

CLAMP FIXTURE	DESCRIPTION
	Designed for mounting on 3/4'' standard or extra heavy pipe—has fixed head and sliding tail
	Similar to above but mounts on 1/2'' standard or extra heavy pipe
	Mounts on 3/4'' pipe but has fixed tail and sliding head—tail and head may be reversed to push instead of pull
	Double bar mounts on 1/2'' pipe—will pull evenly on both sides of the work

Figure 16-15. Clamp fixtures are designed for use on easily available pipe so you can design a clamp in whatever length you need.

double bar design, shown in use in Figure 16-16, is a unique concept that exerts pressure on both sides of the work to prevent any tendency of parts to buckle. These clamp fixtures are especially useful for gluing multipiece slabs. When mounting the fixtures, use one bar that is about 3 inches longer than the other. This will make it easier to "open" the clamp when you must apply it across the work.

Figure 16-16. Double bar clamp fixtures in use on a slab assembly. Pressure is applied equally on both sides of the work.

Other types of clamp fixtures, like the one shown in Figure 16-17, are designed for use on wood bars that you make yourself. The sliding head on the one illustrated is supported by guides so the screw is relieved from any bending strain and will not get out of line. Several types of these fixtures are made for mounting on wood bars of any length that have a cross-section that measures 1¼ × 2½ inches. Others are designed so they can be mounted on a standard two-by-four

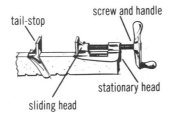

tail-stop
screw and handle
stationary head
sliding head

Figure 16-17. A type of clamp fixture that is mounted on a wooden bar supplied by the woodworker.

Figure 16-18. Clamp fixtures designed for use on wooden bars are usable in other ways—here, as a bench-mounted assembly jig.

of any length. The latter type are made with a head assembly that can be mounted on any flat surface or bench top, as shown in Figure 16–18, to make special clamping jigs for similar assemblies.

An advantage of clamps that have wood bars is that they are less likely to damage finished wood surfaces than clamps made of pipe or steel bars.

C-CLAMPS

C-clamps (Figure 16–19) are available in an endless number of shapes and sizes, allowing applications to vary from straightforward clamping jobs to limitless auxiliary uses. Always use a pad, at least under the swivel, regardless of the style of the clamp. This is suggested for two reasons. First, the swivel will mar the work if it makes direct contact (Figure 16–20). Second, a pad will distribute clamp pressure over a broader area.

CLAMP	NAME	OPENING	DEPTH
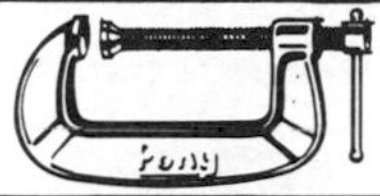	Regular throat	2"–3"	1"–1½"
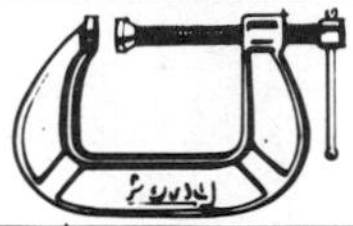	Medium throat	1"–2½"	1"–2½"
	Round frame	5/8'–1¼"	7/8"–1-3/8"
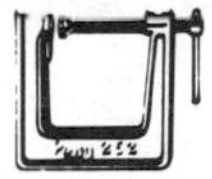	Square frame	1"–1½"	1½"–2"
	Deep throat	1"–2½"	3½"–6¼"
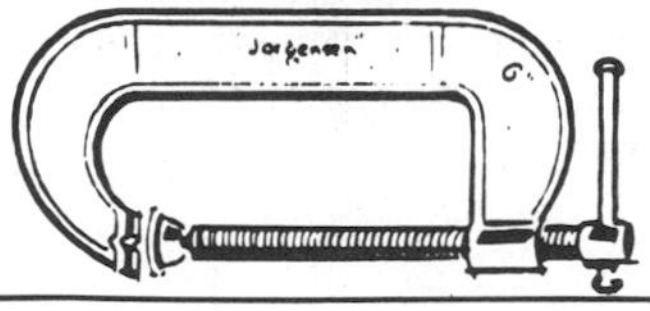	Carriage clamps	2½"–12"	1¾"–6"

TYPE OF HANDLES

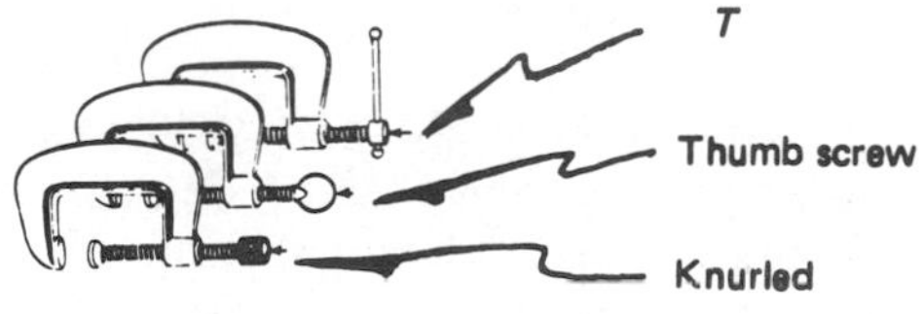

T

Thumb screw

Knurled

Figure 16–19. Sizes and styles of the most common C-clamps.

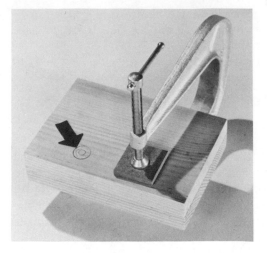

Figure 16–20. C-clamps will mar the work (arrow) unless a pad is used under the swivel. Pads also help to distribute the clamp pressure.

Carriage clamps (Figure 16–21) are usually classified as C-clamps but are made to industrial standards with ribbed cross-sections that will resist considerable side strain. The general design and the bulk of the clamps puts them in the heavy-duty category.

Figure 16–21. Carriage clamps are a type of C-clamp but made to industrial standards for the type of heavy-duty work shown here.

THREE-WAY EDGING CLAMP

A three-way edging clamp looks like a C-clamp (Figure 16–22), but is designed so it can apply right-angle pressure to the edge or side of a workpiece. It is especially useful for installing or repairing edge trim or moldings. Because of the three-screw design, the centered or right-angle screw can be used on or off-center, or the tool can be used as a conventional C-clamp (Figure 16–23).

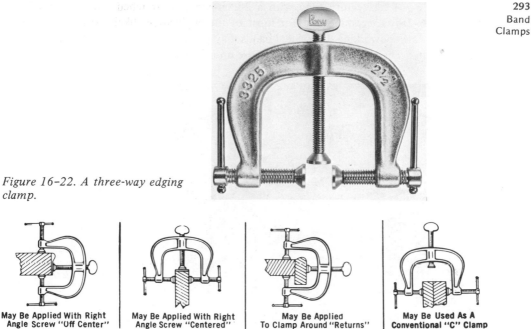

Figure 16-22. A three-way edging clamp.

| May Be Applied With Right Angle Screw "Off Center" | May Be Applied With Right Angle Screw "Centered" | May Be Applied To Clamp Around "Returns" | May Be Used As A Conventional "C" Clamp |

Figure 16-23. Some basic applications of a three-way edging clamp.

BAND CLAMPS

Band clamps (Figure 16-24) solve the special problem of clamping the round or irregular shapes that are often encountered in furniture constructions, pedestals, and segmented forms. With both the light-duty and heavy-duty types, the band is placed about the work and pulled as snug as possible by hand. The final tightening is done by turning the screw or the bolt of the clamp, whichever applies.

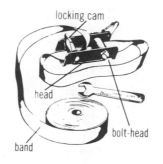

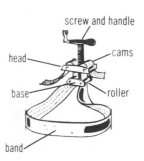

Figure 16-24. The two basic types of band clamps.

For light service, 1" x 15' nylon band

For heavy duty service, available with canvas or steel band; bands are 2" wide, 10', 15', 20', 25', 30', lengths

A heavy-duty type with a 2-inch-wide, prestretched canvas band (Figure 16-25) is recommended for most of the applications likely to be encountered in a woodworking shop. Steel bands may prove more difficult to handle, and can kink. They are recommended for use on round shapes only.

Figure 16-25. A heavy-duty canvas band clamp in use on a frame for an upholstered chair.

Figure 16-26 shows a light-duty band clamp in use doing a repair job on a finished chair. The same application would apply on an original assembly procedure. Some light-duty band clamps are furnished complete with specially shaped steel corners for use when clamping picture frames and the like. The steel corners make it easier to clamp the work and they protect the band as well.

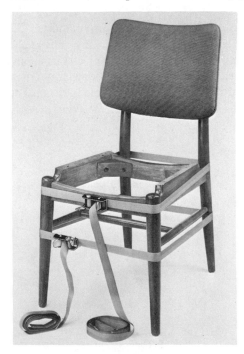

Figure 16-26. Light-duty band clamps being used on a repair job. The same application would apply on the original assembly work.

Edge-clamp fixtures (Figure 16-27) are accessories especially designed to provide pressure at right angles to the axis of a bar clamp. They are used as shown in Figure 16-28 for applying molding, trim or end boards, or applying pressure to the center areas of broad slabs. The double screw design straddles the clamp, applying pressure on both sides of the bar. Be sure to check the thickness of the bar on the clamps you work with. Some edge-clamp fixtures can't be used on bars that are more than 5/16-inches thick.

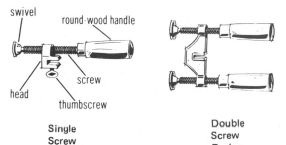

Figure 16-27. Two types of edge-clamp fixtures.

Single Screw Design

Double Screw Design

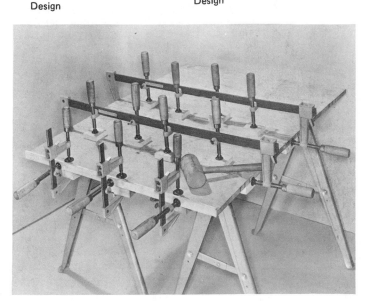

Figure 16-28. The assembly shown here demonstrates two ways to use edge-clamp fixtures.

MITER CLAMPS

The clamp shown in Figure 16-29 is especially designed for mitered, flat casings which are made of material thick enough to bore a 5/8-inch blind hole in the back of each piece. The clamps pull the mating edges tightly against each other no matter what the miter angle. There is little or no tendency for the edges to creep out of alignment.

Figure 16-29. This type of miter clamp requires that blind holes be drilled in the back surfaces of the parts being joined. They may be used regardless of the miter-cut angle.

A more common type of miter clamp is shown in Figure 16-30. A special feature of a device of this type permits you to touch up the joint with a backsaw or dovetail saw, if necessary, after the parts are clamped. Then, after loosening the clamp screws, you can apply glue and butt the cut edges together before retightening the clamps. Since the corner is open, nothing interferes with reinforcing the joint with a mechanical fastener. Once the fastener is in place the assembled pieces can be removed from the clamp. This way, you can work on other corners or other parts without delaying the job.

Figure 16-30. This type of miter clamp is actually a vise that holds parts together for gluing. The joint is exposed so mechanical fasteners can be easily added.

The miter clamp shown in Figure 16-31 has several advantages and is a tool you can make yourself. It applies uniform pressure to all of the joints simultaneously and is adjustable to any frame size within its capacity. Since all joints are visible, you will know immediately whether they are straight and true, and you can easily add a mechanical reinforcement.

The parts you need for making the clamp are shown in Figure 16-32. Work with a good, dry hardwood like maple or oak. Although the length of the arms is called out at 24 inches, you can choose to make them longer or shorter,

*Figure 16–31. A miter clamp you can make yourself is adjustable for various sizes of work. (*Designed by the Adjustable Clamp Co.*)*

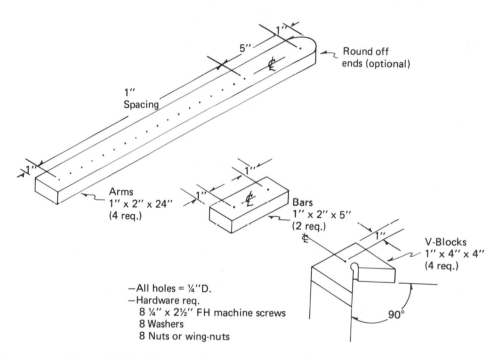

1″
5″
Round off
ends (optional)

1″
Spacing

1″

Arms
1″ x 2″ x 24″
(4 req.)

1″

1″

Bars
1″ x 2″ x 5″
(2 req.)

1″

V-Blocks
1″ x 4″ x 4″
(4 req.)

90°

—All holes = ¼″D.
—Hardware req.
   8 ¼″ x 2½″ FH machine screws
   8 Washers
   8 Nuts or wing-nuts

Figure 16–32. The parts that are needed for the adjustable miter clamp.

basing the decision on the kind of work you plan to do. The best way to make the arms and the bars is to cut the pieces to size and then stack them (holding with clamps), so the holes can be drilled through all at the same time.

A good way to form the *V*-blocks is shown in Figure 16–33. Do a very careful layout and then drill the holes that are called for. Cut out the corners first and then separate the block into the four units you need.

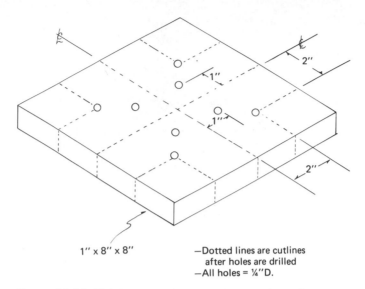

1" x 8" x 8"

—Dotted lines are cutlines
after holes are drilled
—All holes = ¼"D.

Figure 16–33. This is an accurate, easy way to form the V*-blocks. Cut out the corners first. Then separate into four units.*

All of the holes in the arms should be counterbored or countersunk on the underside so the screws will seat flush with the surface of the wood. This way the clamp will lie flat on a bench or wherever it is used.

The photograph (Figure 16-31) shows a handscrew drawing the bars together to apply pressure to the corner joints. If the bars are a considerable distance apart, which can happen if a large frame is being assembled, you can use a bar clamp instead of a handscrew to apply the pressure.

PRESS SCREWS

A common use for press screws is in the construction of veneer press frames like the one shown in Figure 16-34. A tool like this, which you can make yourself, is used to apply wood veneers or materials like plastic laminates

Figure 16–34. Press screws and homemade press frames being used as a veneer press. Note the heavy bed.

to core stock, to clamp inlaid panels, to laminate special components, and even to assemble woodworking components that might require heavy pressure.

The press frames are constructed as individual assemblies, as shown in Figure 16-35. Because the frames are subjected to considerable pressures, they are made of heavy hardwood members held together with substantial bolts. The size of the work you plan to do should be considered when you decide on the size of the frames and the number of them you need. The dimensions given in the drawing are good for average work, but should you decide to modify, be guided by the following general rules.

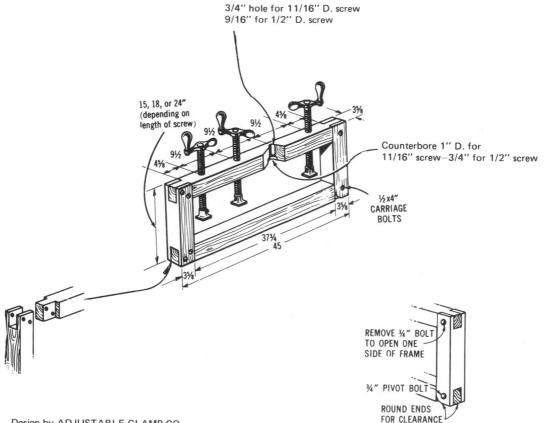

Design by ADJUSTABLE CLAMP CO.

Figure 16-35. Construction details of the press frames. Dimensions may be changed but it is essential that the frames be made to withstand considerable pressures.

Spacing between the press screws should be about 9 inches. In use, the frames should be placed about 9 inches apart, so you will need one frame for each 9 inches of work length. The size of the press screws you use (Figure 16-36) will affect the height dimension of the side members.

Other factors to consider are the distance the screw must travel through the top cross member, the thickness of the work you plan to do, plus the thickness of the bed and the cauls.

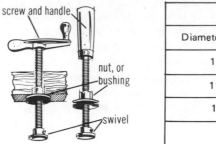

Figure 16-36. Types and sizes of press screws.

Typical Press Screws	
Diameter of Screw	Length of Screw
11/16"	9"
11/16"	12"
11/16"	18"
1/2"	7"

Although the press screws are designed primarily for the purpose described above, there is no reason why they can't be used in the construction of stationary or portable jigs and fixtures for all types of gluing and assembly operations.

HOLD-DOWN CLAMPS

A hold-down clamp, when installed on a bench, as shown in Figure 16-37, can double as a vise to secure parts for assembly procedures. Both regular and heavy-duty types (Figure 16-38) are designed so they can be easily removed from the bench when they are not in use.

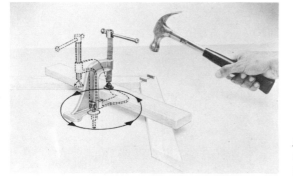

Figure 16-37. A hold-down clamp in use. The tools are designed so they may be mounted when needed.

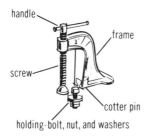

Figure 16-38. Two types of hold-down clamps. Both may be used on either a wooden bench top or a slotted machine table.

A feature of this clamp design is that, unlike a conventional vise which must be situated near a bench edge, this clamp may be located anywhere on a surface. It may also be placed on a slotted machine table, like those found on a drill press, to secure work for drilling or for mortising.

There can be variations in the methods used to mount the clamps so be sure to read the instructions supplied with the tool before mounting them.

SPRING CLAMPS

Spring clamps (Figure 16-39) are like extra, super-strong fingers you can use to hold work in position for short or long periods of time. They can be quickly applied or removed. The clamp pressure is always at the tip of the jaws so you can localize the grip anywhere within the tool's reach. Often, a wood pad is used under the jaws so the clamp pressure will spread over a broader area.

Some types come with specially shaped jaws to grip round objects or have pivoting jaws with serrated edges so they can actually grip around a corner as in a miter joint. Most types are available with protective sleeves over the jaws or the handles, or over both areas, to provide protection for work surfaces and to make handling easier.

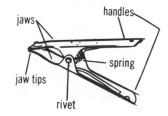

Figure 16-39. The parts of a spring clamp.

Spring clamps come in various sizes, so you have a choice in relation to the work to be held and the amount of pressure you need (Figure 16-40). The springs on some of the larger sizes are powerful enough so you need two hands to open the jaws.

Figure 16-40. Sizes of spring clamps. Larger ones have strong springs and can exert quite a bit of pressure.

SPECIFICATION OF TYPICAL SPRING CLAMPS		
CAPACITY BETWEEN JAWS	LENGTH OF JAWS	REACH ONTO WORK
1″	4″	1¼″
2″	6″	2″
3″	9″	3″
4″	12″	4″

UNIVERSAL CLAMP

The universal clamp is a relative newcomer in the clamp world and is actually a kit of parts (Figure 16-41) that you can assemble in various ways to do a multitude of assembly and gluing work. The tool can do a bar clamp's work without having to span the assembly, which is its major advantage. Thus, it can be used as shown in Figures 16-42 and 16-43 to secure *T*-joints as well as end joints.

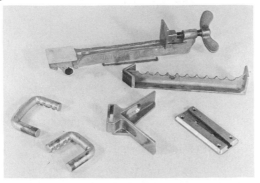

Figure 16-41. The parts of a universal clamp.

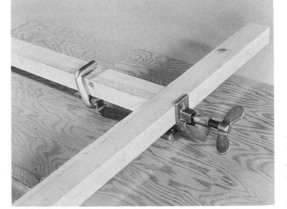

Figure 16-42. A universal clamp organized to hold the parts of a T-*joint. The serrated leg of the* U-*jaw should be placed on a side of the stock that won't be visible.*

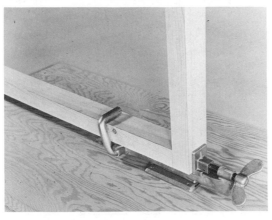

Figure 16-43. Universal clamp holding an end joint. The clamp slips easily in or out of the base which, here, is screwed to the bench top.

The key to this clamp is the interchangeable *U*-shaped jaws that will grip stock from 3/4-inch to 1-5/8 inches thick and which can be inserted on either side of the clamp. Each *U*-shape has a toothed leg that grips the wood. This leg leaves a mark. Place the clamp so the scar will be on a hidden side of the work or use a protective shim between the jaw and the wood.

Figure 16-44 shows how the universal clamp is organized for a miter joint. The miter attachment hooks over serrations in the arm and can be adjusted to accommodate various width materials. The openings in the miter clamp jaws are there so you can drive a screw or a nail while the parts are held firmly together.

The kit includes a special mount for using the clamp on a bench like a vise. It slips out of the mount easily for portable applications.

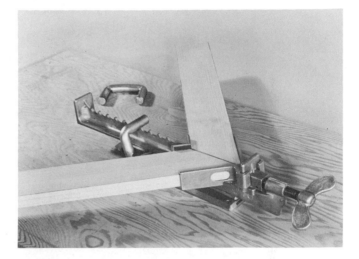

Figure 16-44. Using the clamp to assemble a miter joint. Nails or screws can be driven through the opening in the V-*jaw.*

IMPROVISING

There are times when the right clamp for the job is not available or when the job is peculiar enough so that even a good assortment of standard clamps will not be adequate. Under such conditions the woodworker has no choice but to be creative and imaginative, inventing clamping devices that solve the problem. Often the jig or fixture becomes a permanent tool. Other times it is a quick, makeshift setup that is justified simply because its one-time use solves the problem on hand.

A clamp must apply point or area pressure to keep parts correctly assembled while other work is being done, or to keep surfaces in firm contact until glue dries. The ideas and procedures that are shown in Figures 16-45 through 16-55 have been tested and proven adequate for the jobs being done. They can be used as shown but, more important, they should serve as examples of how to work when you lack a clamp, or how to succeed when the assembly problem is an unusual or rare one.

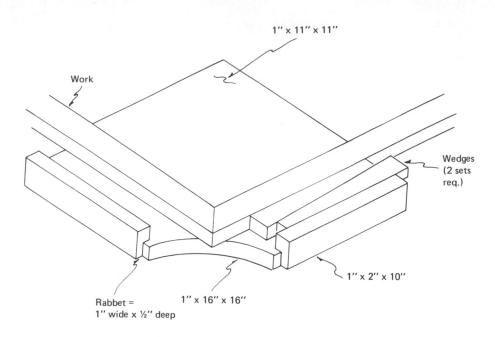

Figure 16–45. A type of mitering jig that you can make yourself. Twin wedges hold the parts in place until the glue dries or until you have driven in nails or screws.

Figure 16–46. A similar type of jig that uses ordinary bolts to provide clamp pressure. Tee-Nuts, pressed into the side pieces, provide threads for the bolts.

304

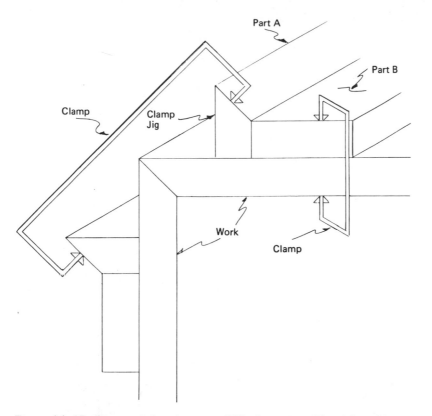

Figure 16–47. Cross and rip miters are difficult to assemble with routine clamping procedures. The idea shown here makes it possible for clamps to span across the corner so parts will pull tightly together. Be sure that parts A and B are joined strongly with glue and screws.

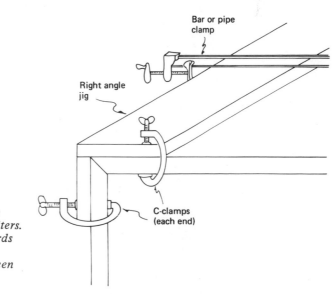

Figure 16–48. This is another way to organize for clamping cross or rip miters. The right-angle jig is simply two boards put together to form a 90-degree turn. Be sure to use wax paper between the jig and the work.

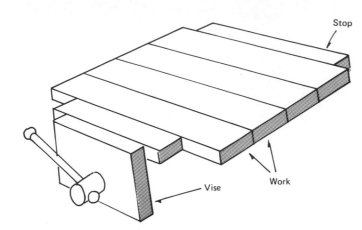

Figure 16-49. How to improvise clamping for a slab assembly. The stop is nailed to the workbench. The bench vise supplies the clamp pressure.

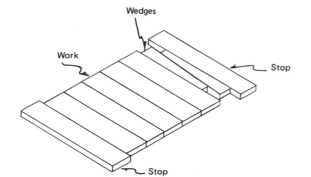

Figure 16-50. Here is another way to do a slab assembly. Two stops are used, each nailed to the workbench. Matched wedges supply the clamp pressure.

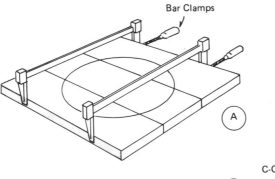

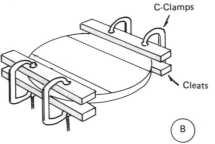

Figure 16-51. Two methods to use when you need a circular part. Assemble the boards and then cut out the piece as in A, or cut the parts first and then assemble as in B. Use bar clamps across the cleats that are held in place with the C-clamps.

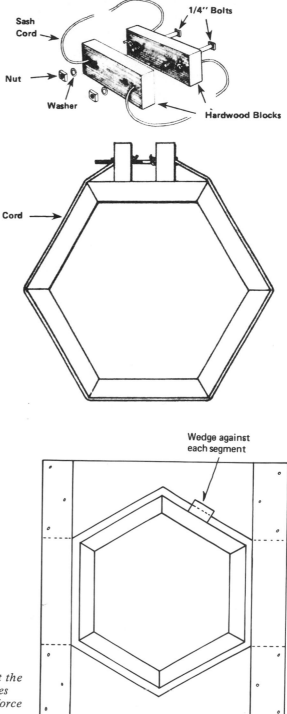

Figure 16-52. An example of the classic tourniquet rope clamp. Here, the rope is pulled tight and knotted. The blocks are pulled together with the bolts to provide the final clamp pressure. A handscrew or a C-clamp can be used in place of the bolts.

Figure 16-53. A special form is made to suit the shape of a segmented assembly. Then, wedges are used against each side of the project to force the corners tightly together.

Wedges

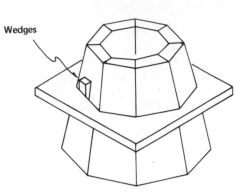

*Figure 16–54. The same idea will
work if the project has sloping sides.
In this and similar situations it's
best to cut the opening for the
project in a single piece of stock.*

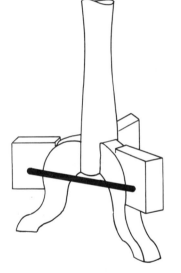

*Figure 16–55. The rope trick again, this time
to clamp legs against a pedestal. The bearing
blocks can be pieces of the scrap which were
removed when the legs were shaped. Always work with sash cord or something similar when you use rope as a clamp. Other types,
like clothesline, may stretch too much.*

Chapter 17

GLUING

A well-fitted joint, correctly glued, will resist stresses that might cause adjacent areas to fail. Glue selection and application should not be approached casually. The craftsmanship you use when forming mating parts could be wasted if you don't follow through on the final step with similar dedication. Parts that go together should stay together, which is why glue is used at all.

GENERAL CONSIDERATIONS

Essentially, glue is a liquid adhesive dispersed in a solvent, usually water, so it can be easily spread. When the joint parts are pressed and held together, the glue and water penetrate the pores of the wood. The glue sticks to the walls of the wood fibers and gains strength as the water evaporates during the setting time.

The speed with which the glue sets and how deeply it penetrates depends on how quickly the water is removed. The strength of the joint and its resistance to outside factors, such as moisture and heat, depends entirely on the nature of the glue. That is one reason why the amount of moisture that is already in the wood can affect both the strength of the joint and the setting time of the glue. Excess moisture can cause a weak joint. Wood that absorbs too much moisture during the gluing operation will swell and then shrink so that stresses will result along the glue line.

Many of our modern glues are designed to minimize the negative effect of conditions which are difficult to control in a small shop. The individual is not likely to have instruments for checking wood moisture content and it's also possible that the shop temperature and humidity may be difficult to control. The best one can do under less than ideal conditions is to attempt to maintain a consistent room temperature and, above all, to be sure that the parts being fabricated and joined are subjected to the same atmosphere. An extreme example of how *not* to work is to make one part from lumber stored in a warm room and the mating piece from lumber taken from an outside storage shed.

309

Some wood species are more porous than others but all are more absorbent at end grain than along edges or on surfaces. The best way to work end grain is to apply a thinned coat of glue almost as you would a sealer and, shortly thereafter, add a second, full-strength coat. A visual check will tell whether the surface is uniformly coated.

It's possible, regardless of where you are using the glue, for some areas to absorb more glue than others. Here too, a visual check will reveal if you should spot-apply additional glue.

So much of the glue we use today is squeezed from a plastic bottle. This tempts many workers to deposit the glue in a wavy bead that they feel will spread adequately under clamp pressure. This is not a good practice. Use a stiff-bristle brush to spread the glue evenly over all mating surfaces.

Don't be frugal with glue but being too generous is wasteful and useless. There should be some squeeze-out when the parts are pressed together, but keep it to a minimum. Remove the excess with a sharp knife or chisel. Then wipe with a lint-free cloth dampened, not soaked, with warm water. Glue that is not removed can cause blemishes and can act as a sealer, preventing stains from penetrating in that area.

Some assemblies are more complex than others. When the job is elaborate, do a dry run first. That is, put the parts together without glue so you can set up a sequence of operations that will facilitate the final procedure. Check to be sure that a joining in one area will not prevent adding another component.

Some glues set more quickly than others. This is not a big factor if the job is small, but on a large assembly it can prove frustrating, if not disastrous, if the glue sets in one area while you are still applying it elsewhere. Glue that sets before the parts are joined is like no glue at all. Many glues set faster at high temperatures. Some shouldn't be used at all at low temperatures, while others are more tolerant. Be sure you read and follow the instructions that are on the container. We must assume the manufacturer knows how to use the glue most efficiently.

Some glues will fill gaps better than others and can be used when joint parts are less than perfect or when a less-than-tight joining is justified to make a very complex assembly easier. A gap-filling glue should not be used to hide poor craftsmanship.

Don't use a water resistant glue when what you actually need is a waterproof product. A picnic table, a patio bench, a dog house, and a fancy mail box need waterproof glue. Inside projects—furniture, built-ins, cabinets, and the like—get by with water-resistant glue. Why make a choice at all? Water resistant glue is cheaper than waterproof glue.

Some glues are more resistant to heat than others. Thermoplastic glues will soften when the temperature goes up to near 160 degrees Fahrenheit (71°C). To be on the safe side, avoid this type of glue if the project will be an enclosure for a heat producing unit like a radiator or a TV set.

Always check components while they are under clamp pressure to be sure the angular relationship is correct. Adjustments can be made before the glue sets, not afterwards. Use temporary braces when necessary to hold parts in alignment. Use clamps during the initial assembly even if the parts will be held together with nails or screws. When similar assemblies must be done, take the time to organize a simple fixture so duplicate operations can be performed in mechanical fashion. This is especially wise when odd-angle relationships are involved.

Try to do gluing jobs in a clean, warm, dust-free area. Contact surfaces should be smooth but not necessarily sanded. Edges smoothed on a jointer or cut with a good carbide-tipped saw blade are pretty close to ideal.

Remember that the chances for joint failure will increase if the parts go together in sloppy fashion or will not mesh without clamp pressure.

KINDS OF GLUE

There are almost as many types of glue as there are joints, but the wide variety is of more interest to the commercial producer and the provider of stock materials than to the individual or the small shop owner. An adequate choice can be made from the assortment of packaged products sold under various trade names. Those that follow are the most common and the most usable. Just be sure to read the label on the container. It will tell the kind of glue, how it should be mixed if necessary, how to apply it, and factors that can affect its efficiency.

Polyvinyl Resin Glue

Polyvinyl resin is a white glue that is popular for general woodworking, and is widely available in convenient plastic squeeze bottles. It is always ready to use but sets best and most quickly at temperatures of 60 degrees Fahrenheit (15.6°C) or higher.

Project parts should be prepared for instant clamping as soon as the glue is spread. Don't use it where you need resistance to moisture or high temperatures. Average clamping time under ideal conditions is from one to two hours, with softwoods requiring the longer periods.

Animal (Liquid Hide) Glue

The glue made from animal hides and bones has always been a favorite for cabinetwork and general woodworking assemblies. It is very strong and does not become brittle, but it is not waterproof and so should not be used on outdoor projects. It will, however, resist heat and mold, and it can supply strength even to poorly fitted joints since it has gap filling qualities. It is available in liquid form, ready to use, or in flake form which must be mixed with water and heated.

Best results are obtained when the temperature of the glue is 70 degrees

Fahrenheit (21°C) or higher. If the room temperature is colder, heat the glue by placing the container in a pan of warm water.

A standard procedure is to apply a thin coat of the glue on mating surfaces and to allow it to become a bit tacky before joining the parts. It needs a longer set time than some other glues, but this can be an asset when you need more time for assembly work. Average clamp time under ideal conditions runs from two to three hours for hardwoods and three to four hours for softwoods.

Casein Glue

Casein glue is a product made from milk curds. It comes as a brownish powder that you mix with water to form a glue with a cream-like consistency. Usually the mixture requires equal parts of powder and water. A good procedure is to mix the material and then to stir it again, about 10 minutes before using. It has a relatively short shelf life after being mixed so don't prepare more than you can use for the job on hand.

Its gap-filling qualities are good, and it can be used at any temperature as long as it is not freezing. But, like almost any glue, it is easier and better to use at warmer temperatures. It has a good degree of moisture resistance but it is not waterproof.

It is often *the* choice for oily woods like yew, teak, or lemon, but it is not used on woods like redwood, oak, or maple because on these species it can cause stains.

Clamping time is about the same as required for animal glue.

Plastic Resin Glue

Plastic resin glue is a urea-formaldehyde material that comes in powdered form and is mixed with water for use. Generally, the correct mixture is two parts of powder to one-half to one part of water. Do not mix more than you can use within two or three hours. It's smarter to prepare only as much as you need immediately.

It is not a good glue to use on oily woods or if the joint mesh is less than perfect. It has considerable resistance to moisture, but it is not considered waterproof.

It's a good glue to use for general woodworking. Joints will be strong but the glue line will be brittle if the joint parts do not fit tightly under clamp pressure.

Best results are obtained when the room temperature is 70 degrees F (21°C) or warmer. Clamping time for both hardwoods and softwoods can be quite long— as much as 16 hours.

Resorcinol Resin Glue

Resorcinol resin glue is a very strong and completely waterproof glue. It is an excellent choice for projects that will be exposed to water such as patio furniture, wooden water containers, boats, and similar projects.

It is a two-component product. One part is resin and the other is a catalyst. When the two materials are mixed together in correct proportion a chemical action occurs and the glue sets. Be very careful when mixing to follow the instructions on the container. Incorrect amounts of catalyst and resin will result in a weak joint. Bench life of the mix is short so only prepare amounts that you can use right away.

The glue leaves a dark line and sets slowly, but it has gap-filling qualities. It will do a better job on poorly fitted joints than most other glues. It should be used at temperatures that are at least 70 degrees; the higher the temperature, the faster the glue will set. Clamping time runs 14 to 16 hours.

Aliphatic Resin Glue

Aliphatic resin glue is a good all-purpose glue for case goods and furniture assemblies, edge-to-edge joints, and face gluing. It is similar to polyvinyl but is preferred by many woodworkers. It is available in plastic squeeze bottles, ready to use. It has good heat resistance, fine spreadability, but is not particularly water resistant.

Good factors in its favor are that it sets quickly and can be used efficiently at any temperature above 50 degrees F. (10°C) even though a higher temperature, about 70 degrees F. (21°C), is preferable. It is a good idea to stir it before use and to apply clamps quickly. Clamping time runs between one and two hours.

Epoxy Cement

Epoxy cement has a separate resin and hardener that must be mixed exactly as explained on the product's label. This is not a general woodworking glue, but is a good choice for bonding dissimilar materials such as metal or tile to wood.

Products like this must be used carefully in well-ventilated areas. Read and obey all the safety instructions.

The epoxy can be used at any temperature but will dry faster with heat. Many jobs can be done without clamping but this will depend on the nature of the work and the product itself. The material will not swell or shrink and is waterproof and oil proof. Some types can be used to fill holes or gaps.

Once it sets, the material can be sanded, filed, drilled, or even machined.

Urea Resin

Urea resin is a resin-catalyst product that sets in seconds under high frequency heat. This quality limits its use in the average woodworking shop. Also, the moisture content of the wood must be low and carefully controlled.

It sets almost colorless and is highly moisture resistant but not waterproof. It is commonly used in factories with special heating equipment for edge gluing.

CONTACT CEMENTS

Contact cement is a special adhesive that is ideal for doing laminations. It is commonly used for bonding plastic laminates to counter tops, but it is also excellent for attaching wood veneers and applying banding to hide plywood edges.

The product comes ready to use and is applied by brush or roller to both surfaces. The word contact must be taken literally. Once the coated surfaces touch they can't be separated or shifted. This calls for very careful placement of parts. A common practice is to place brown wrapping paper between the sheets to be laminated after the cement is dry. The paper is slowly pulled away as the parts are pressed together.

Original products, some still available, were highly volatile and extremely flammable. Some newer types are water-based and are not flammable or toxic. Whatever you use, it is critical that you read and follow all the instructions on the label so you will use the product efficiently and safely.

Contact cements do not require clamping and are moisture resistant. They are easiest to use when the temperature is 70 degrees F. (21°C) or warmer. Be especially careful about the waiting period between application of the cement and assembly of the parts. The product label will tell how long to wait and how to do a simple test to check for readiness. Most times the test is to press a piece of wrapping paper against the coated surface. If the paper doesn't stick, the adhesive is ready.

ILLUSTRATED GLOSSARY

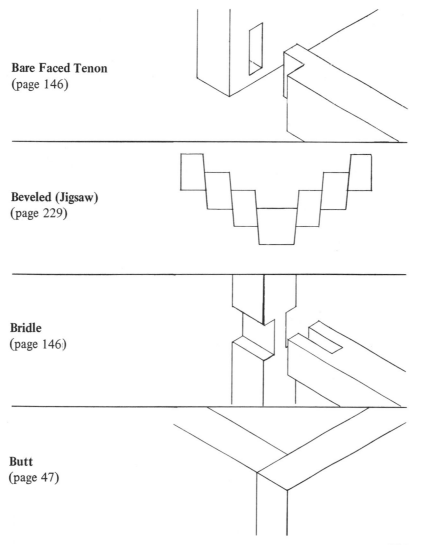

Bare Faced Tenon
(page 146)

Beveled (Jigsaw)
(page 229)

Bridle
(page 146)

Butt
(page 47)

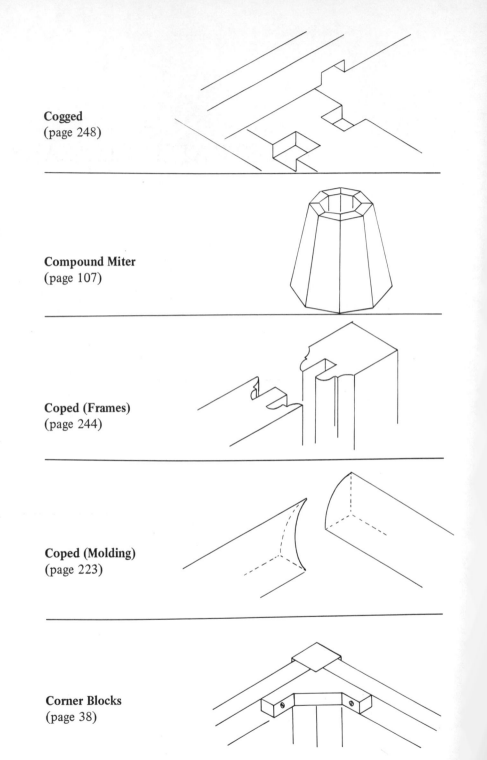

Cogged
(page 248)

Compound Miter
(page 107)

Coped (Frames)
(page 244)

Coped (Molding)
(page 223)

Corner Blocks
(page 38)

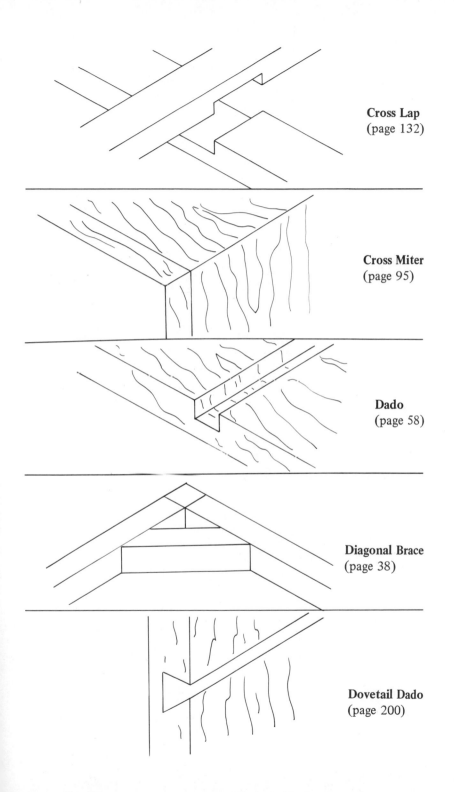

Cross Lap
(page 132)

Cross Miter
(page 95)

Dado
(page 58)

Diagonal Brace
(page 38)

Dovetail Dado
(page 200)

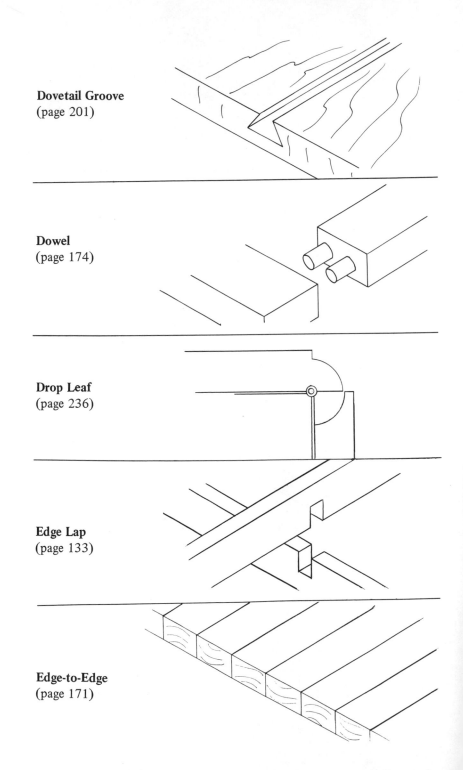

Dovetail Groove
(page 201)

Dowel
(page 174)

Drop Leaf
(page 236)

Edge Lap
(page 133)

Edge-to-Edge
(page 171)

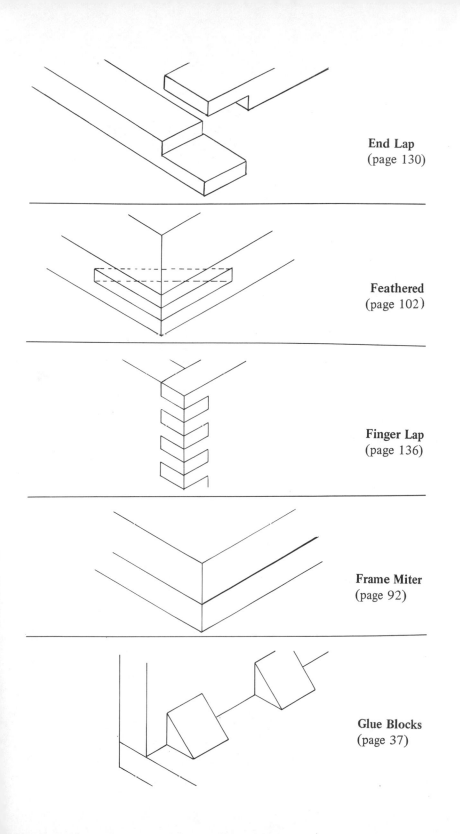

End Lap
(page 130)

Feathered
(page 102)

Finger Lap
(page 136)

Frame Miter
(page 92)

Glue Blocks
(page 37)

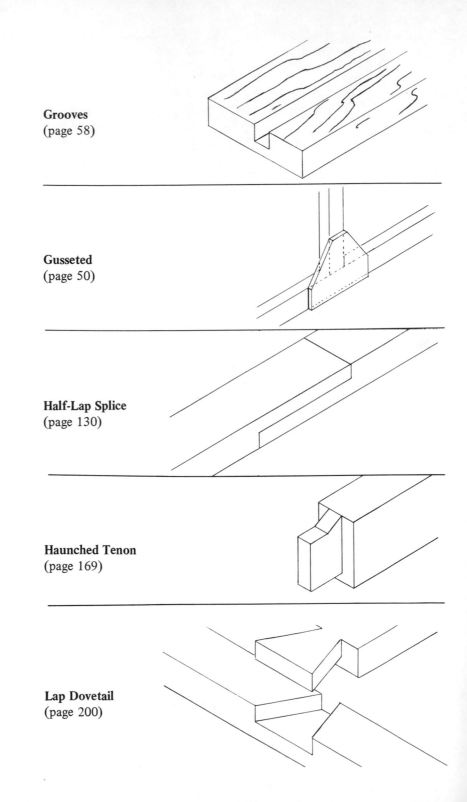

Grooves
(page 58)

Gusseted
(page 50)

Half-Lap Splice
(page 130)

Haunched Tenon
(page 169)

Lap Dovetail
(page 200)

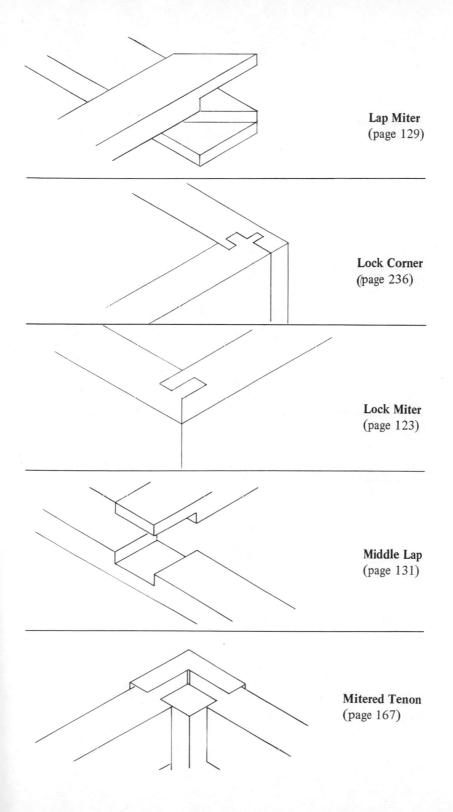

Lap Miter
(page 129)

Lock Corner
(page 236)

Lock Miter
(page 123)

Middle Lap
(page 131)

Mitered Tenon
(page 167)

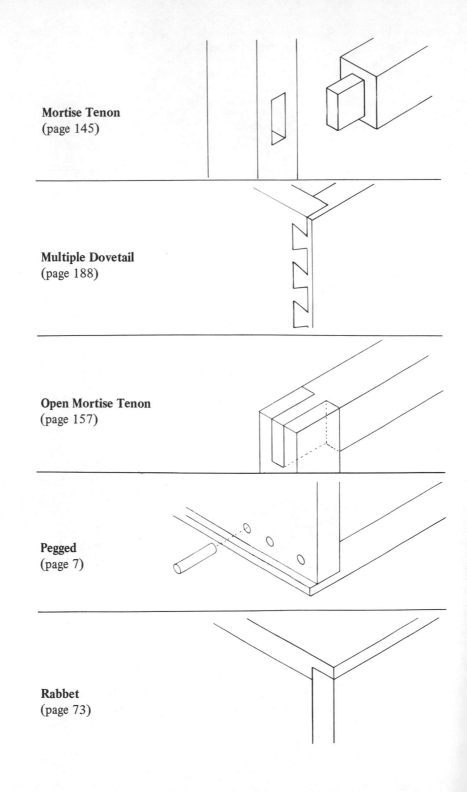

Mortise Tenon
(page 145)

Multiple Dovetail
(page 188)

Open Mortise Tenon
(page 157)

Pegged
(page 7)

Rabbet
(page 73)

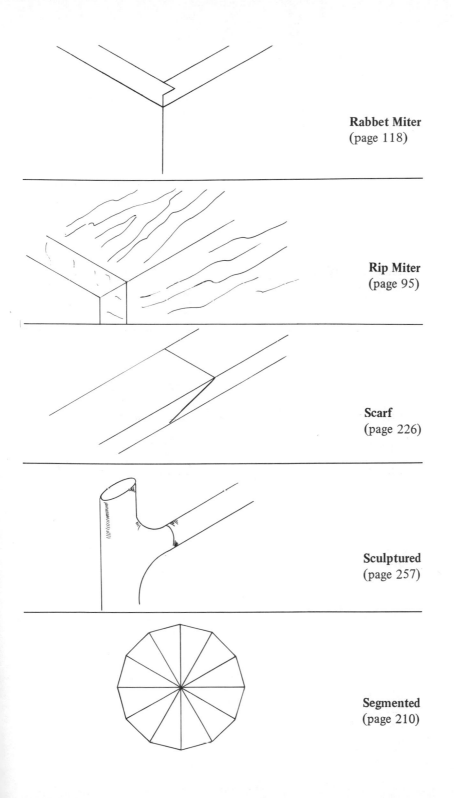

Rabbet Miter
(page 118)

Rip Miter
(page 95)

Scarf
(page 226)

Sculptured
(page 257)

Segmented
(page 210)

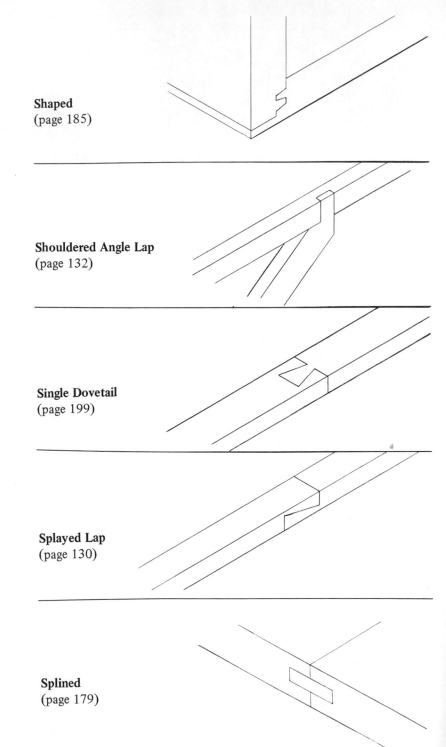

Shaped
(page 185)

Shouldered Angle Lap
(page 132)

Single Dovetail
(page 199)

Splayed Lap
(page 130)

Splined
(page 179)

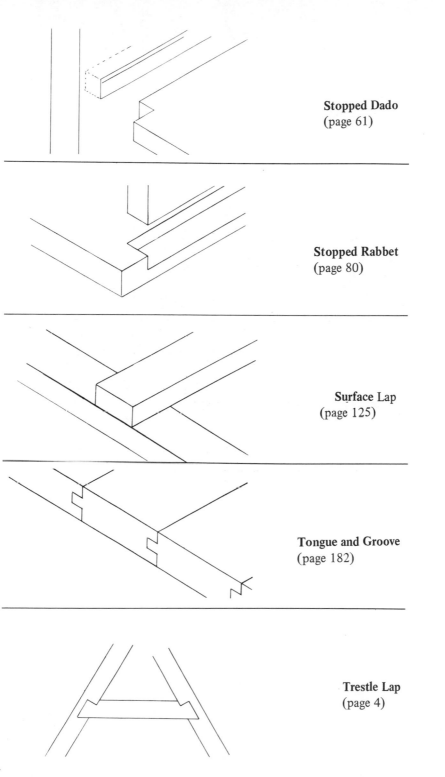

Stopped Dado
(page 61)

Stopped Rabbet
(page 80)

Surface Lap
(page 125)

Tongue and Groove
(page 182)

Trestle Lap
(page 4)

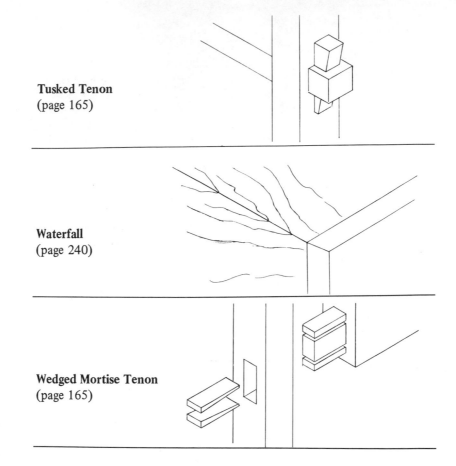

Tusked Tenon
(page 165)

Waterfall
(page 240)

Wedged Mortise Tenon
(page 165)

INDEX

21644

684
DeC

DeCristoforo, R. J.
  Woodworking Techniques: Joints and
Their Applications.

DATE DUE			
OCT 2			